The Gospel of Mark in Context

MATRIX
The Bible in Mediterranean Context

PREVIOUSLY PUBLISHED VOLUMES

Richard L. Rohrbaugh
The New Testament and Social-Science Criticism

Markus Cromhout
Jesus and Identity

Pieter F. Craffert
The Life of a Galilean Shaman

Douglas E. Oakman
Jesus and the Peasants

Stuart L. Love
Jesus and the Marginal Women

Eric C. Stewart
Gathered around Jesus

Dennis C. Duling
A Marginal Scribe

Jason Lamoreaux
Ritual, Women, and Philippi

Ernest Van Eck
The Parables of Jesus the Galilean

Bruce J. Malina and John J. Pilch
Handbook of Biblical Social Values (3rd ed.)

K. C. Richardson
Early Christian Care for the Poor

Douglas E. Oakman
The Radical Jesus, the Bible, and the Great Transformation

Jerome H. Neyrey, SJ
By What Authority?

The Gospel of Mark in Context

A Social-Scientific Reading of the First Gospel

SANTIAGO GUIJARRO

CASCADE *Books* · Eugene, Oregon

THE GOSPEL OF MARK IN CONTEXT
A Social-Scientific Reading of the First Gospel

Matrix: The Bible in Mediterranean Context 14

Copyright © 2022 Santiago Guijarro. All rights reserved. Except for brief quotations in critical publications or reviews, no part of this book may be reproduced in any manner without prior written permission from the publisher. Write: Permissions, Wipf and Stock Publishers, 199 W. 8th Ave., Suite 3, Eugene, OR 97401.

Cascade Books
An Imprint of Wipf and Stock Publishers
199 W. 8th Ave., Suite 3
Eugene, OR 97401

www.wipfandstock.com

PAPERBACK ISBN: 978-1-6667-3419-5
HARDCOVER ISBN: 978-1-6667-2979-5
EBOOK ISBN: 978-1-6667-2980-1

Cataloguing-in-Publication data:

Names: Guijarro Oporto, Santiago, author.
Title: The gospel of Mark in context : a social-scientific reading of the first gospel / Santiago Guijarro.
Description: Eugene, OR: Cascade Books, 2022. | Matrix: The Bible in Mediterranean Context 14. | Includes bibliographical references and indexes.
Identifiers: ISBN 978-1-6667-3419-5 (paperback). | ISBN 978-1-6667-2979-5 (hardcover). | ISBN 978-1-6667-2980-1 (ebook).
Subjects: LSCH: Bible. Mark—Criticism, interpretation, etc. | Bible. Mark—Social scientific criticism.
Classification: BS2585.2 G85 2022 (print). | BS2585.2 (ebook).

Unless otherwise noted, Scripture quotations are taken from Revised Standard Version Bible, copyright © 1989 National Council of the Churches of Christ in the United States of America. Used by permission. All rights reserved worldwide.

Translations of Josephus's works and other classical texts are from the Loeb Classical Library editions.

Acknowledgments

THIS BOOK WOULD NOT have been possible without the support of many people and institutions, and so I would like to thank some of them.

First of all, I express my gratitude to the members of the Context Group for their hospitality, both physical and intellectual, during my stay in the United States when I was a doctoral student. I will never forget their generosity. Among them, Prof. Bruce J. Malina deserves special mention. Although he passed away some years ago, his memory and his teachings continue to inspire me.

I would like to thank my former student Dr. Ana Rodríguez Láiz for allowing me to publish the paper we coauthored on Jesus' anointing. I also express my gratitude to Dr. Cyprian Eranimus Fernandez, who helped me in the preparation of the manuscript. His suggestions have been very useful to improve the original papers and to make them more readable. Finally, I would like to thank Séamus O'Connell, Jessie Rogers, Jeremy Corley, and Luke Macnamara, professors of biblical studies at the Pontifical University, Saint Patrick's College, Maynooth University (Ireland), for their willingness to revise and correct the text. Their attentive reading has helped to improve it and make this book more readable.

I gratefully acknowledge the permission to publish the following articles and essays in revised form:

"La composición del evangelio de Marcos." *Salmanticensis* 53 (2006) 5–33.

"The Politics of Exorcism: Jesus' Reaction to Negative Labels in the Beelzebul Controversy." *BTB* 29 (1999) 118–29.

"Healing Stories and Medical Anthropology: A Reading of Mark 10:46–52." *BTB* 30 (2000) 102–12.

"Why Does the Gospel of Mark Begin as It Does?" *BTB* 33 (2003) 28–38.

Acknowledgments

"The First Disciples of Jesus in Galilee." *HvTSt* 63 (2007) 885–908.

"The 'Messianic' Anointing of Jesus (Mark 14:3–9)." *BTB* 41 (2011) 132–43.

"The Visions of Jesus and His Disciples." In *The Gospels and Their Stories in Anthropological Perspective*, edited by Joseph Verheyden and John Kloppenborg, 217–31. WUNT 409. Tübingen: Mohr/Siebeck, 2018.

"Cultural Trauma, Collective Memory, and Social Identity. The Gospel of Mark as 'Progressive Narrative.'" In *Reading the Gospel of Mark in the Twenty-First Century: Method and Meaning*, edited by Geert Van Oyen, 141–69. Leuven: Peeters, 2019.

Contents

Acknowledgments | *v*

Abbreviations | *ix*

Introduction: The Social Sciences as a Tool for Biblical Exegesis | 1

1. The Composition of Mark's Gospel | 11
2. The Beginning of Mark's Biography of Jesus (Mark 1:1–15) | 31
3. The Galilean Controversies and the Social Identity of Galilean Christianity (Mark 2:1—3:6) | 50
4. The Visions of Jesus and His Disciples (Mark 1:9–11; 9:1–9) | 68
5. Healing Stories and Medical Anthropology (Mark 10:46–52) | 83
6. The Messianic Anointing: Cultural Memory and Jesus' Identity (Mark 14:3–9) | 101
7. The Gospel of Mark as Progressive Narrative: Cultural Trauma, Collective Memory and Social Identity (Mark 11–16) | 119

Conclusion: Why the Context Matters | 145

Bibliography | *149*

Author Index | *163*

Scripture Index | *167*

Abbreviations

AB	Anchor Bible
ABRL	Anchor Bible Reference Library
ANRW	*Aufstieg und Niedergang der römischen Welt*, edited by Wolfgang Haase et al. Berlin: de Gruyter.
AYB	Anchor Yale Bible
Bib Int	*Biblical Interpretation*
BBR	*Bulletin for Biblical Research*
BETL	Bibliotheca Ephemeridum Theologicarum Lovaniensium
BibSem	Biblical Seminar
BR	*Biblical Research*
BTB	*Biblical Theology Bulletin*
BZ	*Biblische Zeitschrift*
BZAW	Beihefte zur Zeitschrift für die alttestamentliche Wissenschaft
BZNW	Beihefte zur Zeitschrift für die neutestamentliche Wissenschaft
CBQ	*Catholic Biblical Quarterly*
CurrBR	*Currents in Biblical Research*
DTMAT	*Diccionario Teológico Manual del Antiguo Testamento*, edited by Ernst Jenni and Claus Westermann. Madrid: Cristiandad, 1978

Abbreviations

EJL	Early Judaism and Its Literature
EKKNT	Evangelisch-katholischer Kommentar zum Neuen Testament
EPRO	Etudes préliminaires aux religions orientales dans l'Empire romain
ETL	*Ephemerides Theologicae Lovanienses*
EvT	*Evangelische Theologie*
ExpTim	*Expository Times*
FRLANT	Forschungen zur Religion und Literatur des Alten und Neuen Testaments
GBS	Guides to Biblical Scholarship
HSM	Harvard Semitic Monographs
HvTSt	*Hervormde theologiese Studies*
JBL	*Journal of Biblical Literature*
JJMJS	*Journal of the Jesus Movement in Its Jewish Setting*
JRS	*Journal of Roman Studies*
JSJSup	Journal for the Study of Judaism Supplements
JSNT	*Journal for the Study of the New Testament*
JSNTSup	Journal for the Study of the New Testament Supplement Series
LCL	Loeb Classical Library
LHBOTS	Library of Hebrew Bible/Old Testament Studies
LNTS	Library of New Testament Studies
LSTS	Library of Second Temple Studies
Matrix	Matrix: The Bible in Mediterranean Context
Neot	*Neotestamentica*
NTAbh	Neutestamentliche Abhandlungen
NovT	*Novum Testamentum*
NovTSup	Supplements to Novum Testamentum

Abbreviations

NTOA	Novum Testamentum et Orbis Antiquus
NTS	*New Testament Studies*
RB	*Revue bibliique*
SANT	Studien zum Alten und Neuen Testaments
SBFA	Studium Biblicum Franciscanum Analecta
SBL	Society of Biblical Literature
SBLSymSer	Society of Biblical Literature: Symposium Series
SBS	Stuttgarter Bibelstudien
SBT	Studies in Biblical Theology
SemeiaSt	Semeia Studies
SNT	Studien zum Neuen Testament
SNTSMS	Society for New Testament Studies Monograph Series
SNTW	Studies in the New Testament and Its World
ST	*Studia Theologica*
SUNT	Studien zur Umwelt des Neuen Testament
TB	Theologische Bücherei
TDNT	*Theological Dictionary of the New Testament.* Edited by Gerhard Kittel and Gerhard Friedrich. Translated by Geoffrey W. Bromiley. 10 vols. Grand Rapids: Eerdmans, 1964–1976
WGRW	Writings from the Greco-Roman World
WMANT	Wissenschaftliche Monographien zum Alten und Neuen Testament
WUNT	Wissenschaftliche Untersuchungen zum Neuen Testament
ZNW	*Zeitschrift für die neutestamentlich Wissenschaft*

Introduction

The Social Sciences as a Tool for Biblical Exegesis

BIBLICAL SCHOLARS AND LAY readers of the Bible have always been aware of the usefulness of knowing the context of biblical texts. Renowned literati and teachers of antiquity, such as Origen and Jerome, who lived in the country of the Bible, report how knowing the geography and culture of those lands helped them to understand the sacred texts. Christians today who journey to the Holy Land have a similar experience when they visit the sites where the episodes narrated in the Bible took place and get in contact with the traditional culture of those regions.

In the critical study of the Bible developed during the last two centuries, knowledge of the biblical context has also occupied a prominent place. Scholars have been interested in the geography of Palestine and the ancient Middle East, and have studied the history of the region in biblical times. They have also described ancient Mediterranean institutions and have considered part of their task to know the results of the main archaeological excavations. All these studies about the material and historical context of the biblical books have contributed to understand them better. For that reason, history, geography, and archaeology belong to the curriculum of theological studies and play a crucial role in the formation of biblical scholars.

In recent years, the study of the original context of biblical writings has undergone a new development thanks to the entry of social sciences into biblical studies. The use of the social sciences in biblical interpretation is not a complete novelty. In the late nineteenth and early twentieth centuries, the so-called Chicago School used social models to interpret ancient Christian texts and reconstruct the history of early Christianity.[1] However,

---

1. On the beginnings of this exegetical school, whose most representative authors are

a systematic application of this new approach has become common only since the *methodological turn* that took place half a century ago. From then on, new methodological approaches have been applied to biblical texts in order to understand them better—whether these approaches call on various forms of literary analysis to interpret the text or on the social sciences to help reconstruct their context.[2]

Various Exegetical Methods for Studying the Bible

The primary purpose of exegesis is to explain the biblical texts, making clear the meaning they had in their original context. By its very nature, exegesis seeks objectivity and, consequently, needs to distance itself from whatever interests or prejudices can compromise this objectivity.

Exegetical methods pursue this goal in different ways. The so-called historical-critical method and the method of literary analysis are the most important ones. The historical-critical method is mainly interested in the diachronic dimension of texts—that is, in their formation process. The method of literary analysis concentrates on the synchronic dimension of texts—that is, on the texts as final products. These two methods are fitting ways to study works that have undergone a complex formation process. As texts, they should be analyzed using literary analysis procedures. Still, their complex formation process requires an analysis of their diachronic dimension as well.

The use of the social sciences to reconstruct the social context of biblical texts has, vis-à-vis these two methods, a complementary function. In relation to the historical-critical method, social-scientific study of the Bible represents a significant expansion of the core concept of *Sitz im Leben*, developed by form critics such as Martin Dibelius and Rudolf Bultmann, who thought that life context played a decisive role in the formation and transmission of oral tradition. Later on, redaction critics developed this concept by applying it to the context from which texts emerged. Nonetheless, both form and redaction critics associated the life context with the *church context*.[3] The use of the social sciences to reconstruct the context of texts expands this notion to include the *social context*. Social context is a

---

Shirley Jackson Case and Shailer Mathews, see Funk, "Watershed."

2. Robbins, "Social-Scientific Criticism."

3. For a synthetic presentation of how these two schools understood the *Sitz im Leben*, see McKnight, *What Is Form Criticism?*

broader category that includes the structures and processes of the groups and cultures in which these texts were produced.

The reconstruction of this social context also has a complementary function to the method of literary analysis. This method analyzes the text to identify its meaning with the help of various literary procedures (e.g., rhetorical, narrative, and semiotic analysis). This approach presupposes that meaning is contained in the text and can be recovered by analyzing its parts. Complete adherence to this axiom tends to disconnect biblical writings from the vital context in which they were born. In turn, reconstructing their context may contribute to recovering the story's world and the social world of the author and his audience.[4]

The use of the social sciences may contribute to making more explicit the context in which biblical texts were composed, thus helping readers today understand the texts' original meaning. These and other methodological procedures are complementary. The methodological complexity of exegesis is not a threat to but an opportunity for potential Bible interpreters, because engaging with this complexity enables them to understand better the text's original meaning.

The Contribution of the Social Sciences

Contextual analysis relies on some basic observations about how the process of reading works and about the social nature of language. The central role that language, texts, and the act of reading play in the theoretical foundation of this type of analysis constitutes the essential characteristic of its methodology. Whereas prior studies analyzed the context as a reality outside the text, which had no intrinsic connection with it (history, archaeology), this recent exegetical approach assumes that there is an intimate relationship between the texts and their social contexts.

The Reading Process

A text is a particular manifestation of language, which is, primarily, a social phenomenon. Those who have explored this relationship between society

---

4. An example of how this approach may contribute to literary analysis can be seen in Rhoads, *Mark as Story*. In the first edition of this book (1982) the authors proposed a narrative analysis of the Gospel without referring to its context. However, in the second edition (1999) this contextual perspective was included.

and language have concluded that language reflects a social group's view of the world (space and time) and of persons and their relationships, as well as the group's view of social values and institutions. Language is the expression of a shared worldview. Consequently, to understand a particular language and the texts that use it, it is necessary to know the worldview of the language users.

This close relationship between language and society appears even more clearly when we consider the process of reading.[5] According to the traditional view, reading is a process by which a person extracts meaning from a text. However, psychosocial studies have shown that reading is an interactive process in which the reader fills with meaning the words and phrases that he or she finds in the text. In the process of reading, in order to interpret a text, the reader applies to the signs (the words and phrases) found in the text the notions that he or she already has about the world, people, or relationships. The meaning is not in the signs themselves but in the social system. Words are receptacles that the reader fills in the process of reading. When text and reader belong to the same society and share the same worldview, the reader can quickly fill words and phrases with the content intended by the writer. However, when the reader does not belong to the same culture as the writer, the reader will tend to fill the words of the text with meanings these words have in the reader's own culture.[6]

The author of the Gospel of Mark and his audience lived in the same culture and therefore shared the same social system. The fact of sharing the same culture facilitated the communication between them because the meaning of the Markan text was not in its words or sentences but in the social system through which these words or sentences made sense. We modern readers are in a different position. We belong to a different culture, and Mark's words do not have for us the same connotations that they had for Mark's original audience. In the first line of his Life of Jesus, the author informs his readers that the story he is about to tell is a gospel, a εὐαγγέλιον (*euangelion*). For us, this word has rich theological overtones that may differ from those it had for Mark's readers. For them, *euangelion* belonged to the vocabulary of imperial ideology. If we do not know this, we may not understand what Mark intended to communicate to his audience when he used the word.

---

5. Regarding the social nature of language and the process of reading, see Malina, "Reading Theory."

6. Malina, "Reading Theory," 8–12.

Introduction

Between Mark's society and ours there is also another significant difference. Cultures can be classified according to their level of contextualization. Those who live in a culture in which the level of contextualization is high share a considerable quantity of unstated information with others in their mileu, whereas those who belong to a culture in which the level of contextualization is low share much less unstated information with others in their mileu. Consequently, texts produced in the first type of culture (a high-context culture) take for granted much information that their potential readers know. In contrast, texts produced in the second type of culture (a low-context culture) offer many more details, because these texts do not presuppose that their potential readers know the details. The Gospel of Mark was written in a high-context society, and so the text presupposes that its original audience shared much information, which then did not need to be spelled out. From the standpoint of readers in low-context societies, this type of text is very much like an incomplete puzzle. If we want to understand it, we need to recontextualize it.

Social Models

For those belonging to low context societies, reading the Bible requires an effort to place its writings in their original social context. We need to recontextualize the fragments, placing them in their original framework. To that end, we should reconstruct the values and behavior patterns shared by those who belonged to ancient Mediterranean culture.

The social sciences are an invaluable tool to accomplish this task. We can reconstruct small portions of that lost world and describe its most characteristic features thanks to them. The main instruments for carrying out this task are social models. A social model is an abstract representation of the value system and the relationships that govern the life of a group. It is something similar to a map. Just as the map is not the territory, the model is not the real world—but as the map helps us to understand the territory, so the model is a useful tool to understand the real world.[7]

Before explaining how social models may contribute to reconstructing the contexts of biblical texts, it might be helpful to know that these models are of two kinds, depending on their point of view. Models can reflect the perspective of those who belong to the culture in which things take place.

---

7. On social models and their usefulness in reconstructing the scenarios presupposed by biblical texts, see Elliott, *What Is Social-Scientific Criticism?*

But, they can also observe that particular culture from the perspective of someone who does not belong to it and wishes to understand what is happening in more universal terms. Models elaborated from the first point of view we call *emic*, while those developed from the second point of view we name *etic*. This terminology comes from linguistics, where it is used to distinguish the system of sounds proper to the native language (phon*emic*) from the universal system of sounds (phon*etic*).

The Gospel of Mark was written in an advanced agrarian society of the Mediterranean region. Consequently, studies of advanced agrarian societies and traditional Mediterranean societies can be useful to reconstruct its context from an *emic* perspective.[8] On the other hand, studies of modern societies or studies that use a more general approach will be helpful to reconstruct that same context from an *etic* perspective. Among the studies collected in this book the reader will find examples of both approaches. *Emic* and *etic* models contribute to better understanding Mark's narrative. Still, when using these approaches, we should remain aware that this gospel, like any other biblical text, was born in a preindustrial society of the ancient Mediterranean.

Studies of advanced agrarian societies show that industrialization was a historic breakthrough of enormous proportions. The Industrial Revolution gave rise to a new society and marked a clear division between preindustrial and industrialized societies. In advanced agrarian societies of past and present, available resources only allow peasants to produce a small surplus, which the rulers appropriate for their use and distribute among their retainers. This fact explains some of the most characteristic features of this type of society: its rigid social stratification, its members' low degree of specialization, its characteristic tension between cities and countryside, and its underdeveloped economy.[9] Production of goods increased enormously in industrialized societies. At the same time, improvements in the transportation of goods and persons gave rise to more intense trade and greater social mobility. All these changes created a new economic system, which essentially reshaped the entire social map. Readers born in an industrialized society must consider all these changes and make an effort to read

---

8. On agrarian societies, see Lenski, *Power and Privilege*, 189–296; Wolf, *Peasants*; Sjoberg, *Preindustrial City*. On Mediterranean culture, see Peristiany, ed., *Honour and Shame*; Gilmore, ed., *Honor and Shame*; Gilmore, "Anthropology of the Mediterranean."

9. Lenski, *Power and Privilege*, 192–210.

the Gospel of Mark, and the rest of the New Testament, in the context of an agrarian society.

Ancient Mediterranean society was a particular type of agrarian society. Comparative studies have shown that the circum-Mediterranean region is an independent cultural area. The different communities bordering the Mediterranean share a series of similarities not found in other cultures. They have the same ecotype, and their inhabitants have lived for centuries in a continuous interaction through war, trade, and culture. This constant interaction has created a set of values and institutions common to them and different from other cultural areas.[10]

Studies of traditional Mediterranean cultures may be helpful for reconstructing the worldview of biblical texts, because the values and institutions of those traditional societies have not undergone very profound changes. Changes affecting the central values and primary institutions of a culture are very slow. Consequently, social groups not yet affected by industrialization may still preserve some of the characteristic features of Mediterranean culture in the first century.[11]

Reading Scenarios

Social models are the starting point and the primary instrument for reconstructing the reading scenarios presupposed by texts. A reading scenario is an abstract representation of a discrete portion of social life. The image comes from the theater, where the scenario sets the context for action and dialogue. In the script of a play, the scenario does not belong to the text but is sketched out in sometimes random introductory notes, which the play's director must adapt. Texts also presuppose a social scenario. When a text is read, the reader or listener spontaneously reconstructs it. Still, when we read ancient texts or texts from another culture, this reconstruction must consider that our social context is different from that in which these texts originated. Therefore, if we want to understand them on their own terms, we need to reconstruct the scenarios they presuppose.

The reconstruction of a reading scenario begins with the selection of an appropriate model. This model will provide an initial representation of one aspect of social life, which should be refined later. The model is adequate when it contributes to explaining the phenomena or the situations

10. Gilmore, "Anthropology of the Mediterranean, 178–79.
11. Malina and Neyrey, "First-Century Personality," 69–72.

about which the text speaks (when the reading scenario has explanatory capacity), and when it allows us to discover aspects of the text and its world that are not evident at first sight (when the reading scenario has heuristic potential). To possess these two qualities, the reading scenario must be elaborated from studies of societies similar to the society presupposed by the text.

Once the pertinent model is identified, we can use it to reconstruct the particular portion of the social life presupposed in the text we want to read. The result will be a first draft of the reading scenario, which we can use to determine the meaning of that particular text in its original context. We may also confront this initial reading scenario with other texts or data contemporary with it. This confrontation has a double objective: it serves to test the pertinence and utility of the models selected and, at the same time, contributes to improving the reading scenario by adjusting it to the concrete situation presupposed by the text.[12] If possible, it might be helpful to confront the model with data external to the text since that helps to reduce the risk of circularity—that is, the risk of constructing a scenario from a text to explain, then, with this scenario, that same text.

This validating process can be repeated until the resulting scenario is refined. This scenario will facilitate reading the text in a social context close to that in which it originated, and recovering the meaning it originally had. So the contextual analysis contributes to explaining the meaning of the text in its original context.[13]

Theme and Content of This Book

The studies collected in this book provide some examples of how the use of models from the social sciences can contribute to a more accurate and considerate reading of the Gospel of Mark. They are revised and updated versions of papers previously published. I have collected them in this book because I am convinced that they can offer some clues to understanding particular aspects of the Gospel of Mark and show the advantages of using appropriate reading scenarios. As will become apparent to the attentive reader, I resort in them to *emic* and *etic* models, sometimes combining both

---

12. This confrontation is realized with the help of the logical process known as *abduction*, which has as its source successive confirmations of an initial hypothesis; see Douven, "Abduction."

13. Neyrey, ed., *Social World of Luke–Acts*; Neyrey and Stewart, eds., *Social World of the New Testament*.

Introduction

types of social models to understand a particular text. I adopt this eclectic approach because I think that exegetical methodology is instrumental, and therefore should serve the purpose of exegesis, which is explaining the original meaning of the text.

The studies are arranged following the sequence of Mark's narrative, but the reader can choose to read them in a different order because each chapter is complete and self-contained. Nonetheless, reading them in the order in which they have been arranged is also a good choice. In any case, I offer here a brief presentation so that the reader can make up his/her mind on how to proceed.

The first chapter has an introductory character. It intends to inform the reader how I understand the compositional process of Mark's Gospel and its historical location.[14] Some aspects, such as the critical role played by the pre-Markan passion narrative, the choice of the biographical genre, and the historical location of the Gospel, lay the foundation for discussion in the following chapters. Hence, it would be advisable to start with this chapter.

The second chapter deals with a particular aspect of Mark's literary genre.[15] In this sense, it complements the previous chapter because it concentrates on the main objection presented to the biographical hypothesis, namely, that the Gospel does not begin narrating the infancy of the protagonist as Hellenistic biographies usually did. This objection to the hypothesis that the Gospel of Mark is a biography has not yet been answered adequately, and I think the reading scenario proposed in this chapter can explain this fact.

The third chapter is unique in this collection because it does not study a Markan text. Instead, its purpose is to reconstruct a collection of controversies used by the evangelist in the composition of his Life of Jesus.[16] I finally decided to include this chapter for two reasons. The first is that it makes present in the book the complex history of the traditions behind Mark's Gospel. The second is that this Galilean collection connects us with the group of Jesus believers who elaborated and transmitted those traditions.

Chapter 4 can be read in connection with Chapter 2 because both of them explore different aspects of Jesus' baptism. This study focuses on

---

14. The first four paragraphs are a revised version of Guijarro, "Composición del evangelio de Marcos." The last paragraph on the historical location of the Gospel is from Guijarro, "Cultural Trauma," 141–46.

15. Originally published as Guijarro, "Why Does the Gospel."

16. Originally published as Guijarro, "First Disciples."

Jesus' vision in that passage and in the transfiguration story.[17] It combines recent *etic* studies on the visual process with the *emic* understanding of the eyes and the visual in traditional Mediterranean societies to construct a reading scenario that helps understand the complexity and significance of visions in the Gospel of Mark.

Chapter 5 goes a step further on the path opened by the previous, in order to grasp the meaning of some unfamiliar aspects of Mark's narrative. If the previous chapter introduces the reader to the world of visions, this one aims at providing readers with adequate lenses to understand Jesus' healings.[18] The way critical exegesis has explained these stories reveals that modern Western readers do not have the appropriate conceptual framework to understand them. Resourcing to medical anthropology, this chapter intends to provide such a conceptual framework.

Chapter 6 concentrates on one momentous event in Mark's narrative: Jesus anointing in Bethany. This is the only place in the whole gospel where Jesus commands those present in the story and those reading or hearing it to remember something.[19] This command invites the reader to consider what is being narrated in the story. Nevertheless, if the reader does not have the right clues, he or she will not be able to grasp the message implied in the woman's action. Once more, having an adequate reading scenario may help to retrieve meanings presupposed in a text produced in a high-context society.

Finally, Chapter 7 proposes reading the last part of Mark's narrative in a scenario that combines historical information about Mark's audience with a social model elaborated to understand how groups deal with the experience of trauma.[20] From a different point of view, the reading proposed in Chapter 7 confirms some of the aspects of Mark's Gospel presented in the first chapter, such as the centrality of the passion narrative in the composition of the Gospel and the importance of contextualizing Mark's Gospel in the aftermath of the Jewish War. Chapter 7 also contributes to explaining the role of the Olivet Discourse (Mark 13) in the Gospel of Mark.

A brief conclusion will illustrate how contextual exegesis can contribute to a better understanding of Mark's Gospel and other biblical texts.

---

17. Originally published as Guijarro, "Visions of Jesus."
18. Originally published as Guijarro, "Healing Stories."
19. Originally published as Guijarro and Rodríguez, "'Messianic' Anointing."
20. Originally published as Guijarro, "Cultural Trauma."

CHAPTER 1

The Composition of Mark's Gospel

Introduction

RESEARCH ON THE GOSPEL of Mark has rightly emphasized the distinctiveness of the passion narrative (Mark 14–16) compared to the rest of the work (Mark 1–13). The differences between these two parts of the gospel are literary and theological. From the literary point of view, the passion narrative has a very concrete setting, a clear chronological framework, a well-balanced plot, and well-defined characters. However, in the earlier part of the Gospel, the geographical and chronological context is more generic, the plot is more diffuse, and the characters less consistent. From the theological point of view, the image of Jesus as the suffering Messiah, which appears progressively in the first part of the narrative, comes to the foreground in the passion story.[1]

The narrative consistency of the passion story suggests that Mark used a passion narrative that circulated in the groups of Jesus believers.[2] Although the canonical Gospel of John and the apocryphal Gospel of Peter report versions of this ancient narrative, scholarly consensus has coalesced around no single reconstruction of it.[3] Despite that, a detailed redactional

---

1. Trocmé, *Passion as Liturgy*, 7–13; Collins, *Beginning of the Gospel*, 100–102.

2. Some authors still contend that the passion narrative is the work of Mark: Linnemann, *Studien zur Passionsgeschichte*; Kelber, "Conclusion."

3. Crossan finds in the Gospel of Peter the oldest version of this story, the so-called Gospel of the Cross. See Crossan, *The Cross that Spoke*. His thesis has been widely contested; see Green, "Gospel of Peter"; and Brown, *Death of the Messiah*, 1332–36.

analysis of the last chapters of Mark allows us to reconstruct the pre-Markan passion narrative.[4]

This reconstruction of the pre-Markan passion narrative can help explain the Gospel's composition because many of the redactional changes introduced by the evangelist are intended to link it with earlier chapters. This observation raises the question of whether in Mark 1–13 there are references to the passion designed to merge both parts. Rhetorically, the redactional changes in Mark 1–13 would function to anticipate (*prolepsis*) some critical aspects of the passion narrative, while the changes in Mark 14–16 would recall (*analepsis*) some aspects of Jesus' activity. These changes would contribute to render the whole story more coherent.

This observation is the starting point of the thesis about the composition of Mark presented in this chapter. My thesis will reveal both Mark's literary originality and its theological import. This chapter will also set the stage for a discussion of the date and location of the Gospel's composition.

Editorial Changes in Mark 14–16

The changes introduced by Mark into the traditional passion story are of three types. First, he added some editorial seams to link independent traditions (Mark 14:1–2, 12, 32). Second, he introduced small additions to some episodes of the traditional story (Mark 14:28, 43, 55b, 61b–62, 72b; 15:10, 21, 22b, 27, 31–32, 39, 40–41, 42b, 43b; 16:7–8). Third, he incorporated into the traditional passion narrative some independent traditions (Mark 14:3–9, 10–12, 22–25, 32–42, 51–52; 15:16–20a).[5] Most of these editorial modifications introduce certain themes characteristic of Mark 1–13 into the passion narrative.

Two additions are clearly intended to link the passion of Jesus with the previous chapters. The first is the promise of seeing him in Galilee after the resurrection (Mark 14:28). The second evokes this same promise in the empty tomb scene (Mark 16:7). Both verses are redactional and break the sequence of the traditional scene.[6] They are relevant because the setting of Jesus' public activity in Galilee is one of the characteristic features of Mark's Gospel. Mark mentions this region in the summaries and editorial seams

---

4. Soards, "Appendix IX."

5. For a fuller discussion of Mark's redactional additions to the traditional passion narrative, see Guijarro, *Jesús y sus primeros discípulos*, 169–87.

6. Marxsen, *Mark the Evangelist*, 70–85.

that provide a uniform geographical framework for traditions that initially did not have such a precise setting.[7] These two mentions of Galilee in the passion narrative serve to unite the first thirteen chapters and the passion narrative.

Mark has pursued this same goal by introducing the scribes into the passion narrative. In their five appearances, they show up together with the chief priests (Mark 14:1, 43, 53; 15:1, 31). The mention of the scribes in 15:1 and 15:31 is evidently redactional. In Mark 14:1, they are mentioned in an editorial summary. In the scene where Jesus' appears before the high priest, the allusion to them is also secondary (Mark 14:53b), as later, only the high priest and the chief priests are mentioned, but not the scribes (Mark 14:55, 60, 63). It is therefore reasonable to think that the mention of the scribes in Mark 14:43 is also redactional and that the pre-Markan passion narrative did not contain any references to the scribes.[8] Still, the scribes are, together with the Pharisees, the main adversaries of Jesus during his public activity (Mark 2:6, 16; 3:22; 7:1, 5). Their mention in the passion narrative evokes the opposition to Jesus during his activity in Galilee, and thus links his passion and that activity.

Editorial changes are another means of linking both parts of the narrative. Some of these involve the disciples. The traditional story casts the disciples in a negative light: the Twelve abandon Jesus (Mark 14:27, 50), Judas betrays him (Mark 14:20–21, 43, 46), and Peter denies him (Mark 14:30, 66–72). Mark intensifies this negative characterization, thus making the passion story the climax of a process of misunderstanding that begins much earlier, in the loaves section (Mark 6:52; 8:14–21), and increases with the announcements of the passion (Mark 8:32; 9:33–34; 10:35–40).[9] In the opening scene of the passion narrative, the disciples are unable to understand the meaning of Jesus' approaching death (Mark 14:3–10), while Judas, one of the Twelve, conspires with the chief priests to hand him over (Mark 14:11–12). In the same way, the account of the prayer in Gethsemane, which was not part of the traditional account (Mark 14:32–42), underlines their incapacity to remain with Jesus in his trials.[10]

---

7. Mark 1:14, 16, 28, 39, etc.; see Marxsen, *Mark the Evangelist*, 52–61.

8. Sanders, *Jesus and Judaism*, 309–17.

9. Campbell, "Why Do You Abandon Me?," 105–10.

10. The protagonists of this episode are the three disciples who accompany Jesus on other special occasions during his ministry (Mark 5:37; 9:2). By mentioning these three disciples, Mark relates the scene of Gethsemane to the preceding ones and the passion of Jesus to his public activity.

The Gospel of Mark in Context

In contrast to the Twelve and their failure, Mark presents a series of secondary characters who behave as faithful disciples.[11] These characters begin to appear already in Mark 1–13,[12] but in the passion story, they are more visible. Their attitude toward Jesus contrasts with his disciples' abandonment, betrayal, and denial at this decisive moment. The woman who anoints Jesus in Simon's house does so in anticipation of his burial (Mark 14:8). Simon of Cyrene takes upon himself the cross of Jesus (Mark 15:21). The centurion confesses Jesus to be the Son of God (Mark 15:39). Joseph of Arimathea, a member of the Sanhedrin, asks Pilate for Jesus' body (Mark 15:42–47). Finally, a small group of women witnesses his burial and goes to his tomb (Mark 15:40–41; 16:1–8). The attitudes of these secondary characters recall Jesus' teaching about discipleship: taking up the cross (Mark 8:34) or serving (Mark 9:35; 10:43, 45). Mark introduces most of these secondary characters in the passion story, portraying them as exemplary disciples (Mark 15:40–41, 43b). This presentation of the secondary characters shows his interest in giving continuity to a paradox that begins during Jesus' ministry: his close disciples abandon him while others follow him.[13]

Finally, the most relevant modifications are those that Mark introduces in his characterization of Jesus. In the traditional passion narrative, Jesus is acclaimed as "Son of Man" (Mark 14:21) and "King of the Jews" (Mark 15:2, 9, 12). Mark, however, introduces other titles used in earlier chapters to identify Jesus: "Master" (Mark 14:14 = 4:38; 5:35; 10:17; 12:14, 19, 32); "Rabbi" (Mark 14:45 = 9:5; 11:21), and above all the title that summarizes his Christology: "Messiah Son of God." This title appears in a strategic passage: the process before the Sanhedrin. Jesus is accused of having announced the temple's destruction (Mark 14:57–58), but he does not respond. Then, the High Priest asks him about his identity: "Are you the Messiah Son of the Blessed One?" (Mark 14:61). This question is not related to the previous accusation but makes sense in the context of the evangelist's presentation of Jesus in the preceding chapters.[14] Moreover, this question and Jesus' answer constitute the culmination of the long and enigmatic

---

11. Malbon, *In the Company of Jesus*, 189–225.

12. Peter's mother-in-law (Mark 1:29–31); the demon-possessed man of Gerasa (Mark 5:18–20); the Syrophoenician woman (Mark 7:24–30); the blind man Bartimaeus (Mark 10:46–52); and the widow (Mark 12:41–44).

13. On the characterization of the disciples see Tannehill, "Disciples in Mark," 134–57; see also Malbon, *In the Company of Jesus*, 41–69.

14. Perrin, "High Priest's Question."

presentation articulated around the so-called Messianic secret.[15] Jesus' identification with the "Son of the Blessed One" (Mark 14:61b) is closely related to the centurion's affirmation that recognizes Jesus as "Son of God" (Mark 15:39). Again, this scene is a significant addition to the traditional passion narrative, which constitutes, together with the preceding one, the climax of Jesus' presentation. Mark interweaves his presentation of Jesus during his public ministry with the revelation of his identity in the passion.

From the above analysis, we may conclude that Mark intended to link the passion story with the preceding chapters. He edited the traditional passion narrative, adding some minor details such as the references to Galilee and the mentions of the scribes. However, his editorial work can be seen even more clearly in the way he continues to present Jesus and the disciples, so that the revelation of true discipleship and of Jesus' true identity takes place precisely in this last part of the narrative.

Allusions to the Passion in Mark 1-13

In close correspondence with the editorial modifications introduced by the evangelist in the final part of the narrative, several allusions anticipate and announce Jesus' passion in the chapters that narrate Jesus' activity.

The first explicit reference to the future passion of Jesus appears at the conclusion of the Galilean controversies (Mark 2:1—3:6). The concluding verse is an editorial addition: "The Pharisees went out and immediately conspired with the Herodians against him, how to destroy him." The decision to kill Jesus is not a consequence of the preceding discussion. Still, it anticipates Jesus' passion (Mark 3:6 = Mark 15:1). This anticipation has been hinted at in the preceding controversies by two subtle allusions: one names the reason for Jesus' eventual condemnation ("He blasphemes" [Mark 2:7 = Mark 14:29]), and another (from Jesus' own mouth) points to his coming death ("when the bridegroom is taken away from them" [Mark 2:20]).

The second group of allusions to the future passion of Jesus is to be found in the so-called passion announcements (Mark 8:31–32; 9:31; 10:33–34). While these announcements are very similar in content, the third, which is the most detailed, reproduces the plot of the passion story point by point: "He will be delivered to the chief priests" (Mark 14:10.

---

15. This question tries to define Jesus' messianism by excluding other ways of understanding it: Marcus, "Mark 14:61."

43–50); "they will condemn him" (Mark 14:53–65); "they will hand him over to the Gentiles" (Mark 15:1–5); "they will mock him . . . they will spit on him . . . they will scourge him" (Mark 15:15–20); "they will kill him" (Mark 15:21–32); "he will rise again" (Mark 16:1–8). The best explanation for this phenomenon is that the author of Mark's Gospel composed the third passion announcement with the passion narrative in mind, in order to link the public activity of Jesus with it.

In the context of these predictions, there are also other references to Jesus' death. After his transfiguration, Jesus asks his disciples not to tell anyone what they have seen "until the Son of Man has risen from the dead" (Mark 9:10). This injunction is part of an exchange that has little to do with the preceding account of the transfiguration (Mark 9:11–13) and therefore should be attributed to the evangelist's editorial work. Likewise, after the third passion announcement, Jesus asks James and John, "Are you able to drink the cup that I am about to drink and be baptized with the baptism with which I am about to be baptized?" (Mark 10:38). This sentence alludes to Jesus' future death, and the consequences it will have for the disciples. Finally, in the words addressed to the disciples after the request of the James and John, Mark introduces a saying of Jesus that underlines the salvific value of his death (Mark 10:45), thereby reinforcing the allusions to the passion within this section of the Gospel.

There are also two allusions to his passion in the context of Jesus' activity in Jerusalem (Mark 11–13). The first establishes a close relationship between the inevitability of Jesus' eventual passion and death and his temple activity: "The scribes and the chief priests heard him and sought how they could kill him" (Mark 11:18 = 14:1). The second allusion, the parable of the wicked tenants, announces the connection between angry authorities and Jesus: "They killed him and threw him out of the vineyard" (Mark 12:8). These references to Jesus' impending death appear in the context of the controversies triggered by his activity in the temple (Mark 11:27—12:40). In this way, Mark relates the opposition to Jesus' teaching and activity with the immediate cause of his passion, merging the perspectives of the traditions he wished to combine (i.e., the traditions about Jesus' teaching and healing on the one hand, and the traditions about Jesus' passion and death on the other hand).

In addition to these explicit anticipations of Jesus' death, other allusions bind together both parts of the gospel narrative. Some have to do with the figure of John the Baptist, whose arrest and death anticipate the passion of Jesus, as three editorial passages show (Mark 1:14; 6:17–29; 9:11–13). These editorial changes describe John's arrest and death in terms of Jesus' passion.[16] As Jesus' forerunner, John announces the destiny of Jesus. In this way, the evangelist not only prepares readers for the passion narrative but also links Jesus' activity (Mark 1–13) with his passion (Mark 14–16).

Some editorial changes or additions in respect to the disciples also help unify both parts of the narrative. Judas Iscariot is introduced as "the one who handed him over" (Mark 3:19, my translation), thereby anticipating Jesus' arrest, where Mark describes him as "the one who handed him over" (Mark 14:44, my translation). On the other hand, by identifying the seed falling among the rocks with those who "when tribulation and persecution come upon them because of the word, . . . are immediately scandalized" (Mark 4:17, my translation), Mark anticipates the reaction of the disciples in the passion (see Mark 14:27. 29. 50). The disciples' lack of understanding after Jesus' three predictions also anticipates the reactions of the Twelve in the passion narrative. After the first announcement, Peter "rebukes" Jesus, urging him not to follow the way of the cross (Mark 8:32b). After the second, the disciples begin discussing who is the greatest (Mark 9:33), and after the third, James and John seek a place of honor in his kingdom (Mark 10:35–40). This manifest incomprehension (Mark 9:32) prefigures the complete failure of the disciples at the moment of the passion, which Mark underlines, as we have seen above.

This analysis of allusions to the passion in Mark 1–13 corroborates our conclusion in studying the editorial changes in Mark 14–16. The references to the plot against Jesus and to his future passion and death, as well as the particular presentation of John the Baptist, and the passages in which the fates of both, John and Jesus, are related to the ultimate fate of the disciples, are indications of Mark's editorial work. Allusions to the passion narrative in Mark 1–13 prepare readers for the decisive moment of the drama it narrates (in chapters 14–16).

The Composition of Mark's Gospel

The preceding analysis argues that the author of Mark's Gospel sought to relate the account of Jesus' public activity to a preexisting narrative of Jesus' passion. This observation offers an interesting clue in investigating

16. On the editorial aspects of the Baptist's presentation, see Marxsen, *Mark the Evangelist*, 27–40.

the composition process of this gospel. The most common explanation of this process assumes that Mark used fluid traditions, along with some collections of controversies, miracles, parables, and instructions, in addition to a traditional passion story, to create a more developed narrative about Jesus.[17] The existence of a traditional passion story is also the starting point for the explanation I propose. Still, before presenting my proposal, it would be appropriate to mention other possible explanations. I mention two that represent the extremes on a spectrum which allows for a number of more nuanced explanations.

Etienne Trocmé proposes the first explanation. Although his study on the formation of Mark's Gospel had limited reception, the results of the analysis on the relationships of Mark 1–13 and Mark 14–16, and other studies on the literary arrangement of Mark 1–13, invite us to look at his proposal again. According to Trocmé, there were two editions of the Gospel of Mark. The first one included only the first thirteen chapters, while the second was an enlarged edition that contained the passion narrative. The task of Mark's final editor would have consisted of combining these two compositions.[18]

Trocmé's main argument for postulating the existence of a first edition of Mark containing only Mark 1–13 relies on a comparison with the other two Synoptic Gospels. This comparison shows that while Matthew follows Mark closely throughout the story, Luke separates from him in the passion narrative. The word agreements of Luke with Mark, which in the rest of the Gospel are approximately 50 percent, go down to 27 percent in the passion narrative. The best explanation for this fact is, according to Trocmé, that the version of Mark used by Luke did not contain a passion narrative. Trocmé's hypothesis is confirmed if we examine the relationships between Mark 1–13 and Mark 14–16. In Mark, the passion narrative is so different from the remainder of the Gospel that it can be considered a *disturbing appendix*, which the author of the second edition would have tried to connect to the longer story by inserting into that longer story (Mark 1–13) some geographical references that are absent in Luke.[19]

Some observations of Jens Schröter about the structural similarities between Mark 1–13 and the Q Document support Trocmé's thesis. Schröter has noted that the narrative structure of Q coincides with that of Mark

---

17. Marcus, *Mark 1–8*, 56–69.
18. Trocmé, *Formation de l'Évangile* [ET = *Formation of the Gospel*].
19. Trocmé, *Formation de l'Évangile*, 169–203.

1–13. Both compositions begin with the presentation of the Baptist, followed by Jesus' baptism and temptations (Q 3:2b—4:14 = Mark 1:1–13), and both conclude with the announcement of the coming of the Son of Man (Q 17:23—22:30 = Mark 13).[20] The fact that there was another contemporary composition, called Q, with the same narrative pattern as Mark 1–13 supports the hypothesis of a first edition of Mark containing only the first thirteen chapters.

This explanation of Markan formation, attractive as it is in light of Schröter's observations, has, however, a weakness that makes it implausible. As the above discussion has shown, the task of the author of the Gospel did not consist of joining two preexisting literary blocks but of composing a narrative of Jesus' public activity, and of joining that composition to a preexisting passion story, which he also modified in order to make it the conclusion of his story.

At the other end of the spectrum from this position, we find the position of Werner Kelber.[21] He contends that the gospel author is responsible for the composition of the entire work, including the passion narrative. In three theses, Kelber summarizes the results of the studies gathered in the volume edited by him:[22] (a) the main Markan themes and also many of the secondary ones converge in Mark 14–16; (b) this means that Mark 14–16 is a theologically inseparable and homogeneous part of the Gospel as a whole; (c) therefore, it is necessary to question the traditional thesis of a pre-Markan passion narrative.

From these three conclusions, we can deduce three other theses about the composition of the Gospel: (a) there are no significant differences between Mark 14–16 and Mark 1–13, and therefore what we know about the literary genesis and composition of Mark 1–13 may be applied to Mark 14–16; (b) no pre-Markan tradition has exercised a decisive influence in the composition of Mark; (c) Mark's literary achievement consisted in composing what he calls "the gospel" from multiple and diverse units of tradition.

As Larry Hurtado and others have shown, Kelber's explanation of Mark's composition process and our three deductions above do not explain why the evangelist has preserved some traditions that are at variance with

---

20. Although Schröter's purpose was not to explain the composition process of Mark, his observations reveal the existence of a traditional pattern shared by Q and Mark 1–13: Schröter, *Erinnerung an Jesu Worte*, 436–58. For a reconstruction of the content and the order of the Q Document, see Robinson et al. eds, *Critical Edition of Q*.

21. Kelber, "Conclusion."

22. See Kelber, ed., *Passion in Mark*.

his theological vision. On the other hand, Trocmé's redactional analysis of the Gospel and Schröter's observations about Mark's relationship with Q reveal that those traditions were adapted to the situation and interests of the author and recipients of Mark's Gospel. Therefore, the Gospel of Mark is not, at least from a literary point of view, a *revolutionary* document, but an *evolutionary* composition: that is, a narrative that followed a path already open.[23]

The explanation I have proposed, namely, that Mark composed the first thirteen chapters from independent traditions in order to complement a preexistent passion narrative, falls somewhere between these two extremes.[24] It acknowledges the existence of pre-Markan compositions, ascribing to the final writer the task of editing them to compose an original work. In this respect my proposal does not differ from the prevailing view. However, the redactional analysis presented in the previous pages emphasizes two elements that render my proposal more precise. First, my proposal attributes to the pre-Markan passion story a decisive role in the composition of the Gospel. Second, it argues that Mark used a previously existing temporal pattern to shape the traditions of Jesus' public activity. The evangelist's task consisted of assembling the passion story with the traditions gathered in the preceding chapters to compose a new work. This process explains the differences elaborated in the analysis of the two literary blocks of Mark. In Mark 1–13, the editorial work integrated various traditions and collections to construct a narrative with a geographical and temporal framework, consistent characters, and a narrative plot. In Mark 14–16, however, the evangelist's writing activity did not entail articulating a story based on previous traditions but in rewriting an already existing narrative.

Mark's Literary Genre and Its Implications

The result of the editorial work carried out by Mark is a coherent narrative, which derives its character from its literary and theological point of view. In recent years, narrative studies on Mark have shown convincingly that this

---

23. Hurtado, "Gospel of Mark."

24. This proposal is in agreement with the much-quoted sentence of Martin Kähler, who more than a century ago suggested that the Gospels could be described as "passion narratives with detailed introductions" (Kähler, *Sogenannte historische Jesus*, 60).

gospel is what might be termed a good story.²⁵ The process that produced this new formulation of the traditions about Jesus entailed creating a new narrative and, more precisely, composing a biography of Jesus. Creating a narrative implied integrating into a coherent story traditions that originally had diverse forms. A miracle story or even an anecdote already had a basic narrative structure, but these were not stories. The inclusion of these small, independent traditions within a larger setting to form a plot in which events were linked together and characters were better defined produced a developed story. On the other hand, composing a biography implied articulating such a story according to a specific literary genre pattern—Greco-Roman biography, or *bios*.

As far as we know, the author of Mark's Gospel was the first to create a comprehensive narrative about Jesus. Before Mark, traditions about him had been assembled into collections of similar literary units (miracles, controversies, parables) or into more complex collections of sayings and teachings.²⁶ In this context, the passion narrative was a remarkable exception, and the importance that Mark accorded to it invites us to consider the possibility that it may have served as a model for the composition of his gospel. In the passion narrative we already find an initial portrayal of the characters, which Mark expanded and developed. An example of this is the presentation of the disciples. In the passion narrative there was already a negative characterization of the Twelve. Mark developed it by editing the individual traditions included in Mark 1–13 and reworking the traditional passion narrative. In this way, starting from an initial portrayal, he constructed a complex collective character. The traditional passion story also had a narrative plot, which Mark took as a model for articulating independent traditions in the first part of his narrative (Mark 1–13).

In composing his narrative (*diēgēsis*), Mark followed the directions given by contemporary rhetoricians. He intended to produce a particular type of narrative, a biography, which the Greek called *bios* and the Latin *vita*. Ancient biographies were short stories. They generally consisted of a succession of anecdotes that revealed the moral character of the protagonist, and usually covered three periods of the protagonist's life: his birth and

---

25. Rhoads et al., *Mark as Story*; Dewey, "Survival of Mark's Gospel."

26. Some of these collections were incorporated by Mark into his gospel and are easily identifiable: controversies (Mark 2:1—3:6; 11:15—12:40), parables (Mark 4:1–34), and miracles (Mark 4:35—5:43; 6:45—8:10); see Kuhn, *Ältere Sammlungen*.

education (noble origins), his public activity (noble actions), and the end of his life (noble death).[27]

Mark's Gospel was the first Christian writing to follow the pattern of ancient biographies.[28] Although this tendency to shape the tradition about Jesus in biographical form is already visible in the Q Document, which includes numerous anecdotes about him, that composition was only an embryonic form of biography.[29] However, by linking the passion story with the traditions of Jesus' public activity, Mark composed the first comprehensive biography of Jesus.

In the Q Document, as in Mark 1–13, Jesus' activity is placed between John's preaching, announcing the "coming one" (Q 3:7–9. 16b–17 = Mark 1:2–7), and Jesus' final discourse, which announces the coming of the Son of Man (Q 17:23—22:30 = Mark 13). Mark uses this pattern, but he adapts his story to the pattern of the *bios* by incorporating the passion narrative with its emphasis on the protagonist's death. By including the passion in his narrative about Jesus, the evangelist modified the traditional outline that places Jesus' activity between the two comings (Mark 1–13) and articulated his story according to the biographical pattern, which emphasized the importance of Jesus' death (Mark 1–16). This change signaled a decisive step in adapting Jesus' traditions to ancient biographies since one of their most characteristic traits was narrating the story of the protagonist's death.[30]

The incorporation of the passion story introduced an essential change in the way Jesus' public activity was understood. This activity was transferred from an eschatological framework to a historical one. Within the tripartite pattern of ancient biographies, Jesus' public activity is set in the context of his life. This new outline breaks the continuity between the first coming and second coming of Jesus, thus creating a new framework to preserve his words and deeds as historical events. With the introduction of the biographical outline, the words and actions of the earthly Jesus were placed in the past. This fact, in turn, gave rise to the category of memory as the

---

27. The reference work on the biographical genre of the Gospels is Burridge, *What are the Gospels?* On the three parts of ancient biographies see Frickenschmidt, *Evangelium als Biographie*, 240-350.

28. Keith, *Gospel as Manuscript*, 73–99.

29. Downing, "Genre for Q."

30. Frickenschmidt, *Evangelium als Biographie*, 303–50.

recollection of a significant past. This category, which was not so crucial in the Q Document, is central to the biography of Jesus composed by Mark.[31]

The composition of Mark's Gospel was a decisive step in adapting Jesus tradition to the model of ancient biography. The result, however, was limited. Some years later, Matthew and Luke saw the need to adjust Mark's Life of Jesus to the prevailing model of ancient biographies. It is not by chance that both included an account of Jesus' childhood (infancy narratives) and expanded the events after his death (resurrection stories).[32] The most important of the two biographical elements added to Mark's biography of Jesus by Matthew and Luke was the first (infancy narratives). As stated above, ancient biographies usually began narrating the birth and education of the protagonist. In so doing, they intended to show that he came from an honorable lineage, that he was born in a famous place, and that he had received an adequate education. However, Mark's Gospel introduces an adult Jesus, who comes from Galilee to the Jordan to be baptized by John (Mark 1:9). We cannot presume that Mark began his story this way because he lacked information about Jesus' origin, for Mark knew well that Jesus was from a Galilean village called Nazareth (Mark 1:9; 14:70). He also knew Jesus' mother's and brothers' names (Mark 6:3). Consequently, Mark could have started his Life of Jesus by mentioning all this. Still, Mark began his story narrating the activity of an adult Jesus because he knew that the primary purpose of the beginning of a biography was to inform the audience about the protagonist's honor, and the information he had about Jesus' origins did not highlight his honor. As I will try to show in the next chapter, Mark chose a different path for revealing, at the beginning of his biography, Jesus' honorable origins.

These observations confirm that the editorial work carried out by Mark to link the story of Jesus' activity (Mark 1–13) with the story of his passion (Mark 14–16) not only intended to give greater literary unity to his narrative. Mark's editing also helped to present the traditions of Jesus using a new literary pattern. Therefore we can conclude that Mark composed a *bios*, an ancient biography, about Jesus, and that Mark did so taking the traditional passion narrative as the starting point and model for his undertaking.

---

31. This different perspective explains why narrative material dominates in Mark, while Q contains mostly discursive material. Jacobson, *First Gospel*, 62–67.

32. Frickenschmidt, *Evangelium als Biographie*, 460–97. Keith, *Gospel as Manuscript*, 100–130.

Mark's literary achievement had a theological relevance that should be stressed. In the previous stages of tradition, the focus was on the teachings and actions of Jesus. At that initial stage, gospel tradition was similar to rabbinic tradition. However, when those memories about Jesus were included in the framework of a biographical narrative, interest focused on Jesus himself. This is not to say that previous tradition was not interested in Jesus. However, the adoption of the literary genre of ancient biography (*bios*) introduced a change decisive in the development of Christology.[33] The primary purpose of ancient biographies was to praise the honor of their protagonists. What mattered were not the actions or teachings but the moral qualities and honor of the protagonist. For that reason, the characterization of the protagonist was very important. The adoption of this literary genre brought with it a significant theological turn that implied a higher concentration on Jesus. Jesus himself, the enigma of his person, which Mark tries to decipher through a progressive revelation of his identity, appeared then in new light: Jesus was not only the author of prodigious teachings and actions (Mark 1–13), or the martyr who suffered unjustly (Mark 14–16), but the Son of God (Mark 1–16).

The Time and Place of Composition

The composition of Mark's Gospel as described above took place in a specific rhetorical situation. A rhetorical situation may be defined as "the set of related factors whose interaction create and control a discourse." The related factors that configure a rhetorical situation are three: exigence, audience, and constraints. Exigence refers to "some kind of need or problem that can be addressed and solved through rhetorical discourse." Audience refers to "those who can help resolve the exigence." Finally, constraints are contextual factors (e.g., persons, events, situations) that affect the achievement of the rhetorical discourse.[34] The following discussion of the time and place of composition of Mark's Gospel intends to explore some aspects of the situation that generated and controlled its discourse.

Traditional wisdom holds that the Gospel of Mark was composed in Rome in the second half of the first century. The identification of this location is based on information that Eusebius supplies in the fourth century, claiming to have received it from Papias, the bishop of Hierapolis, who had

---

33. Burridge, "Gospel Genre."
34. Grant-Davie, "Rhetorical Situations," 265–66.

lived in the first half of the second century. According to Eusebius, Mark was the secretary or interpreter of Peter and wrote down his memories of Jesus (*Ecclesiastical History* 3:39,15). Papias does not say that this happened in Rome, but the fact that 1 Pet 5:13 seems to locate both Peter and Mark in the empire's capital suggests the connection. The critical study of the Gospel of Mark has provided additional internal data to support this external evidence, which favors a Roman origin. Critics find support for this hypothesis in Mark's use of some Latinisms (Mark 12:42; 15:16), in the fact that he has to explain a Jewish custom (Mark 7:3–4), and in the atmosphere of hardship, which could reflect the persecution of Emperor Nero, narrated by the Roman historian Tacitus (*Annales* 15.44.2–3).[35]

Still, in recent decades, scholars have uncovered a particular apologetic bias implied in relating Mark's Gospel with Peter and Rome.[36] They have also noticed the limited value of the internal data adduced in favor of this connection. This critique of the traditional view has given way to another proposal that locates the composition of Mark near Palestine, in the region of Syria. This proposal, which was until recently the opinion of a minority, has been reinforced with solid arguments and is worthy of serious consideration.

The main arguments in favor of the Syrian location of the Gospel of Mark were presented by Gerd Theissen and Joel Marcus thirty years ago.[37] Both authors independently arrived at the conclusion that the Jewish War and its impact on the regions near Palestine was the life context of the Gospel's composition. In the following years, other authors have corroborated this conclusion with new data and created a new consensus. This consensus underlines, above all, the close connection between the story of Mark and the Jewish War, even if the exact identification of the place of composition is still a matter of debate. Nevertheless, most authors who relate the Gospel

---

35. For the arguments in favor of a Roman origin, see Hengel, *Studies in the Gospel of Mark*, 1–30; Incigneri, *Gospel to the Romans*. Recently Shaw, "Myth of the Neronian Persecution," has cast serious doubt on the very existence of the Neronian persecution.

36. It is no coincidence that the connection between Peter and the city of Rome was established at the beginning of the second century, that is, when Christian communities were debating about which Jesus books contained the true gospel and when some of the books received the titles that conferred them apostolic authority; see Hengel, *Studies in the Gospel of Mark*, 64–84.

37. Theissen, *Lokalkolorit und Zeitgeschichte*, 271–84 [ET = *Gospels in Context*]; Marcus, "Jewish War." A year before the publication of Theissen's book, the relationship of Mark with the Jewish War was set out in detail in Schenke, *Markusevangelium*, 11–48, but this work had little impact on the academic discussion.

of Mark with the Jewish War are of the view that it was composed in the region of Syria, and in an environment where the impact of the Jewish War was keenly felt.[38]

The primary evidence that connects the Gospel of Mark with the Jewish War is found in the final chapters of the Gospel (Mark 11–16) and, more specifically, in the Olivet Discourse (Mark 13). In the narrative framework of this discourse, Jesus announces the destruction of the temple (Mark 13:1–2) but not its future reconstruction, as in other similar sayings (Mark 14:58; John 2:19). These other sayings are undoubtedly traditional, but the saying in Mark 13:2 reflects the evangelist's redactional activity, as it makes reference to only the first half of the traditional statement (destruction), and not the second (rebuilding).[39] On the other hand, the announcement of the adversities that the disciples will suffer (Mark 13:9–13) describes a situation that occurred during the war, when many disciples had to appear before Jewish and Roman courts (Mark 13:9, my translation: "to Sanhedrins and synagogues . . . before governors and kings") or were accused by their relatives, thus creating a social disintegration similar to what, according to Flavius Josephus, prevailed during the war (*Jewish War* 2.461–464).[40] Likewise, the reference to the "abomination of desolation" placed where it does not belong (Mark 13:14), which initially may have referred to the profanation of the temple during Caligula's reign, appears in this context as a clear allusion to the defilement of the temple in the years before its destruction.[41] These allusions suggest that the whole discourse refers to the events of the war and reflects their impact on the Gospel's audience.[42]

An essential argument to link the Gospel of Mark with the Jewish War is the attitude toward the temple reflected in the narrative. In the central part of a characteristic sandwich composition, Mark narrates Jesus'

---

38. Theissen places it in the Syrian region (Theissen, *Lokalkolorit und Zeitgeschichte*, 260–61 [ET = *Gospels in Context*]), and Marcus in the Decapolis (Marcus, "Jewish War," 460–62); Roskam locates it in Galilee (*Purpose of the Gospel of Mark*, 94–113). Some recent studies, however, explain the references to the war as part of a rhetoric that proposed an alternative to Vespasian's ascent, and situate the composition of the Gospel in Rome: see Gelardini, *Christus Militans*, 3–22.

39. Theissen, *Lokalkolorit und Zeitgeschichte*, 271. Kloppenborg, "*Evocatio Deorum* and the Date of Mark" sees in this statement a reflection of the ritual by which the defeated nations were separated from their protective gods.

40. Theissen, *Lokalkolorit und Zeitgeschichte*, 281–84.

41. Theissen, *Lokalkolorit und Zeitgeschichte*, 272; Marcus, "Jewish War," 447.

42. Collins, "Apocalyptic Rhetoric"; Balabanski, "Mark 13."

expulsion of the merchants and money changers from the temple (Mark 11:15–17). He also explains the meaning of Jesus' performance by means of a combined quotation that includes a reference to Isaiah and another to Jeremiah: "My house shall be called a house of prayer for all the nations [Isa 56:7], but you have made it a den of brigands [Jer 7:11]" (Mark 11:17, my translation). This combination of scriptural quotations that the Gospel of Mark presented as words uttered by Jesus reflects the events in Jerusalem in the years preceding its destruction. The word used in this saying to identify those expelled by Jesus is not *kleptēs* (robber), which would be the most suitable term in Greek to refer to the merchants and the money changers mentioned before, but *lēstēs* (brigand), which is the term used by Flavius Josephus to refer to the revolutionaries in the war against Rome. Josephus explains how during the first years of the war, some groups of *lēstai* (brigands) entered Jerusalem and occupied the temple, defiling the worship and transforming the sanctuary into a place of business (*Jewish War* 4:135–157). The description of the temple as a "den of brigands" better fits this situation than it does the expulsion of the merchants and money changers reported by Mark.[43]

The allusion to the Jewish revolutionaries who occupied the temple reveals the significance of the first part of the citation attributed to Jesus. The contrast between the temple as a "house of prayer for all the nations" and its current situation as a "den of brigands" reflects the situation in Jerusalem during the first years of the Jewish War. In that period, groups of bandits who occupied the city and its temple, driven by their nationalistic zeal, succeeded in banning sacrifices for the Gentiles. This ban was critical, as, according to Josephus, it triggered the war (*Jewish War* 2.409).[44]

The episode of Jesus' action in the temple reflects a negative attitude toward the sacred place that permeates the rest of Mark's narrative. The temple is described as an outdated—even idolatrous—institution (made by human hands), which is to be destroyed. The negative evaluation of the temple in turn explains the announcement of a new temple (Mark 14:58)—an announcement also made during the war by some sectarian Jews. All of this supports the hypothesis that Mark was composed near Jerusalem around the time of the Jewish revolt.[45]

---

43. Marcus, "Jewish War," 448–56; see also Lücking, "Zerstörung des Tempels," 150–57.

44. Marcus, "Jewish War," 448–52.

45. Wardle, "Mark, the Jerusalem Temple and Jewish Sectarianism."

Locating the writing of the Gospel in the proximity of Jerusalem is also consistent with one striking feature of Mark: its resistance to characterizing Jesus as the "Son of David." In Mark, this designation is linked to Jesus' activities in or near Jerusalem: on his way from Jericho to the holy city (Mark 10:47–48), when he enters the city (Mark 11:9–10), and during his teaching in the temple (Mark 12:35–37). Mark's reluctance to assign this title to Jesus is evident in the first two passages. In the first a blind man uses it, while in the second, those who acclaim Jesus as Son of David will later abandon him. In the third scene, Jesus openly disagrees with a dynastic vision of his messianism. When the chief priests ask him about the origin of his authority (Mark 11:28), he does not refer to his familial connection with David. Instead, he tells a parable in which he identifies himself as "the son" (Mark 12:1–12). Mark's Gospel is markedly restrained in its designation of Jesus as Son of David. This reluctance is remarkable in that the other Gospels, as well as ancient Christian tradition, evince no difficulty in designating Jesus thus. On the contrary, they see in this title an essential trait of Jesus' identity. This unusual feature of Mark's story reflects the situation of the Gospel's audience in the aftermath of the Jewish War, during which time associating with a Davidic messiah would have triggered the kind of retaliation that many Jews suffered during the war and afterwards.[46]

Recently, Christopher Zeichmann proposed an additional argument in favor of the location of Mark's Gospel in Syria. Studying the use of Latin words in Greek texts in the context of code-switching habits during the first century CE in Rome, Syria, and Palestine, he concludes that Mark's Latinisms are better located in a provincial setting than in Rome. Thus, a traditional argument in favor of a Roman provenance can end up being an argument against it. Zeichmann has also proposed a precise date for the composition of Mark. In an insightful analysis of the taxation episode (Mark 12:13–17) in the context of contemporary coinage circulation and tax policies, he concludes that the denarius, which plays a crucial role in the episode, did not circulate in Palestine until after the war. This fact leads to the conclusion that the Gospel of Mark could not have been written before 71 CE.[47]

These arguments have convinced most scholars that the Gospel of Mark was composed in the shadow of the Jewish War. The impact of this

---

46. Marcus, "Jewish War," 146–49. See also Rodríguez Láiz, *Mesías hijo de David*, 43–107, and 242–50.

47. Zeichmann, "Loanwords or Code-Switching?"; Zeichmann, "Date of Mark."

event on groups of Jesus believers helps identify some aspects of the exigence and the constraints of the rhetorical situation that led to its composition. The choice of the *bios* genre to preserve and transmit the memory of Jesus is in keeping with such a rhetorical situation, as one of the primary purposes of ancient Lives was to present a model for their audience, and Mark's addressees needed a model to imitate.[48]

Conclusion

In this introductory chapter, I have tried to show that Mark's rewriting of the traditional passion narrative (Mark 14–16), as well as his composition of the preceding section of his gospel (Mark 1–13), was aimed at producing a unified and coherent story about Jesus. Analysis of the editorial modification evidenced in Mark 14–16 has shown that the evangelist reworked a traditional passion narrative to make it the narrative conclusion of his preceding account. Likewise, the study of the proleptic references to the passion in Mark 1–13 has confirmed this tendency to blend both literary blocks.

Mark intended to include the traditions about Jesus within the framework of a coherent narrative and wanted to articulate them along the lines of a literary genre known in his context. The literary pattern he used to integrate the words and actions of Jesus in the first part of his narrative and the way he combined the first part with the passion narrative suggests that Mark wanted to compose a Life of Jesus. The work that we know as the Gospel according to Mark received this title some decades later in order to express more clearly that it contained the good news about Jesus. From this perspective, the term *gospel* refers to its theological import, not to its literary genre. From a literary point of view, Mark's Gospel was a specific type of Hellenistic Life.

Mark's literary achievement introduced a new perspective through the process of receiving and transmitting the traditions about Jesus. Before Mark, memories about Jesus were transmitted independently or in more or less elaborate collections. Mark integrated these traditions into an extensive narrative that followed the model of ancient biography. This literary project had significant theological implications because this new form of recalling and transmitting the traditions about Jesus focused on Jesus' person and identity.

48. Capes, "*Imitatio Christi*."

The christological focus resulted from an increasing interest in Jesus' identity, which was somehow intrinsic to Jesus tradition. Nevertheless, Mark's decision to compose a Life of Jesus might have been triggered by the need to present his audience with a means of coping with the challenging situation in Syria and Palestine during and after the Jewish War. The role played by the passion narrative in the composition process, as well as the prominent place it occupies in Mark's narrative, suggests that this rhetorical situation contributed to the composition of a Life of Jesus.

Matthew and Luke followed Mark's example. Both undertook the task of rewriting his Life of Jesus to complete it and adapt it to the model of Hellenistic biographies. Still, the credit for having composed the first biography of Jesus belongs to Mark, and it is to him that we must attribute one of the most remarkable and lasting literary and theological achievements of nascent Christianity.

CHAPTER 2

The Beginning of Mark's Biography of Jesus

(Mark 1:1–15)

Introduction

IN THE PREVIOUS CHAPTER, I concluded that Mark intended to write a *bios*—a Life of Jesus—and discussed some features of his narrative that support this conclusion. Nonetheless, I also observed that the beginning of his gospel apparently does not follow the model of Hellenistic biographies. This is a significant feature because beginnings play an essential role in narrative texts. They connect readers and hearers to the text and prepare them to understand the story that follows.[1] Mark's beginning also intends to introduce his readers/hearers to the story of Jesus, but compared to Hellenistic biographies and the other two Synoptic Gospels, it does so in a peculiar way. Both Matthew and Luke narrate Jesus' birth and tell about his genealogy. Mark, instead, begins his story by describing Jesus' baptism and temptations.

Research on the beginning of Mark's Gospel has made use of different models of literary analysis to understand it.[2] Similarly, the use of social-science models has produced a more profound knowledge of the social

---

1. On the functions of the Gospel's beginnings, see Malbon, "Ending at the Beginning."

2. Scholars usually distinguish between (1) narrative analysis (e.g., Rhoads et al., *Mark as Story* [3rd ed.]; Boring, "Mark 1:1–15"; Mell, "Jesu Taufe"; Naluparayil, *Identity of Jesus*), (2) structuralist analysis (e.g., Malbon, *Narrative Space*), (3) rhetorical analysis (e.g., Dormeyer, "Mk 1,1–15 als Prolog"), and (4) reader-response analysis (e.g., Sankey, "Promise and Fulfilment").

context of the beginning of Mark's Gospel.³ In the path already opened by these studies, this chapter intends to answer a fundamental question: Why does the Gospel of Mark begin as it does?

The Unusual Beginning of Mark's Gospel

Mark's beginning displays some peculiar traits, which distinguish it from the rest of the Gospel. In these initial verses, John the Baptist plays a prominent role to the point that he can be considered the early narrative's protagonist. On the other hand, the events narrated occur in an imprecise time ("Then," and "In those days") and are located in geographical areas with symbolic connotations (the desert, the Jordan River). Moreover, most of the events described at the start of Mark's Gospel are unusual phenomena (skies parting; a voice from heaven speaking; and the Spirit, Satan, and angels making appearances).⁴ Scholars agree on the peculiarity of this beginning but disagree as to the length and literary nature of this *beginning* of the Gospel.

Regarding its length, two proposals have gained widest acceptance: one places the end of this beginning at Mark 1:13, and the other at Mark 1:15. The first proposal, mainly based on observations about the narrative, considers the peculiar associations of time and space in Mark 1:1–13, as well as the fact that Jesus appears in these verses as a passive character.⁵ The second proposal is grounded on the literary structure of these verses, which includes a prologue (Mark 1:1–3) and a parallel presentation of John (Mark 1:4–8) and Jesus (Mark 1:9–15). The unity of this beginning is reinforced by the mention of the keyword "gospel" at the start and the end, and by the repetition of the same literary pattern in the presentation of John and Jesus: "appeared . . . baptize . . . in the wilderness . . . proclaim."⁶ Both these proposals point to the transitional character of Mark 1:14–15, which is, at the same time, the end of the first and the beginning of the second part of Mark's story of Jesus. In what follows, I will take Mark 1:1–15 as the beginning of the Gospel.

The second point of disagreement concerns the literary nature of this beginning. It is often referred to as the *gospel prologue*, although usually this

---

3. McVann, "Reading Mark Ritually"; van Eck, "Baptism of Jesus"; DeMaris, "Possession Good and Bad."
4. Marcus, *Mark 1–8*, 137–39.
5. Malbon, *Narrative Space*, 72–75.
6. Boring, "Mark 1:1–15"; Klauck, *Vorspiel im Himmel?*, 19–34.

designation has no technical sense. Only Detlev Dormeyer has suggested using it in a technical sense.[7] According to him, Mark's prologue is similar to that of other ideal biographies in Roman and Hellenistic literature: the main topics of the narratives are announced at the beginning by way of oracles and revelations according to the pattern of Homer's *Odyssey* (1:1–21). However, both the identification of the Gospels with this literary genre and the relationship between the beginnings of those works and that of Mark's Gospel are far from convincing.[8]

From another perspective, Hans-Joseph Klauck has compared the beginning of Mark with the *proemium* or *exordium* of literary speeches, whose main goals were appealing to the benevolence of the reader and introducing the topics the discourse will cover. In the end, nonetheless, Klauck decides not to go all the way with his argument and keeps the traditional designation of *prologue*.[9]

These two proposals either neglect or pay little attention to the recent discussion about the literary genre of Mark, which has stressed its similarities with Hellenistic biographies. This lack of attention in these two proposals to connections between Mark and ancient biographies may be due to the fact that the beginning of Mark differs from the beginnings of typical ancient biographies. Still, this initial observation needs to be assessed in more detail by comparing the beginnings of ancient Lives with Mark's Life of Jesus.

After a detailed comparison between the Gospels and some of these ancient biographies from earlier, contemporary, and later times, R. A. Burridge and others have concluded that the Gospels belong to this genre, which includes a vast repertoire of narratives about the lives of different characters.[10] Burridge's study shows that ancient biographies were different from today's biographies. Actually, Mark's contemporaries did not call them biographies but Lives (*bios* in Greek, *vita* in Latin). The life was a literary genre somewhere between history and praise.[11] Applying the names used by ancient rhetoricians, we may describe Lives as narratives (*diēgēsis*)

---

7. Dormeyer, "Mk 1,1–15 als Prolog," 199–203.

8. Burridge, *What Are the Gospels?*, 99–100.

9. Klauck, *Vorspiel im Himmel?*, 34–35, notes that Mark 1:14–15 is closely related to what follows, and proposes to understand these verses as a kind of proposition, which closes the *exordium*, announcing the theme of the *narratio*.

10. Burridge, *What Are the Gospels?*, 218–19; see also Frickenschmidt, *Evangelium als Biographie*, 210–350.

11. Burridge, *What Are the Gospels?*, 61–69.

that portrayed the character of a person with a praising touch (*egkōmion*). This definition matches Luke's description of his Gospel and other similar narrative writings (Luke 1:1: *diēgēsis*).[12] In his discussion about the Gospels as biographies, Burridge mentions some common traits that ancient Lives share with the Gospels. Among them, two are especially relevant for our purposes: first, the presence both in ancient Lives and in the Gospels of a title or an introductory formula, and, second, the preoccupation both in ancient Lives and in the Gospels with opening subjects—the ancestry, birth, and education of the human subject under consideration.

Although Mark 1:1 may be taken as a title, it is clear that the rest of Mark's beginning is not a preface or prologue akin to those found in contemporary Lives.[13] At the beginning of these Lives, the author informs readers about the method used in composing his work, enhances the character's relevance, and mentions the addressees (Luke 1:1–4; Philo, *Life of Moses* 1:1–4). However, we do not find this kind of information in the beginning of Mark's Gospel. In fact, the most peculiar feature of the beginning of the Gospel of Mark is the lack of information about Jesus' ancestry, birth, and education. This is a salient feature, for the rest of his gospel does contain numerous similarities, both in form and content, with the Hellenistic Lives. The beginning seems to be an exception, which both Matthew and Luke tried to adjust by composing an infancy narrative of Jesus.[14]

This observation takes us back to our original quest: Why did Mark begin his gospel as he did? Why did he not follow the pattern of the Hellenistic Lives? Before answering these questions, we will supplement Burridge's statements by comparing the beginnings of some contemporary Lives to identify their salient traits. We will consider a brief but significant selection of six ancient biographies. All of them date back to a time between the first century BCE and the first century CE. They were written in different languages by authors in various places: the *Life of Atticus*, by Cornelius Nepos; and the *Life of Agricola*, by Cornelius Tacitus—both written in Latin; and the *Autobiography* of Flavius Josephus; the *Life of Moses*, by Philo of Alexandria; the *Life of Demonax*, by Lucian of Samosata; and the *Life of Cato the Younger*, by Plutarch, written in Greek.

---

12. See Neyrey, *Encomium for Jesus*.

13. Burridge, *What Are the Gospels?*, 193–95.

14. Burridge, *What Are the Gospels?*, 249, points out that Matthew and Luke represent with respect to Mark a second stage that tries to bring this gospel closer to the genre of Hellenistic Lives. For a complementary view, see Keith, *Gospel as Manuscript*, 100–130.

The Beginning of Mark's Biography of Jesus

The following table shows how they deal with the three topics usually covered by the beginnings of Hellenistic and Roman Lives:

	Ancestry	Birth	Education
Atticus (Cornelius Nepos, *Life of Atticus* 1:1–4)	He was born of the most ancient family in Rome. His father was a great administrator of his house, rich, and cultivated.	Not mentioned	Educated by his father and later on by other teachers. Cicero was his classmate.
Agricola (Cornelius Tacitus, *Agricola* 4–5)	Both his paternal and maternal ancestors were distinguished.	Not mentioned	In his youth, he devoted himself to the study of philosophy. Later on, he received military training.
Josephus (Flavius Josephus, *Autobiography* 1–12)	From a priestly family on his father's side and a kingly family on his mother's side. He was born in Jerusalem, the greatest Jewish city.	Not mentioned	He received instruction in different groups. Finally he become a Pharisee.
Moses (Philo of Alexandria, *Life of Moses* 1:5–31)	Parents' noble origin. Seventh generation since arriving in Egypt.	Not mentioned	He was educated in Pharaoh's palace. He learned the customs of his time.
Demonax (Lucian of Samosata, *Demonax* 3–4)	From Cyprus. Outstanding wealth and social level.	Not mentioned	Teachers (Agatobulus, Epictetus) and comprehensive education (poetry, philosophy, gymnastics...)
Cato Minor (Plutarch, *Cato Minor* 1–4)	Distinguished ancestors.	Not mentioned	Educated in his maternal uncle's house, a well-known man, He showed excellent qualities during his training.

A striking feature of this sample of ancient Lives is that all lack a birth account. Actually, Lives including this aspect were an exception.[15]

---

15. Of the ten studied by Burridge, only two narrate the birth: the funerary eulogy of Evagoras written by Isocrates (fifth century BCE), and that of Apollonius written by Philostratus (third century CE); see Burridge, *What Are the Gospels?*, 146 and 178.

Therefore, only the references to ancestry and education should be considered characteristic elements of the beginnings of Hellenistic Lives.

To understand why Lives used to begin this way, we should keep in mind that they were encomiastic narratives, a peculiar kind of narratives somewhere between the *diēgēsis* and the *egkōmion*. Thanks to the information provided by ancient rhetoricians, we know the features of these two basic literary genres. We know even the procedure followed in composing them, for both were part of the preparatory exercises (*progymnasmata*) that well-to-do young people learned during their training for public life.[16]

Rhetoricians agree that the praise of a person (usually male) must begin by informing the audience of his ancestry and education. We can confirm this by briefly examining what three contemporary writings say in praise and in narration. These writings are the *Rhetorica ad Herennium*, an anonymous rhetorical treatise from the first half of the first century BCE; the introduction to the *Life of Epaminondas*, written by Cornelius Nepos around 50 BCE; and Aelius Theon's *Progymnasmata*, composed toward the end of the first century CE.[17]

> To the external circumstances belong such as can happen by chance, or by fortune, favorable or adverse: descent [*genus*], education [*educatio*], wealth, kinds of power, titles of fame, citizenship, friendships, and the like, and their contraries. (*Rhetorica ad Herennium* 3:10)

> External circumstances: Descent—in praise: the ancestors of whom he is sprung; if he is of illustrious descent, he has been their peer or superior; if of humble descent, he has had his support, not in the virtues of his ancestors, but in his own. Education—in praise: that he was well and honorably trained in worthy studies throughout his boyhood. (*Rhetorica ad Herennium* 3:13)

> Therefore I shall speak first of his family [*genus*], then of the subjects which he studied [*disciplinae*] and his teachers, next of his character, his natural qualities, and anything else that is worthy of record. Finally, I will give an account of his exploits which many writers consider more important than mental excellences. (Cornelius Nepos, *Life of Epaminodas* 1:4)

---

16. On the purpose and pedagogy of the preparatory exercises, see the excellent introduction by Patillon and Bolognesi in Théon, *Progymnasmata*, xvi–xxiii; on the education process, see Cribiore, *Gymnastics of the Mind*, 221–30.

17. Translations of ancient texts are from the Loeb Classical Library.

The properties of the person are origin (*genos*), nature, training, disposition, age, fortune, morality, action, speech, (manner of) death, and what followed death. (Theon, *Progymnasmata*, 78; in Kennedy, ed., *Progymnasmata*, 28)

External goods are, first, good birth, and that is twofold, either from the goodness of (a man's) city and tribe and constitution, or from ancestors and other relatives. Then there is education, friendship, reputation, official position, wealth, good children, a good death. (Theon, *Progymnasmata* 110; in Kennedy, ed., *Progymnasmata*, 50)

	Ad Herennium	Cornelius Nepos	Théon (*diēgēsis*)	Théon (*egkōmion*)
ANCESTRY	*Genus*	*Genus*	*Genos*	*Eugeneia*
EDUCATION	*Educatio*	*Disciplinae*	*Agōgē*	*Paideia*

The information provided by these ancient writers confirms that Lives usually began by informing their audience about the ancestry and education of the protagonist. This is precisely what Matthew and Luke do at the beginning of their gospels.[18] Despite the brevity of the descriptions of ancient rhetorical texts, the fact that they agree about the information that should be provided at the beginning of Lives indicates that people knew that literary pattern. Now, if Mark knew that this was the customary way to begin a biography, the question of why he did not follow it becomes all the more intriguing. Was it perhaps due to a lack of data? It seems that it was not the case. Mark knew that Jesus came from a Galilean town called Nazareth (Mark 1:9) and considered him a Galilean (Mark 14:70). Mark was familiar with the name of his mother and the names of his brothers, although he does not mention the name of his father or of his sisters (Mark 6:3). Mark might know something about Jesus' education since we are told that Jesus was a *tektōn* (Mark 6:3)—that is, a craftsman who worked with wood, stone, and similar materials.[19]

With all this information, Mark could have begun his Life of Jesus by discussing Jesus ancestry and education. However, he did not, and we may ask why. From other sources, we know that Jesus' origins triggered puzzlement and even criticism among his contemporaries. Nazareth was a little town from which nothing good could come (John 1:46), and Judean people had a negative view of Galileans (John 7:52). Consequently, introducing

---

18. Neyrey, *Honor and Shame*, 90–105; Neyrey, *Encomium for Jesus*, 18–49.
19. Meier, *A Marginal Jew* 1:278–85.

Jesus as a native of Galilee would not have been an appropriate way to enhance his honor or status.[20] On the other hand, it is surprising that Mark calls Jesus "the son of Mary" (Mark 6:3) and not "the son of Joseph," as do the other two Synoptics (Matt 1:16; Luke 4:22). The mention of Mary's name has led many to think that the name of Jesus' father was unknown to Mark.[21] Finally, we know that being a nonspecialized artisan was unworthy of a noble person.[22]

Jesus' humble origin, from a marginal family in an unknown village, may have been an issue for Mark when writing his Life of Jesus, for those narratives aimed to praise their protagonists by reporting their noble origins and excellent education. Most characters in the contemporary Lives were distinguished people belonging to noble families, who could boast noble ancestry and education. However, the information available to Mark about Jesus' origins did not allow him to write a beginning of this kind.

The praising goal in Lives, especially of their beginnings, may have prevented Mark from following the pattern of the genre at the beginning of his Life of Jesus. Nonetheless, this is only a partial answer to our question. This answer only explains why the beginning of Mark's Gospel does not fit the pattern of ancient Lives, but it does not explain why he chose to begin it as he did.

In this connection, it might be helpful to keep in mind the purpose of ancient Lives. Burridge has identified seven possible goals: to praise the protagonist, present him as an example, inform about him, defend him from accusations, preserve his memory, entertain, or instruct.[23] Some of these goals are explicit in the Lives mentioned above: praising the protagonist (Tacitus, *Agricola*. 4; Philo, *Life of Moses* 1:3); defending him from accusations (Josephus, *Autobiography* 1:6); presenting him as a model (Lucian, *Demonax* 2); preserving his memory (Lucian, *Demonax*. 2; Philo, *Life of Moses* 1:3); or informing about him (Philo, *Life of Moses* 1:1).

---

20. Neyrey, *Honor and Shame*, 56–57.

21. Some authors have suggested that by referring only to his mother, Mark could harbor some doubts concerning Jesus' legitimacy; however, this might have not been the case because, as Ilan, "Man Born of Woman," 23–45 has shown, the use of matronymics was not uncommon among Jews at the time of Jesus.

22. Cicero, who is representative of contemporary views, mentions among the most dishonorable those who work for others with their own hands (*De officiis*. 1:150). Some comments in the Gospels reflect the same mentality (Matt 13:55: "Is this not the son of the carpenter?").

23. Burridge, *What Are the Gospels?*, 149–52.

Mark is likely to have pursued some of these goals in writing the beginning of his gospel, although he may have done it in a different way. Praising Jesus and defending his honor seem to have been important goals for him. Both purposes were related, for to present Jesus as an honorable person necessarily implied defending him against the reactions provoked by his humble origin. Mark combines these two purposes—the laudatory and the apologetic—that have the same goal: to show that Jesus was an honorable person.

To understand Mark's initial presentation of Jesus, we should keep in mind that he carried out this task in the context of his culture. Therefore, we need to reconstruct the scenario shared by the author and audience of Mark's Gospel. In what follows, I will propose three such reading scenarios. The first one will concentrate on how honor was perceived in ancient Mediterranean society and how it could be acquired. The second one will explain how rituals of status transformation work. Finally, the third scenario will briefly describe how the initiation of holy men occurs in traditional cultures. Each one of these reading scenarios will show a particular aspect of the context presupposed by the beginning of Mark's Gospel.[24]

Revelation and Defense of Jesus' Honor

Honor was, and still is, the core value in Mediterranean culture. This is something verified by anthropological studies,[25] which have contributed to a better understanding of the New Testament in recent years.[26] On the other hand, rhetorical works on praise are a native source of information about the importance given to honor in Greco-Roman culture.[27] According to Jerome H. Neyrey, the praising discourse, the *enkōmion*, epitomizes what modern anthropological studies say about honor in the Mediterranean world. This fact illustrates the substantial agreement between ancient

---

24. The first and third scenarios are *emic* because they use models from societies similar to that of Mark and his audience. The second one is an *etic* scenario based on a cross-cultural model. On these two types of reading scenarios, see the Introduction to the present book (pp. 5–6).

25. Peristiany, ed., *Honour and Shame*; Gilmore, ed., *Honor and Shame*.

26. Malina, *New Testament World* (Rev. ed.), 28–62; Malina and Neyrey, "Honor and Shame."

27. Malina and Neyrey, *Portraits of Paul*, 18–63.

rhetoricians and today's anthropologists.[28] The primary purpose of ancient eulogies was to show and praise a person's honor, which was also the primary goal of Hellenistic Lives. Therefore, an adequate understanding of the concept of honor in the Mediterranean culture may throw light on the way Mark has carried out his task of showing and defending Jesus' honor.

Honor may be defined as a person's awareness of his or her worth, together with the public recognition of the person's worth by other people. Of these three elements (an awareness of worth, a claim of worth, and public recognition of worth), the third one is the most important since in the end it is public recognition that determines a person's honor. It is up to others to say who is honorable and to what extent.[29] Now, one of the most distinctive features of the first-century Mediterranean world is its constant search for honor, recognition, and praise. Some philosophers even considered *philotimia* (love, desire, the search for honor) as the quality distinguishing human beings from animals:

> For indeed it seems to me, Hiero, that in this, man differs from other animals—I mean, in this craving for honor (*philotimia*). In meat and drink and sleep and sex, all creatures alike seem to take pleasure; but love of honor is rooted neither in the brute beasts nor in every human being. But they in whom is implanted a passion for honor [*timē*] and praise [*epainos*], these are they who differ most from the beasts of the field, these are accounted men (*andres*) and not mere human beings [*anthropoi*]. (Xenophon, *Hiero* 7:3)

Honor was the most precious good in the ancient Mediterranean culture, and the search for it conditioned every social interaction. However, like all goods, whether material or immaterial, honor was limited. Therefore, if an individual or a family increased their honor, they did so at the expense of someone else's honor. Consequently, the search for public recognition and praise took place within a highly competitive (i.e., an agonistic) atmosphere.[30]

---

28. Neyrey, *Honor and Shame*, 83–88.

29. Bourdieu states: "The point of honor is the basis of the moral code of an individual who sees himself always through the eyes of others, who has need of others for his existence, because the image he has of himself is indistinguishable from that presented to him by other people" (Bourdieu, "Sentiment of Honor," 211).

30. This agonistic character of traditional Mediterranean society surfaces in Jesus' controversies with his adversaries. For an orderly presentation of the various aspects of honor in the ancient world, see Neyrey, *Honor and Shame*, 14–32.

The Beginning of Mark's Biography of Jesus

In Jesus' world, there were two ways to obtain honor: to receive it from those who could bestow it, or to earn it by one's actions. Honor received from others was *ascribed honor*, while *acquired honor* was honor earned by one's efforts. The first one was by far the more important in the ancient world. As a rule, it depended on the family one was born into, for family was the store of shared honor.[31] It could also be bestowed by those invested with authority. On the other hand, an individual acquired honor by actions, either in competition among equals or in response to benefits received.[32]

The Gospels often refer to Jesus' honor, even if Mark avoids the actual term for honor (*timē*). Most of Jesus' actions, especially his teaching and miracles, are understood as acts of beneficence by people who in turn respond by giving him praise and recognition: people are astounded; his fame spreads (Mark 1:27–28). We can get an idea of Jesus' increasing honor by looking at the response of Pharisees and other religious or political groups (Sadducees, Herodians), who perceive his growing honor as a threat to theirs, and who question his actions (Mark 3:22). Controversies, so frequent in the Gospels, are honor contests in which Jesus defeats his adversaries. All these actions and the underlying claims imply that Jesus has some ascribed honor. Nevertheless, in Mark's view, this honor does not come from his family but from his intimate relationship with God. Therefore, the main goal of the beginning of Mark's "life" of Jesus is to reveal the origin of Jesus' ascribed honor.

Several elements reveal this honor in the opening verses (Mark 1:1–3). In Mark 1:1, leaving aside the title "Son of God," which might be a later addition,[33] Jesus is acclaimed as Messiah; that is, he is introduced as (God's) Anointed. These opening verses also state that the beginning of his ministry agreed with what Isaiah foretold, thus applying to him an announcement that initially referred to God himself: "Prepare the way of the Lord." With sober but accurate strokes, Mark depicts Jesus as God's Anointed One who fulfills what God had promised through the prophets.

The introduction of John the Baptist (Mark 1:4–8) also stresses Jesus' honor. What Mark says about John confirms that he is a true prophet, and therefore a person with honor. His actions take place in the desert by the Jordan, locations that are related to the events of Israel's exodus from

---

31. Guijarro, *Fidelidades en conflicto*, 117–25.

32. Malina and Neyrey, *Portraits of Paul*, 27–29; Malina and Neyrey, "Honor and Shame," 27–32.

33. Head, "Text-Critical Study of Mark 1:1"; Croy, "Where the Gospel Text Begins."

Egypt.³⁴ Mark's characterization of John supports Mark's claim that God has sent him to prepare him the way, as Isaiah's reference in Mark 1:2–3 also affirms. Both the Baptist's garments and his diet point in the same direction since they reveal that he is a prophet. John's honor is confirmed by the response of the inhabitants of Jerusalem and all Judea, who come to him in great numbers to receive his baptism of repentance. Nevertheless, Mark's presentation of John as a prophet is not meant to praise him but to enhance Jesus' honor, presenting Jesus as the "Stronger One," who will baptize, not with water, but with Holy Spirit.³⁵ John cannot confer any honor upon Jesus, but John can acknowledge and proclaim the greatness of the honor God will bestow on him.

From a literary point of view, Jesus' presentation (Mark 1:9–15) parallels John's (Mark 1:4–8). However, the presentation of Jesus confirms what has been said previously. The critical moment is the vision after Jesus' baptism, in which Jesus' ascribed honor is finally revealed. Mark presents Jesus as (God's) Anointed, as the Lord whose way John the Baptist is preparing, and as the Stronger One who will baptize with Holy Spirit. Next, the Holy Spirit comes down upon Jesus, and God himself declares that he is his Son. In Mark's view, Jesus' true identity is revealed in his baptism. The main character in Mark's story is not just a man named Jesus, who comes from Nazareth in Galilee (Mark 1:9), but rather God's Son, who is filled with his Spirit (Mark 1:10–11). In Jewish society, God was the supreme source of honor. Therefore, the words pronounced by the heavenly voice confer upon Jesus the highest ascribed honor one could think of. These words are the culmination of all previous statements, and in them the revelation of Jesus' identity reaches its climax.³⁶

This presentation of Jesus corresponds to the cultural values of the society where the author of the Gospel and his audience lived. In a society based on honor, only those born in an honorable family can claim public recognition. If an individual born in a lowly family requests this kind of recognition, his authority and his actions will be attributed to an evil spirit unless an extraordinary event empowers him to claim authority

---

34. Malbon, *Narrative Space*, 72–75.

35. Marcus, *Mark 1-8*, 153–58.

36. In a recent monograph, Helen Bond comes to the same conclusion: Bond, *First Biography*, 128–31. See also Peppard, *Son of God in the Roman World*, 93–124.

and recognition. Jesus, born into a low-status family of artisans, has no legitimacy as a public figure. However, if he is God's Son, his legitimacy is undeniable.[37]

The following two scenes—the temptation narrative (Mark 1:12–13) and the beginning of Jesus' public ministry in Galilee (Mark 1:14–15)— confirm the soundness and truth of what has been previously revealed about Jesus. This is precisely the function of the temptation account, where Jesus is put to the test in the wilderness. Jesus' victory over Satan confirms that he is God's Son. Therefore, he can act as the herald of the "good news of God," announcing the coming of the "reign of God," asking for repentance and faith from those who listen to him (Mark 1:14–15). Only a person endowed with such power by God could do so.

This reading of Mark 1:1–15 as a narrative revealing Jesus' ascribed honor shows that the climax of this beginning is the presentation of Jesus (Mark 1:9–15). This presentation includes three scenes: baptism (Mark 1:9–11), testing (Mark 1:12–13), and the inaugural mission (Mark 1:14–15). Now, these three episodes are interrelated and describe what is known by anthropologists as a *status-transformation ritual*. Mark depicts Jesus' transformation in these scenes and shows how a Galilean peasant becomes the herald of God's kingdom. In the following section, we will explore this process in order to understand Mark's presentation of Jesus.

The Status-Transformation Ritual

Status-transformation rituals have the function of enacting and confirming a person's passing from one status to another in a socially significant way. Like all rituals, they cross those boundaries that societies use to classify individuals, things, time, and space. All cultures possess this kind of social maps, which shape their purity systems. In Jesus' world, God's holiness was the measure to separate what was pure and impure. This holiness was symbolized in the Jerusalem temple. The city and its temple, where God dwelled, were the basis of and the measure for classifying people and objects.[38] In this social map, an artisan born of a family living in an unknown Galilean village was far from what was expected for God's Anointed One. Therefore, Mark's presentation of Jesus intends to show that Jesus the

---

37. Malina and Rohrbaugh, *Commentary on the Synoptic Gospels*, 177.
38. Neyrey, "Clean/Unclean," 91–93.

Galilean artisan was the Son of God, by describing the process through which his status was transformed.

According to Victor W. Turner, the status transformation process has three stages: separation, liminality, and aggregation. Separation involves being detached from the ordinary course of life by distancing oneself from those people with whom one lives and going to a place and time different from the normal. Liminality is the threshold state of the one who has been separated from the ordinary course of life and who undergoes the initiation process (the *initiand*). In this intermediate state, the initiand is dispossessed of former status and somehow must die to achieve new status. During this ambiguous period, the common attributes of the initiand are stressed, originating a peculiar social bond, which Turner calls *communitas*. Finally, aggregation involves incorporating the initiand into society with the new status acquired through the ritual process. The ritual process requires the participation of an elder, who plays the role of mystagogue. There are also some ritual symbols that play essential roles at different points in the process.[39]

In Mark 1:9–15, we find all the elements of the ritual process.[40] Jesus plays the role of the initiand; the mystagogues are John the Baptist and, above all, God's Spirit; and there are ritual symbols: baptism, the Jordan River, the voice from heaven, and the desert. There are two basic movements in the narrative, corresponding to the beginning and the end of the initiation process. The first one signals the moment of separation: "In those days Jesus came from Nazareth of Galilee and was baptized by John in the Jordan" (Mark 1:9). The second one refers to the moment of aggregation: "After John was arrested, Jesus went to Galilee preaching the good news of God" (Mark 1:14, my translation). There is an intermediate period during which Jesus' status is transformed (the period of the vision during his baptism and the temptations). Let us consider in more detail the three moments of Jesus' status-transformation process.

The first stage—*separation*—is briefly described, but the narrative contains all the characteristic elements: Jesus moves from Galilee to Judea, from his village to a place in the desert by Jordan's banks, where John is baptizing. There is, therefore, a detachment that happens for Jesus (from his family and fellow villagers). Likewise, he goes to a different place endowed

---

39. Turner, *Ritual Process*, 94–130; McVann, "Rituals of Status Transformation," 335–41.

40. Van Eck, "Baptism of Jesus."

with great symbolism (the desert, the Jordan River), and things happen according to time that is very different from time in the ordinary course of life. Jesus goes to Judea to undergo John's baptism, a status-transformation ritual based on the confession of sins and a rite of immersion (Mark 1:4–5). In this first stage, John acts as the elder, and the baptism is the ritual symbol. However, in Mark's view, the rite of baptism is just the beginning of the upcoming liminal period.

The intermediate stage, characterized by *liminality* and *communitas*, begins with the vision of the heavens tearing, the Holy Spirit coming down on Jesus like a dove, and a heavenly voice speaking to him; and the intermediate stage continues with Jesus' sojourn in the wilderness (Mark 1:10–13). Both the space and the time of these events are highly symbolic: Jesus comes out of the Jordan, the heavens open, the Spirit leads him to the desert, and he stays there for forty days. The account recalls the forty years spent by the people of Israel in the desert, and Elijah's stay in Mount Horeb for forty days. The desert is indeed one of the most common places where status-transformation rituals take place.[41] It is a space and a time of a religious, not a profane character, where Jesus loses his previous status and acquires a new one. Therefore, through this process, Mark has revealed Jesus' identity (the source of his ascribed honor) and has established him as the herald of God's reign.

The liminality of this stage may be perceived in the ambiguity of Jesus' status and the new relationships he establishes. Although the voice from heaven declares he is God's Son, his identity will not be revealed until his testing period ends. Therefore, ambiguity is a mark of all this period in which Jesus has no connections with other human beings, while he interacts with beings belonging to another realm of existence. The Spirit comes upon him and becomes his guide and leads him to the desert. The voice from heaven declaring him as God's Son also belongs to this supernatural realm, where both Satan and the angels live. In Mark's narrative, Jesus establishes these relationships with beings belonging to the supernatural world in order to show that he is not a human being like others.

Jesus' relation to the Spirit and his confrontation with Satan in this early stage of the gospel narrative anticipate his later confrontations with evil spirits. Mark gives his readers a key to understanding the meaning of the exorcisms, which Jesus himself will explain in the controversy with the Pharisees later in the narrative (Mark 3:22–30). When confronting demons,

---

41. Turner, *Ritual Process*, 95.

Jesus acts with the power of God's Spirit, because his exorcisms are a sign of a more profound confrontation.[42] In presenting Jesus as he does, Mark is claiming Jesus' honor as God's Son, a status that endows Jesus with power over the unclean spirits.

The ritual process ends with Jesus' aggregation; with his return to the society he left, but now with a new status (Mark 1:14–15). He left Nazareth to undergo a baptism of repentance and now comes back to Galilee as the herald of God's reign. There is a movement from sacred to secular space: from the wilderness and the Jordan to Galilee. At the same time, Jesus moves from sacred to secular time: from the forty days in the desert to the moment of John's arrest. After the ritual process, Jesus' newly acquired status enables him to preach with authority the imminent arrival of God's reign and to request faith and repentance. This new authority of Jesus as God's Son will appear soon in his actions. Mark summarizes these actions in the next episodes of his narrative: the call to the first disciples (Mark 1:16–20), the day at Capernaum (Mark 1:21–39), his activity in all Galilee (Mark 1:40–45), and his controversies (Mark 2:1—3:6). Jesus manifests his ascribed honor in his acts of beneficence, and this honor increases through his confrontations with those who question him.

The ritual process underlying Jesus' presentation at the beginning of Mark's Gospel fulfills two important goals: it reveals the source of Jesus' ascribed honor and defends him against the accusations of being possessed by Satan. The source of Jesus' ascribed honor is revealed in the vision after his baptism, when he is declared Son of God, while his victory over Satan shows that he acts by the power of God's Spirit.

Jesus' status transformation, as Mark presents it, takes place through a process similar to that undergone by holy men in traditional cultures. The ascribed honor Mark claims for Jesus is the one characteristic of holy men. Therefore, as Mark presents it, Jesus' ritual process of status transformation from an unknown artisan to a holy man is similar to ritual initiations of holy men in other cultures. The model of these rituals will help us determine more precisely why Mark began his gospel as he did.

---

42. See Guijarro, "Politics of Exorcism." Jesus' baptism and temptations could have been formulated in the light of the accusations made against him of casting out demons with the power of Beelzebul. Mark, by presenting him in this way, would be responding to these accusations and claiming Jesus' honor as the Son of God with power over the spirits.

The Beginning of Mark's Biography of Jesus

Jesus' Initiation as a Holy Man

The figure of the holy man is familiar to many preindustrial societies. Although this figure has its distinct features in each culture, it is possible to identify some common features that characterize holy men from a social viewpoint. Anthropologists have studied especially the figure of the shaman as the prototype of the holy man. A shaman may be defined as a person able to access and control the spiritual or divine realm so that it favors the community he belongs to.

Some years ago, Marcus Borg suggested that "the initiation sequence in the spiritual world (baptism), followed by the temptation or testing in the desert has surprising similarities with the information we possess about charismatic figures in different cultures."[43] Pieter Craffert and John Pilch have developed Borg's suggestion. Considering how the shaman is presented in different cultures, Craffert uses the term *shamanic complex* to refer to the general typology of this social figure. According to him, this typology "is made up of a configuration and some features (experience of altered states of consciousness) and some social functions (such as healing, mediation, prophecy, exorcism, and possession of spirits) flowing from such experiences."[44] John Pilch, in turn, considers the relevance of the fact that the shaman can enter into an altered state of consciousness.[45]

The call and subsequent initiation of a holy man are crucial for the rest of his life. Given his social prominence, the process by which a person becomes a holy man is highly ritualized and occurs through a status-transformation ritual. This status-transformation ritual shows remarkable similarities with what we find at the beginning of Mark. Therefore, by comparing Mark 1:1–15 with the holy man's call and initiation process, we may understand better the meaning of Mark's beginning.

Pilch identifies six features in the call of a shaman:[46]

1. Contact with the spirit (through possession or adoption);

2. Identification of the possessing or adopting spirit;

3. Acquisition of the necessary ritual skills;

---

43. Borg, *Jesus*, 43, and 53 n17, where he quotes several works on shamanism.
44. Craffert, "Jesus and the Shamanic Complex," 324.
45. Pilch, "Altered States of Consciousness," 106; on altered states of consciousness, see Chapter 4 of the present book (pp. 71–73).
46. Pilch, "Altered States of Consciousness," 107.

4. Guidance by the spirit and a real-life teacher;

5. Growing acquaintance with the possessing or adopting spirit; and

6. Ongoing experiences of altered states of consciousness.

Most of these features appear in the baptism narrative, which corresponds to Jesus' call. The vision after his baptism and his temptation in the desert, which takes place after a long fasting period, are typical forms of altered states of consciousness. At the same time, Jesus' testing in the desert confirms successful initiation.[47] These elements, used in different cultures to describe the initiation of holy men, have in Jesus' case culturally specific connotations. As we have seen, these connotations come from symbols that evoke the founding history of God's people (the desert, the Jordan River), and, above all, the oracles of the prophets, holy men par excellence in Israel's history). Moreover, Jesus' presentation as a holy man in the Gospel of Mark depends on the social and cultural conditions of first-century Palestine. It is within this framework that Jesus' new status may be grasped.

Conclusion

The unusual beginning of Mark's Gospel compared to other contemporary Lives has led us to ask why those Lives begin by narrating the origin and education of their protagonists, while Mark does not. This inquiry has revealed that Mark did not begin his gospel talking about Jesus' origin and education because the available data were not fitting to reveal his ascribed honor. His author, nonetheless, did not abandon this goal but tried to do it differently.

To start with, Mark used several traditions about the beginnings of Jesus' ministry to reveal the origin of his ascribed honor. This is the primary goal of the prologue, containing an announcement attributed to Isaiah (Mark 1:1–3), and of the presentation of John the Baptist, pointing toward the revelation of the "Stronger One" (Mark 1:4–8). Yet, in Jesus' presentation, this honor is fully revealed when he is proclaimed Son of God, endowed with the Spirit, and made herald of God's reign (Mark 1:9–15). Jesus' honor derives not from his human ancestry but from his intimate relationship with God.

---

47. Craffert, "Jesus and the Shamanic Complex," 334; Pilch, "Altered States of Consciousness," 108–9.

The Beginning of Mark's Biography of Jesus

On the other hand, the presentation of Jesus (Mark 1:9–15) follows the pattern of a status-transformation ritual. The three steps characteristic of this kind of process are clearly signaled. First, Jesus' separation from his village and his social connections (his departure from Nazareth). Second, the initiation period in the Jordan and the desert, with the help of John the Baptist and under the guidance of the Spirit. Third, the aggregation, namely, his return to Galilee as God's herald, announcing the imminent arrival of God's reign. Through this process Jesus' identity is transformed and revealed.

This status-transformation ritual displays some characteristic elements of the initiation of the holy man in traditional cultures. During his initiation, the holy man experiences altered states of consciousness (the vision after baptism and the testing in the desert). He attains a familiarity with the divine world, which enables him to act in favor of his community. Mark describes the initiation process by which Jesus becomes aware of his being Son of God and the broker through whom God will act as a patron for his people.

We may conclude, then, that although the beginning of Mark's Life of Jesus differs from other similar Lives, yet he attains the goal of informing his readers about Jesus' ascribed honor. In the opening verses of his gospel, readers and hearers get to know that Jesus' ancestry goes back to God, and that he has received an intense education under the guidance of the Spirit through this initiation process. Therefore, the beginning of Mark's Gospel is not an obstacle to classifying the whole Gospel as a Life of Jesus.

CHAPTER 3

The Galilean Controversies and the Social Identity of Galilean Christianity

(Mark 2:1—3:6)

Introduction

THE ALMOST COMPLETE SILENCE of both Christian and non-Christian sources regarding the Jesus movement in Galilee is a striking and intriguing fact. Galilee was the main center of Jesus' activity, and so it is reasonable to think that his disciples would have continued there the movement he began. How, then, are we to explain the fact that so little information has come down to us about these Galilean disciples?

The lack of sources about the Galilean followers of Jesus explains why scholars have tried to identify the writings that may indirectly testify to the existence of such groups of disciples there.[1] In line with these studies,

---

1. Lohmeyer, *Galiläa und Jerusalem*, saw in the tradition of the resurrection appearances and the accounts of the Gospels a reflection of the existence of two centers of Christianity in Palestine: one in Jerusalem, and another in Galilee. Somewhat later, Elliott-Binns, *Galilean Christianity*, 33–53, based his reconstruction of Galilean Christianity on the Letter of James, which, according to him, was written in Galilee. Other studies have searched for information about these first Galilean disciples of Jesus in pre-Gospel traditions. Kloppenborg Verbin, *Excavating Q*, 214–61, and others situate the composition of Q in Galilee, thus making this document the primary source for the reconstruction of the Jesus movement there before the Jewish-Roman war. Others, including Schenke, *Urgemeinde*, 203–16, have tried to reconstruct the Jesus movement in Galilee from oral traditions, especially the popular miracle tradition.

the present chapter seeks to analyze the collection of the so-called Galilean controversies (Mark 2:1—3:6) to identify the group of disciples that preserved and transmitted these memories of Jesus, observing how they constructed their identity in confrontation with other groups.

This study will concentrate on the background of Mark's Gospel, whose author incorporated these controversies in his Life of Jesus. In Mark's narrative, these brief stories help define Jesus and his disciples' behavior against that of the scribes and Pharisees, most probably because the groups of Jesus followers for whom this gospel was written were living in a context in which they also had to legitimate their conduct.[2]

The Pre-Markan Collection of the Galilean Controversies

The first step in our research will be to identify the collection of controversies used by Mark in the composition of Mark 2:1—3:6. This section comprises five small units. However, not all of them were in the pre-Markan collection. Heinz-Wolfgang Kuhn includes in this collection only the first four units, arguing that in the first and the fourth, the title Son of Man (Mark 2:10, 28) does not have eschatological overtones as in the rest of the gospel.[3] Mark likely added the last story (Mark 3:1–5) to give the collection the form of a balanced triptych.[4] He also added the sentence that functions as a conclusion to this series of controversies (Mark 3:6) to relate the initial opposition to Jesus in Galilee to the rejection he will experience in Jerusalem later in his narrative.

However, a closer analysis shows that the first and the last stories share some traits that distinguish them from the other three. First, in these two narratives, the disciples do not intervene, whereas in the others they play a crucial role. Second, the discussion in these two controversies concentrates on Jesus' power and not on his or the disciples' behavior, as the other three stories do. Third, only the first and the last controversies include a miracle. Moreover, only the first and last controversies feature explicit allusions to

---

2. An additional argument that favors this connection is the importance of Galilee in the Gospel of Mark. As Willi Marxsen pointed out in his pioneering study, placing Jesus' activity in Galilee is one of the most characteristic features of Markan redaction; see Marxsen, *Mark the Evangelist*, 52–61.

3. This title is not used again in Mark until the first announcement of the passion (Mark 8:31). From that point on, it is used with relative frequency and always with an eschatological meaning: see Kuhn, *Ältere Sammlungen*, 81–89.

4. Dewey, "Literary Structure," 115–16.

Jesus' passion. In the first one, Jesus is accused of blasphemy, as he will be in the later interrogation before the high priest (cf. Mark 2:7 and Mark 14:64). In the last episode, he is invited to cure on the Sabbath so that he can be accused of unlawful activity, just as he will later be accused before Pilate (cf. Mark 3:2 and Mark 15:3–4). This agreement between passages is especially relevant to determine the history of the composition of this controversy collection, because the use of passion vocabulary in Mark 1–13 reveals the evangelist's redactional activity.[5] Therefore, it is quite probable that Mark included the first and the last controversies in order to create a triptych whose centerpiece is the traditional collection of controversies (Mark 2:13–28).[6] The location of this triptych at this precise point and the connections between these controversies and Jesus' passion should also be attributed to Mark.

In addition to this major redactional activity, there are three other minor interventions in the preexisting controversy collection. Two of these episodes bring "the people" onto the scene. The most recognizable appearance of "the people" is the one in 2:15 because it is introduced by an explicative *gar* (for, because) in the enclitic (second) position, which is characteristic of Mark's style: "for there were many of them who were following him." The other appearance of "the people" is in 2:13: "all the multitudes were coming to him." Both additions serve to play down the importance of the disciples and to widen the circle of Jesus followers.[7] A third minor redactional intervention can be found in 2:22, where to the saying about the wine and the wineskins the redactor added the following commentary: "but one puts new wine into new wineskins," thus insisting on the theme of new wine, to which Jesus will refer again in the account of the Last Supper (Mark 14:25).[8]

After identifying Mark's redactional work, we should determine if the pre-Markan composition shows any indications of reelaboration. This information would be useful for ascertaining the perspective and the intentions of the group of disciples that gathered the single stories to form this little collection.

---

5. See Chapter 1, above; see also Rolin, *Controverses dans l'Évangile de Marc*, 126–27.

6. Gnilka, *Evangelium* 1:131–32; Marcus, *Mark 1–8*, 213–14.

7. Rolin, *Controverses dans l'Évangile de Marc*, 122. The widening circle of followers reveals the increasing importance of the local communities; see Roh, Familia Dei *in dem synoptischen Evangelien*, 145–63.

8. Rolin, *Controverses dans l'Évangile de Marc*, 123.

The Galilean Controversies

The account of the calling of Levi that is now included in the first story (Mark 2:13–14), is an independent tradition.[9] It was added to the original controversy, together with the saying about calling sinners, thus providing it with a new framework that related Jesus' attitude toward sinners and tax collectors to his mission.[10] In the second controversy, two sayings of Jesus were added that initially had nothing to do with the question about fasting (Mark 2:21–22). These sayings do not show any sign of Markan redaction, and therefore should be considered part of the pre-Markan collection.[11] Last, in the third story, the argument about David and his men (Mark 2:25–26) originally had no relationship with the question asked by Jesus' adversaries, and therefore probably was not part of the original controversy.[12] This kind of argument is not characteristic of Mark, so we must conclude that it belongs to the pre-Markan composition.

From these observations, we can identify three phases in the composition process of the Galilean controversies. In the first one, the three controversies were transmitted independently and had a similar form (Mark 2:16–17; 18–20; 23–24, 27). In a second phase, these three stories were grouped because of their formal and thematic similarities and, more importantly, because they respond to the same practical necessities. In the process of being grouped, they were probably expanded by adding secondary elements like the calling of Levi and the reference to Jesus' mission in the first controversy (Mark 2:14–15a. 17c), the sayings of commentary in the second (Mark 2:21–22), and the argument about the transgression of David in the third (Mark 2:25–26). It would have been also at this point when an introduction would have been added, in order to place these controversies "by the seashore," (Mark 2:13) and when the christological

---

9. This story is inspired by the calling of Elisha (1 Kgs 19:19–21), and has the same literary pattern as other calling accounts (Mark 1:16–18; 19–20). See Guijarro, *Fidelidades en conflicto*, 170–74.

10. POxy 1244, fol. 2, col. 2, has preserved a version of this controversy lacking the calling of Levi (Mark 2:14–15) and the saying about the mission of Jesus (Mark 2:17b): "Now when the scribes, Pharisees and priests saw him, they were angry that he was reclining in the midst of sinners. But when Jesus heard, he said: Those who are healthy have no need of a physician . . ." (Bernhard, *Other Early Christian Gospels*, 116–17).

11. The Gospel of Thomas has preserved both the sayings (log. 47c) and the pronouncement story (log. 104), but in different logia and without any relationship between them.

12. Though in Lev 24:5–9 it is said that the loaves of bread were presented on the Sabbath, the act of eating them is not a transgression of the Sabbath, but rather a transgression of the law according to which only the priests could do such a thing (1 Sam 21:1–7).

argument in the third controversy (Mark 2:28) acquired a closing function. Finally, in a third phase, the redactor of Mark's Gospel would have added the first and last controversies (Mark 2:3–12 and 3:1–5), thus creating a triptych characteristic of his style. At this point, the collection was set in Capernaum (Mark 2:1–2) to draw a contrast with the positive reception of Jesus' message and miracles during his first stay in Capernaum (Mark 1:21–39). The conclusion (Mark 3:6), which connects the whole composition with the passion narrative, also belongs to this last compositional stage.

According to the preceding observations, the preexisting collection of the Galilean controversies used by Mark can be reconstructed as follows:[13]

Setting

13 And he [Jesus] went out again by the seashore

First Controversy

14 As he passed by, he saw Levi, the son of Alphaeus, sitting in the tax booth, and he said to him: "Follow me." And he got up and followed him.

15 And it happened that he was reclining at the table in his house and many tax collectors and sinners were dining with Jesus and his disciples . . . 16 And when the scribes of the Pharisees saw that he was eating with the sinners and tax collectors, they said to his disciples: "Why is he eating with tax collectors and sinners?" 17 And hearing this, Jesus said to them: "It is not those who are healthy who need a physician, but those who are sick; I did not come to call the righteous, but sinners."

Second Controversy

18 John's disciples and the Pharisees were fasting, and [some] came and said to him: "Why do John's disciples and the disciples of the Pharisees fast, but your disciples do not fast?" 19 And Jesus said to them: "Can the attendants of the bridegroom fast while the bridegroom is with them? So long as they have the bridegroom with them, they cannot fast. 20 But days will come when the bridegroom is taken away from them, and then they will fast in that day. 21 No one sews a patch of unshrunk cloth on an old garment; otherwise, the patch pulls away from it, the new from the old, and a worse tear results. 22 No one puts new wine into old wineskins;

---

13. What follows, with slight modifications, is from the New American Standard Bible (NASB).

otherwise, the wine will burst the skins, and the wine is lost and the skins as well."

Third Controversy

23 And it happened on the Sabbath that he was passing through the grain fields, and his disciples began to make their way along while picking the heads of grain. 24 The Pharisees were saying to him: "Look, why are they doing on the Sabbath what is not lawful?" 25 And he said to them: "Have you never read what David did when he was in need, and he and his companions became hungry; 26 how he entered the house of God in the time of Abiathar, the high priest, and ate the loaves of the offering, which is not lawful for anyone to eat except the priests, and also gave to those who were with him?" 27 Jesus said to them: "The Sabbath was made for man, and not man for the Sabbath. 28 So the Son of Man is Lord even of the Sabbath."

Having completed the reconstruction of the pre-Markan collection, we now ask whether this reconstructed collection can be located in Galilee.

The Location of the Galilean Controversies

A first clue about the original setting of the collection is found in their location "by the seashore." This way of referring to Lake Kinnereth reflects a local perspective because only in its immediate vicinity is the name "sea" applied to a lake.[14] If Mark 2:13 was added when the pre-Markan collection was formed, as suggested above, this location could be a clue that the collection was composed in Galilee.

This initial suggestion can be tested by examining the characters and the topics discussed in the controversies. The characters are, on the one hand, "Jesus' disciples" and, on the other, "the scribes of the Pharisees," "John's disciples," and "the Pharisees." The topics of discussion refer to some of Jesus and his disciples' behavior that their adversaries judge to be reprehensible: "eating with tax collectors and sinners," "not fasting," and "doing what is not lawful on the Sabbath." The collection of controversies could have been composed in Galilee only if the presence of Pharisees was significant there and if these questions of ritual purity and Sabbath observance were relevant in the region.

---

14. Theissen, *Lokalkolorit und Zeitgeschichte*, 112–15 [ET=*Gospels in Context*].

Concerning the presence and influence of Pharisees in Galilee during the first century CE, the information we have is not very conclusive. What can be deduced from the references in Josephus, Paul's Letters, and the Gospels is that there were Pharisees in Galilee. They were not part of the governing class, nor did they belong to the local aristocracy, but were "a minor and probably relatively new social force, struggling to influence people toward their way of life," a fact that "would explain why they were in constant conflict with Jesus and other proponents of traditional piety different from their own."[15]

As for the context of Jewish observance that these controversies reflect, there is information of great interest in the archaeological excavations of recent years. Discoveries from these excavations show that Galilee's cultural and religious profile, especially in the domestic sphere, was very similar to that of Judea in the Roman period.[16] Jonathan L. Reed has identified four archaeological markers of Jewish identity that can be found both in Judea and in Galilee: the abundance of stone vessels, the existence of ritual baths (*miqvaot*), the secondary burials within ossuaries in loculi tombs, and the absence of pig bones.[17] These indicators, which reveal the Jewish character of Galilee, are closely related to the topics discussed in the controversies between Jesus and the Pharisees.

We have, therefore, three pieces of evidence that support the location of the pre-Markan collection of controversies in Galilee: their location by the seashore, the characters mentioned in them, and the questions discussed. Although not all of them carry the same weight, together they allow us to propose a reasonable hypothesis. The most conclusive piece of evidence speaks to the Jewish character of Galilee and the concern about identity and religious practices there. That is, the issues raised in these controversies fit very well with such concerns. Hence, although this controversy collection could have been composed either in Judea or in Galilee, the latter is more likely because the Christian community in Jerusalem was known for its observance of traditional Jewish practices.[18] One additional argument in favor of the Galilean location of these controversy episodes is the

---

15. Saldarini, *Pharisees, Scribes and Sadducees*, 295, see also 291–97.

16. Reed, *Archaeology and the Galilean Jesus*, 28–43; Chancey, *Greco-Roman Culture*, 221–9.

17. Reed, *Archaeology and the Galilean Jesus*, 43–53. For the Jewish character of Galilee and the ideology behind the Hasmonean repopulation, see Freyne, "Geography of Restoration," 289–311.

18. Guijarro, "Primera generación," 108–19.

growing consensus about the Syrian origin of Mark's Gospel. For if Mark was composed in the Syro-Palestinian region, the geographical proximity would easily explain why traditions from Jerusalem (such as the passion narrative) were combined with traditions from Galilee (such as the collection of controversies, whose reconstruction has been proposed above).[19]

The Construction of a New Social Identity

The Galilean controversies are especially interesting for getting acquainted with the groups of Jesus followers that preserved and transmitted the traditions that Mark included in his Life of Jesus, because in these stories the disciples' identity and way of life play an essential role. In the second and third controversies, for example, what triggers the discussion is the disciples' behavior (not fasting, in 2:18; doing things unlawful on the Sabbath, in 2:24). Even though in the first controversy the primary object of discussion is Jesus' behavior (eating with tax collectors and sinners, in 2:16), the disciples are also seated at the table (2:15). What is discussed in these controversies, then, is the behavior of Jesus and his disciples, and it is likely that those who brought together these stories exhibited that kind of behavior as well and wanted to continue the behavior in front of other groups. If this is the case, then the pre-Markan collection likely reflected the group identity of the disciples who composed and transmitted it.

An argument in favor of Galilee as the social location for these controversies derives from the fact that they were transmitted in an informally controlled way. This mode of transmission preserves the essential characteristics of a story while adapting it to new situations. According to Kenneth Bailey, this kind of oral transmission is typical of traditions that a particular group considers relevant for its identity.[20] Unlike poems and proverbs (which are transmitted in a fixed and inflexible manner), and unlike irrelevant bits of news (which are transmitted with much freedom), the memories of persons and events that are important for the identity of a group are transmitted with fidelity both to the tradition and to the new

---

19. On the location of Mark in the Syro-Palestinian region, see the last section in Chapter 1 of this book (pp. 24-29).

20. The main characteristic of this type of transmission resides in the way it is controlled; it is not controlled by those seen as professionals (formal control), but by the group (informal control); see Bailey, "Informal Controlled Oral Tradition," 42-45.

situation, and therefore with a certain degree of flexibility.[21] Behind this collection of controversies, there is a group that recalls events from the life of Jesus to strengthen its identity by differentiating itself from other groups.[22]

To understand how a group constructs and consolidates its social identity, I will use here some basic concepts developed in the field of social psychology.[23] Social identity can be defined as "that part of an individual's self-concept which derives from his knowledge of his membership of a social group (or groups) together with the value and emotional significance attached to that membership."[24] This general definition of social identity needs to be adapted to different cultural contexts, bearing in mind that the content and relevance of this part of the individual's self-concept is culturally defined. Mediterranean culture had a pronounced collectivist orientation, which implies that the act of belonging to a group went a long way in determining an individual's identity.[25] Individuals in that culture shared a dyadic understanding of personality and therefore understood themselves (and defined others) as part of a group whose shared identity defined much of the individual's identity.[26]

According to the above definition, social identity has three interrelated dimensions: a cognitive dimension, by which the individual knows the identity markers shared by members of the group; an evaluative dimension, achieved by the comparison with other groups; and an affective dimension, which involves emotional attachment to the group. In what follows, I will consider the cognitive and the evaluative aspects because they are more visible in the controversies. The affective dimension is not so evident but can be inferred by observing the two other dimensions.

The cognitive dimension of social identity is constructed through categorization. Categorization is one of the human mind's primary resources.

---

21. According to Bailey, the situation in the rural zones of Palestine before the Jewish-Roman war in 66–70 CE was especially apt for this type of transmission ("Informal Controlled Oral Tradition," 50). See also Guijarro, *Jesús y sus primeros discípulos*, 23–24.

22. Theissen, *Lokalkolorit und Zeitgeschichte*, 126–31, raises the question of the function of the pronouncement stories and concludes that they "define social identity . . . and tend to have a socially demarcating function" (123–24) [ET = *Gospels in Context*].

23. Tajfel, *Human Groups and Social Categories*, 254–67. Esler has been the first to apply the theory of social identity to the study of ancient Christian texts; see his excellent summary of social identity theory in Esler, *Conflict and Identity in Romans*, 19–39.

24. Tajfel, *Human Groups and Social Categories*, 255.

25. Triandis, *Individualism & Collectivism*, 43–80.

26. Malina and Neyrey, "First-Century Personality," 72–83.

It is a process by which differences are minimized, and similarities are enhanced between diverse objects to reduce their diversity to manageable cognitive proportions. In social life, this resource plays an essential role in the patterning of behavior and the maintenance and creation of social values, norms, and beliefs characteristic of a group (identity descriptors). The most visible result of categorization in social life is the creation of stereotypes, which are abstract representations of the categories that define a group.[27]

The evaluative dimension of social identity is achieved through comparison. Groups become aware of their value when they compare themselves with other groups. This comparison is usually dominated by favoritism towards the in-group and by negative evaluation of the out-group or out-groups.[28] Individuals need to have a favorable view of their group because this positive view contributes to their positive perception of themselves. In first-century Mediterranean society, which had a collectivist orientation and the core value of which was honor, this evaluative dimension of social identity was achieved through public confrontation in a situation like the one presupposed in the controversies.[29] In such a context, the positive evaluation of the in-group in its confrontation with the out-group is highly intensified because of the importance of group affiliations for understanding individual identity.[30]

In addition to these synchronic aspects of social identity, there is also a diachronic dimension by which groups establish a relationship with persons and events in the past or the future to define or reinforce their identity. In traditional cultures, such as the one in which Jesus and his disciples lived, this diachronic dimension was strongly oriented toward the past and was closely related to cultural memory. Cultural memory is a form of collective memory that concentrates on fixed events of the past relevant to the group identity. According to Jan Assmann, it includes "that body of re-usable texts, images, and rituals specific to each society in each epoch,

---

27. According to Tajfel: "social stereotypes consist of assigning certain traits in common to individuals who are members of a group and also of attributing to them certain differences in common from members of other groups" (Tajfel, *Human Groups and Social Categories*, 115). On categorization see also Tajfel, *Human Groups and Social Categories*, 132–34.

28. Tajfel, *Human Groups and Social Categories*, 256–59.

29. Malina and Neyrey, "Honor and Shame," 29–32 and 38–41.

30. Triandis, *Individualism & Collectivism*, 68–72.

whose cultivation serves to stabilize and convey that society's self-image."[31] The first groups of Jesus' disciples shared with other Judean groups a cultural memory shaped by the epic traditions of Israel, and reference to it was a privileged means for constructing their group identity.

The Social Identity of the Galilean Disciples

The preceding observations about how groups construct and maintain their social identity can help explain how the group of Jesus' disciples that gathered and transmitted the Galilean controversies constructed their social identity. In the three stories, the categorization of the in-group and out-group(s) is indeed visible. In all of them, too, there is a tendency to create and maintain a positive identity through comparison, and in two of them we find references to Israelite cultural memory. I will now examine these three indicators of group identity construction, starting with categorization.

As stated above, categorization works by selecting a few traits that the group members have in common to transform them into descriptors. In the controversies, this process is visible in the definition of the groups that appear in them: Jesus' disciples as the in-group, and his adversaries as the out-group(s).

The first characteristic of the in-group highlighted in the controversies is the condition of being Jesus' disciples, which all the members share (Mark 2:15, 16, 18, 23). The positive value of this group identity descriptor comes from the positive value attached to Jesus in the three stories. In the first one, Jesus appears as a prophet with authority, whose invitation draws a tax collector away from his table. He is also presented as a physician whose task is to care for those who have some ailment. The fact that both images appear together is not a coincidence since in the Jewish tradition, the model of the healer who acts as an intermediary between God and the patient was the prophet Elijah, precisely the one whose actions are here recalled.[32] In the second story, Jesus is presented as the bridegroom who is now with his friends but later will be taken from them. This image also had connotations in the Jewish tradition, which represented God as the husband of Israel and the wedding feast as an expression of the time of salvation (Hos 2; Ezek

---

31. Assmann, "Collective Memory," 132.

32. The calling of Levi follows the literary pattern of the calling of Elisha (1 Kgs 19:19–21). Jesus performs the role in Mark that Elijah played in 1 Kings, see Guijarro, *Fidelidades en conflicto*, 170–74.

The Galilean Controversies

16). Finally, in the third story, Jesus is presented as the Son of Man, the Lord of the Sabbath. In the pre-Markan controversies, this self-designation evokes the theology of creation: Jesus is the man par excellence for whose service the Sabbath was instituted.[33] The social identity of the disciples is thus defined by their association with Jesus, who is presented as someone with the authority to legitimize a new pattern of behavior.

This general description of the shared identity is illustrated by some actions distinctive to the group. In the first controversy, Jesus is "eating with sinners and tax collectors" (Mark 2:16); in the second, the disciples "do not fast" (Mark 2:18), and in the third they do "what is not lawful on the Sabbath" (Mark 2:24). These three actions have to do with laws that established what could be eaten, with whom it was permitted to share food, and when one should eat or abstain from food. To understand the meaning of these behaviors, we should keep in mind that in traditional cultures, meals are ceremonies that contribute to the strengthening of group boundaries. Eating the same foods, or eating with some persons while avoiding others, or abstaining from eating on some days . . . all these behaviors contributed to defining the identity of groups. Meals display crucial aspects of group identity.[34]

In Second Temple Judaism, especially after the Maccabean period, dietary prescriptions were a decisive element in defining the identity of different groups. All these groups used dietary rules to define and strengthen their boundaries, distinguishing between those who belonged to the group and those who did not, in order to define their respective identities.[35] In the Galilean controversies, the categorization of the disciples is achieved by stressing two identity descriptors shared by them: their association with Jesus and the way they eat. The second descriptor has an intense local tone that confirms the setting of the controversies in a Galilean social context. This behavior not only defines the group's identity in which it was transmitted but also helps to place this group in a precise context: that of the flourishing of diverse groups within Judaism.[36]

---

33. In Mark this title generally has an apocalyptic overtone derived from Dan 7, and is applied to Jesus, especially in the passion narrative. In this passage and in Mark 2:10, however, it does not have this connotation, but instead underlines Jesus' connection with other human beings. See Marcus, *Mark 1–8*, 246.

34. On meals as ceremonies and their contribution to group identity, see Neyrey, "Ceremonies in Luke–Acts," 362–68.

35. Baumgarten, "Finding Oneself in a Sectarian Context," 127–30.

36. Baumgarten, *Flourishing of Jewish Sects*, 125–47.

The second resource that groups use to define their identity is comparison. Group comparison is governed by a positive assessment of the in-group and a negative evaluation of the out-group(s). The out-group with which the in-group of Jesus' disciples is comparing itself is the same in the three controversies: "the scribes of the Pharisees" (Mark 2:16); "the disciples of the Pharisees" (Mark 2:18); and "the Pharisees" (Mark 2:24), even though in the second instance "the disciples of John" are also mentioned (Mark 2:18). The fact that these groups are mentioned without further explanation indicates that the original audience of the controversies was familiar with them. They were, in fact, groups that were well known in the first-century Palestinian context.[37]

In the controversies, the scribes of the Pharisees would not sit at the same table as sinners and tax collectors (Mark 2:16). It is expressly stated that the Pharisees and the disciples of John practiced fasting (Mark 2:18). Implicit is also the fact that they observed the Sabbath. Their adherence to certain norms associated with food is a descriptor of their group identity. For them, as was the case with other Judean groups, the observance of such purity laws related to meals was an instrument for establishing boundaries and distinguishing their members from other Judeans.[38]

The controversies present three different confrontations between this group and the group of Jesus' disciples. Still, given their thematic coherence and the centrality of the food laws in the Judaism of that day, the collection has an exemplary and representative character. Therefore the three stories can be considered as three examples of the same attitude. The confrontation occurs clearly within the framework of Israelite dietary laws, which seem to be shared by all. There is no argument as to whether or not it is lawful to practice table fellowship with non-Judeans. At stake here are certain practices intended to single out groups within Judaism. In this framework, criticisms addressed to Jesus' disciples by their adversaries contain a negative evaluation of their identity.

The answers to these accusations in the earliest version of the controversies reflect popular wisdom and common sense: "it is not those who are healthy who need a physician, but those who are sick" (Mark 2:18a); "while the bridegroom is with them, the attendants of the bridegroom do not fast,

---

37. Baumgarten, *Pharisees, Scribes and Saducees*, 277–97.

38. Baumgarten, "Finding Oneself in a Sectarian Context," 131–39, identifies a spectrum that situates Banus and John the Baptist at the most radical practicers, the Essenes or the Qumran sect as strict observers, and the Pharisees as the most moderate observers of food laws.

do they?" (Mark 2:19a); "the Sabbath was made for man, and not man for the Sabbath" (Mark 2:27). Nevertheless, when these anecdotes were gathered into a more elaborate composition, this positive evaluation of the disciples' behavior was reinforced with arguments grounded on Jesus' mission: "I did not come to call the righteous, but sinners" (Mark 2:17b), and on his lordship over the Sabbath: "The Son of Man is Lord even of the Sabbath" (Mark 2:28). The basis for the positive evaluation of the in-group was the person and authority of Jesus.

The analysis of intergroup comparison in the Galilean controversies reveals a situation in which the identity of the in-group was threatened and a positive differentiation needed to be constructed. The stress laid on food laws that served to define sectarian groups in Palestinian society reflects this strategy of distinction, as does the marked favoritism toward the in-group achieved through the close attachment of its members to Jesus.

The third resource in the process of group identity construction is the appropriation of cultural memory. In the context of the first groups of Jesus' disciples, this was achieved through reference to persons and events of the epic past of Israel. In the controversies, there is, in fact, one explicit reference to the story of David and his men, who ate the loaves that only the priests were allowed to eat (1 Sam 21:2–7; Mark 2:25–26). In the story of Levi's calling, there is also a reference to the calling of Elisha by Elijah (1 Kgs 19:19–21; Mark 2:14). This allusion to Elisha's calling by Elijah, together with the reference to Jesus' mission in Mark 2:17b, is intended to present Jesus as a prophet sent to heal those in need and to call sinners. In the cultural memory of Israel, Elijah was remembered as the prophet who gathered a group of itinerant disciples and performed miracles (1 Kgs 17—2 Kgs 2; Sir 48:3–5).[39] Both aspects appear in the first controversy, where the reference to Elijah characterizes Jesus as a prophet with authority. But Elijah was also remembered for his association with Gentiles (1 Kgs 17:7–24, recalled in Luke 4:25–26), a behavior that Jesus and his disciples also analogously echo when they eat with sinners and tax collectors. Thus, the implicit but evident reference to Elijah in the first controversy establishes continuity between the attitude of Jesus and his disciples toward sinners and Elijah's attitude toward Gentiles.

Similarly, the allusion to David's story establishes a relationship between the behavior of David and his men and that of Jesus' disciples. The original anecdote, as noted above, had nothing to do with the observance

---

39. Öhler, *Elia im Neuen Testament*, 1–30.

of the Sabbath, for although Lev 24:5–9 prescribes that the loaves should be presented on the Sabbath, in 1 Sam 21:2–7 David and his men are supposed to break a cultic prescription according to which only the priests were allowed to eat the loaves of the offerings. Nevertheless, recalling this story in the context of the controversy about Sabbath observance serve to identify the disciples' behavior with the behavior of one of the most important characters in the cultural memory of Israel.

It is worth noting that according to the composition process of the Galilean controversies sketched above, these two references to the cultural memory of Israel most probably were added when the controversies were grouped. This means that the Galilean controversies witness to the existence of a group of Jesus' disciples that was struggling to construct a (new) identity within the framework of Israelite tradition.

The Historical Setting

The construction of a new social identity that can be observed in the pre-Markan collection of the Galilean controversies permits going one step farther and ask whether it is possible to identify the context and contours of the group of disciples portrayed in them. I will seek to accomplish this by addressing three questions: What factors could have favored the appearance of such a group? Who were the adversaries against whom they were defining their identity? And what was the group of those first disciples like?

Earlier in this chapter, when describing the categorization process, I pointed out the importance of the cultural context to understand group identity formation. In the context of the first groups of Jesus disciples in Galilee, there was a factor that must have affected its definition as a group, namely, the flourishing of Jewish sects after the Maccabean period.[40] According to Albert I. Baumgarten, this phenomenon has its roots in the *enclave culture* that developed in the Babylonian exile and was later transferred to Palestine. Initially, it was a *national enclave* whose objective was to differentiate Israelites from other peoples. The transfer of this *enclave culture* to the sectarian groups that emerged at that time was a consequence

---

40. The term *sect* is used here in the technical sense it has in sociological studies. It can be defined as "a voluntary association of protest, which utilizes boundary mechanisms to distinguish between its own members and those otherwise normally regarded as belonging to the same national or religious entity" (Baumgarten, *Flourishing of Jewish Sects*, 7).

of the failure of Maccabean policy to maintain Judean identity over against the surrounding Hellenistic culture. Many Judean groups "coped with the new situation by forming little enclaves, smaller and more secure, to replace the larger, national enclave threatened with disintegration."[41] In any case, there were diverse sectarian groups in Palestine in the Second Temple period, and they defined their identities by establishing differences between themselves and other Judeans.

The first groups of Jesus' disciples emerged in a context in which other Judean groups were reacting to the threat of disintegration and claiming the Israelite inheritance. These groups defined their identity in contrast to other groups already well-established. In the Galilean controversies, the Pharisees are the primary opponents. However, it is reasonable to ask whether these Pharisees represent the Pharisees in general or Pharisees who had joined the Jesus movement. At a time when Judean groups of Jesus disciples had not yet neatly defined their boundaries, Pharisees who had joined the Jesus movement likely continued to live as Pharisees.

There is some evidence of an influential group of Pharisees in the Jerusalem community of Jesus disciples. This group, associated with James, triggered a conflict in the Antiochian community due to their understanding of table fellowship (Gal 2:11–15).[42] If the influence of this group could make it to Antioch, we can presume that their impact was even greater in Galilee, not just because of geographical proximity but also because Galilee was very close to Jerusalem in terms of religious practice. It is, therefore, reasonable to think that the adversaries of those who composed and transmitted the pre-Markan collection of controversies would have been not the Pharisees in general but Christian Pharisees connected with the Jerusalem community. If this was the case, then the controversies reflected a conflict between different groups of Jesus disciples trying to define their identities in different ways.

This information is relevant for discovering what the group of those first disciples was like. Above all, it was a group that tried to construct its identity against other, more established groups. This trait, evident in the controversies, implies that the Jesus group behind the triptych of controversy episodes was not an aggregate of individuals. Rather they were a

---

41. See Baumgarten, "Finding Oneself in a Sectarian Context," 146, also 140–47; and Baumgarten, *Flourishing of Jewish Sects*, 81–113, where he shows how these groups used delimitation strategies (food, clothing, and so forth) to distinguish themselves from other Israelites.

42. Wedderburn, *History of the First Christians*, 89–120.

group in the process of defining their shared identity against mainstream Judean groups and other groups of Jesus disciples. They were an active reform group that, like other reform groups, included individuals from the social stratum of the retainers, who occupied an intermediate echelon in the social ladder.[43]

The identity of this group of Jesus disciples was defined by its connection with Jesus, whom they recognized as a model for their behavior, and about whom they expressed a series of convictions and beliefs. The image of Jesus that appears in the controversies implies an acknowledgment of his mission, an interpretation of the meaning of his death, and the recognition of his authority.[44] The Christology of this group, which presupposes an acknowledgment of Jesus' status as sent by God, subject to his will, and clothed in his authority, is the element that defined the identity of its members.

Jesus' actions also defined this group's identity. In the controversies, this behavior reflects the position of the group regarding food laws. This fact is especially telling, as such laws played a central role in defining the identities of contemporary Judean groups. In contrast with other groups, which promoted a more rigid distinction concerning Gentiles and Hellenized Judeans, this group had a more flexible attitude: they could sit at the table with sinners and were not strict in the observance of fasting and Sabbath restrictions. The controversies are, therefore, representative of the attitude of the group toward outsiders.

Conclusion

The identification of a group of Jesus disciples in Galilee proposed in this study is based on the reconstruction, location, and dating of the pre-Markan collection of the Galilean controversies. This reconstruction is grounded in a redactional analysis of the Markan text and is, therefore, hypothetical.

---

43. On the Pharisees see Saldarini, *Pharisees, Scribes and Sadducees*, 35–49. Miquel Pericás, "Movimiento de Jesús," 101–108 suggests with convincing arguments that the group of disciples who composed the Q Document also belonged to the social group of the retainers.

44. The mission of Jesus was understood against the background of the prophetic mission of Elijah, the healing prophet evoked in the first controversy (Mark 2:17b). The meaning of his death was expressed indirectly in the use of the passive form as belonging to God's plan (Mark 2:20: "when the bridegroom is taken from them"). Finally, his authority was connected to his identity as the Son of Man (Mark 2:28).

THE GALILEAN CONTROVERSIES

Nevertheless, the confluence of literary and contextual arguments makes it plausible.

The construction of a shared identity reflected in this collection of controversies fits well in the context of Second Temple Judaism. The flourishing of Jewish sects was a typically Palestinian phenomenon that helps explain the emergence of the first groups of Jesus disciples in the region. In this context, the group of disciples behind the Galilean controversies represents a concrete form of the following of Jesus in Galilee during the first generation. They were a reform group that preserved the tradition of the sayings of Jesus and his pronouncement stories because they found in them a means to define their identity as a group.

This group was building a shared identity through confrontation with other similar groups. The hypothesis presented in this chapter is that the Galilean group behind Mark's controversy episodes had in view other group(s) of Jesus' disciples of Pharisaic observance—disciples whose indirect description fits well with what we know of the Jerusalem community. This observation reveals the richness and plurality of Christian beginnings in Judea and Galilee. At the same time, the fact that the author of the Gospel of Mark incorporates these controversies into his Life of Jesus some years later is a telling sign of this gospel's connection with the Galilean tradition and of the author's interest in preserving a particular memory of Jesus.

CHAPTER 4

The Visions of Jesus and His Disciples

(Mark 1:9–11; 9:1–9)

Introduction

THE CONCENTRATION OF VISIONARY experiences around the Easter events, along with the importance of such events for the Christian faith, has shaped how the Gospel visions have been understood and explained. However, Easter appearances are not the only context in which such experiences are reported to have taken place in the beginnings of Christianity. The Gospels also mention other episodes of visions experienced by Jesus alone (Mark 1:10–11 par; Luke 10:18) or by his disciples (Mark 9:4–7 par), as well as sayings that announce future visions (Mark 13:26 par; John 1:51). Although the contents of these visions and their protagonists differ, the experiences narrated are very similar.

The purpose of this chapter is to examine the visionary experiences of Jesus and his disciples reported in the Gospel of Mark in light of neurosciences and cultural studies to understand the meaning they had for Mark's original audience.

The Traditional Interpretation of Visions, and Its Limits

The modern understanding of the visions of Jesus and his disciples have been shaped by the critical study of the Easter narratives. A widespread explanation of the Easter visions affirms that they belong to a process aimed at overcoming the cognitive dissonance caused by the death of Jesus. According to this explanation, his disciples, confused by that traumatic event, went through a process of reflection to integrate that experience. Their visions would have been the outcome of this reflective process.[1]

From a different perspective, the visions have been explained as hallucinations triggered by complex psychological processes. In the apostle Peter's case, for example, the vision of the Risen Lord would have been the result of an intense grieving process resulting from his denial, while the apostle Paul's visions could be explained as evidence of having overcome his guilt for past stubborn opposition to Jesus followers.[2] Finally, from a literary point of view, which accounts for the distance between the event and the story, visions are seen as literary elaborations aimed at awakening the reader's hope that the expectations dashed by the death of Jesus will nevertheless be fulfilled.[3]

Although these explanations differ, they all are informed by modern presuppositions and strive to integrate the data provided by biblical texts with the ontology of the Western culture. According to this perspective, visions result from processes of reflection, psychological activity, or literary creation, and interpreting them as actual events is naive or prescientific. However, we may ask if this cognitive framework is adequate to understand the visual experiences reported in ancient texts.

These texts belong, in fact, to a different culture, and presuppose a different cognitive framework. To explain the difference between modern Western cultures and cultures with a different cognitive system, anthropologists talk about *monophasic* and *polyphasic* cultures. Monophasic cultures value cognitive experiences that take place during normal waking phases. In contrast, polyphasic cultures also derive knowledge from visions, dreams, and other such experiences without drawing distinctions between this knowledge and knowledge acquired in everyday life. Like many other cultures, ancient Mediterranean culture was polyphasic, whereas modern Western culture is monophasic.[4]

When approaching the visions reported in the Gospels, we cannot forgo our worldview or the way we think. However, we are aware that those visions presuppose a different cognitive system. This seeming ambiguity is

1. Müller, *Entstehung des Glaubens*, 61–66.
2. Lüdemann, *Auferstehung Jesu*, 72–128.
3. Focant, *Évangile selon Marc*, 596.
4. Craffert, *Life of a Galilean Shaman*, 394–95.

usually solved by adopting two extreme positions: intercultural universalism or cultural relativism. The first option would try to explain the phenomenon with categories that are valid for all cultures. In contrast, the second option would accept as accurate the explanation given in the native culture. Nevertheless, it is also possible to overcome this ambiguity by adopting an eclectic approach. This third option acknowledges the complexity of intercultural dialogue and, accepting the multidimensional character of reality, strives to blend the two preceding options.[5]

In this study, I will adopt such an eclectic approach to explain the visions of Jesus (and his disciples) reported in the Gospel of Mark. Accordingly, in what follows, I will try to combine the native understanding of visions with the universalistic explanation of Western culture. In other words, I will try to blend the *emic* and the *etic* perspectives creatively.[6]

Visual Perception

Before defining this blended approach to visions more precisely, it might be useful to recall some characteristics of visual perception; a process extensively studied in neurosciences and psychology.

Vision is a complex process that involves the sensory perception of our eyes and the constructive ability of our brain. The human eye's ability is minimal and, because of that, it can only handle a small portion of the visual stimuli produced by the objects it sees. Compact information obtained by the human eye must be processed and expanded later by our brain through a complicated procedure. The human brain uses the previously acquired, verified, and stored information to broaden the limited information received via the optic nerve. Our brain uses this previously stored information to reconfigure the data obtained by the eye and transmitted by the optic nerve, thus blending personal experience and acquired cultural schemes.[7]

The act of seeing is an interactive process that involves both external stimuli and the activity of our brain, which through memory, stores a vast amount of information. One can then say that seeing is a hermeneutical activity because what we see is ultimately the result of our brain's

---

5. Lloyd, *Being, Humanity*, 1–4; Craffert, "Re-Visioning Jesus."

6. On the distinction between *emic* and *etic* models, see the Introduction to this book (pp. 5–6).

7. Stone, *Vision and Brain*.

The Visions of Jesus and His Disciples

interpretation of the stimuli it receives.[8] This interpretation—it should be emphasized—is determined by previous personal experience and, above all, by cultural clues acquired in the socialization process. Cultural patterns are, therefore, a key element in the visual process.

The visual process is usually triggered by external stimuli, but the process can also occur without any external input. Polyphasic cultures do not distinguish between these two kinds of visions, but monophasic cultures do. In monophasic cultures, vision is triggered by an external stimulus that typically takes place in a waking state. In contrast, hallucination is the visual process not triggered by an external stimulus that usually occurs in other consciousness states.[9] In both cases, however, the hermeneutic activity involved in the visual process is the same. This observation allows studying the visions as a complex phenomenon in which cultural expectations play an essential role.

States of Consciousness

In monophasic cultures, which favor knowledge acquired in waking phases, there is only one reliable form of consciousness, the so-called ordinary consciousness. Consequently, visions, dreams, and other experiences that do not take place in this state of consciousness are explained as psychological constructions and therefore are considered unreliable forms of knowledge. These presuppositions determine the *etic* interpretation of visions as hallucinations. In contrast, in polyphasic cultures, which typically accept the existence of various states of consciousness, visions, dreams, and the like, belong to everyday consciousness and can be the source of experience and knowledge. These presuppositions, in turn, shape the *emic* interpretation of visions.

8. As Macknik et al. state, "The truth, as amazing as it may seem, is this: it is our brain that builds reality, both visually and otherwise. What you see, hear, feel and think is based on what you expect to see, hear, feel and think. In turn, expectations are based on the totality of the memories and previous experiences" (*Sleights of Mind*, 21). "Our eyes only tell us part of what we are able to 'see'; the rest is the work our brain through a real labyrinth of stages" (*Sleights of Mind*, 24).

9. Although the phenomenon is more complex, this broad definition will suffice for our purposes. Sacks concords that "precise definitions of the word *hallucination* still vary considerably, chiefly because it is not always easy to discern where the boundary lies between hallucinations, misperception, and illusion. But generally, hallucinations are defined as perceptions arising in the absence of any external reality." (Sacks, *Hallucinations*, vii).

In this study, I will attempt a dialogue between these two perspectives. Such a conversation will stimulate an approach to the phenomenon of visions with a respectful and critical attitude at the same time. This dialogical perspective can be labeled as *derived etic* because it is an *etic* insight that has been modified to access a phenomenon that in Mark's Gospel is reported in *emic* terms.[10] Such a perspective is the one adopted by recent studies on altered states of consciousness. Anchored in the scientific tradition of Western culture, such studies include a cultural sensitivity that allows a considerate approach to the visionary experiences of other cultures.[11]

An altered state of consciousness can be described as a human experience in which feelings, perceptions, cognitions, and emotions are modified so that the individual's relationship with his body, his identity, the environment, people, space, and time changes.[12] Such states allow people to access dimensions of reality that are not accessible to everyday consciousness. They can take different forms (sleep, hypnosis, trance, possession, sky journeying, among others). These various forms of consciousness are defined as *altered* in comparison with the standard or normal state of consciousness. The term is purely descriptive and has no negative connotations: it designates a state of consciousness other than the normal one.

In this context, it should be noted that although it is spontaneously perceived as natural in monophasic cultures, the so-called common state of consciousness is an arbitrary construction based on our way of perceiving reality. A person's ordinary consciousness is configured during the process of enculturation, through which individuals in various stages of their lives assume the features of what their culture considers consensus reality.[13] In constructing this consensus reality, every human group makes a selection, suppressing aspects or possibilities that do not belong to their everyday consciousness. However, in polyphasic cultures, the possibilities not selected in the ordinary state of consciousness are often selected as relevant in other states of consciousness, which are defined as different or altered' in the sense mentioned above.[14]

---

10. Pilch, *Flights of the Soul*, 1–13.

11. The pioneering study by Tart, *States of Consciousness*, remains a key reference. See also Cardeña and Winkelman, eds., *Altering Consciousness*.

12. This definition is based on Pilch, *Flights of the Soul*, 148.

13. Tart, *States of Consciousness*, 33–50.

14. Tart, *States of Consciousness*, 42.

Moreover, polyphasic cultures, which assume different states of consciousness, have culturally structured ways to induce the transition from the normal state to various altered states. This process, which can be observed only in monophasic cultures in the transition from wakefulness to sleep or in cases of hypnosis and meditation, is easily triggered in polyphasic cultures, using relatively simple techniques.

The transition from one form of consciousness to another has three phases. In the first phase, the baseline state, usually the normal state of consciousness, is structured.[15] The second phase is a period of unstable transition, in which the baseline state is destructuralized. Finally, the destructured state of consciousness is restructured in the third phase and acquires a new configuration.[16] In this process, there are two transitions: one in which the configuration of the baseline state of consciousness is destabilized, and another in which the new configuration of consciousness is restructured. In the first transition, to induce a destabilized state of consciousness, it is necessary "to disrupt enough stabilization processes to a great enough extent that the baseline pattern of consciousness cannot maintain its integrity." In the same way, in the second transition, sufficient stimuli should be applied to "push disrupted psychological functioning to the new pattern."[17]

Studies on altered states of consciousness provide a suitable model for understanding the visual experiences narrated in the Gospels.[18] In this framework, visions are not understood as the visual expression of a process of reflection, the result of a psychological construction, or the symbolic formulation of theological ideas. Instead, they can be considered actual experiences from which knowledge can be gained.

The Cultural Grammar of Jesus' Visions

To understand the visions reported in the Gospels, we should remember that both the visual process and the configuration of altered states

---

15. The basic state of consciousness can be defined as "an active, stable, overall patterning of psychological functions which, via multiple stabilization relationships (loading, positive and negative feedback, and limiting) among its constituent parts, maintains its identify in spite of environmental changes" (Tart, *States of Consciousness*, 70).
16. Tart, *States of Consciousness*, 51–87.
17. Tart, *States of Consciousness*, 71–72.
18. Pilch, *Flights of the Soul*, 109–23.

of consciousness are cultural constructions. As we have seen above, the culture of a group shapes the complex process performed by the human brain in the act of seeing. By the same token, cultural presuppositions and perceptions configure the various states of consciousness. Consequently, to understand the Gospels' visions, we should become acquainted with their cultural grammar, that is, with the motifs, forms, and expressions that those visions had in ancient Mediterranean culture. In that culture, visions were closely related to religious experience. Actually, they were a fundamental expression of that experience. In his study on the irrational among the Greeks, Eric Dodds recognizes the importance of these events in the Hellenistic world:

> It is likely that these [visions] were commoner in former times than they are today since they seem to be relatively frequent among primitives, and even with us, they are less rare than is often supposed. They generally have the same origin and psychological structure as dreams, and like dreams, they tend to reflect traditional culture patterns. Among the Greeks, the most familiar type is the apparition of a god or the hearing of a divine voice that commands or forbids the performance of certain acts.[19]

In Second Temple Judaism, visions were also related to religious experience. In a book titled *The Visionary Mode*, Michael Lieb has identified an essential visionary tradition that originated in the vision of Ezekiel (Ezek 1–3). The purpose of this vision, which takes place in a state of ecstasy, is to see the glory of God. It is, therefore, the *visio Dei* to which every mystical experience tends.[20] Ezekiel's vision was the starting point and the constant reference of a long visionary and mystical tradition that had different expressions in Judaism and Christianity.[21] In the pre-Christian Jewish tradition, Ezekiel's vision inspired various visionary experiences. The visions described in the book of Zechariah (Zech 1–6), for example, are most likely a reenactment of that original vision.[22] These visions, in turn, together with those of Ezekiel, seem to have influenced those described in the book of Daniel and in the first book of Enoch, as well as those narrated in the book of Revelation (Rev 4–5).

---

19. Dodds, *Greeks and the Irrational*, 116.
20. Lieb, *Visionary Mode*, 15–26.
21. According to Pilch, *Flights of the Soul*, 30–47, Ezek 1–3 has the features of an experience in an altered state of consciousness.
22. Tiemeyer, *Zechariah and His Visions*, 13–17.

The Visions of Jesus and His Disciples

In later Jewish tradition, this visionary trajectory received a name and acquired a cultural formulation. It was known as the tradition of the *Merkabah* (Sir 49:8), the celestial chariot of the divine throne, whose vision could be experienced by practicing the works of the *Merkabah*.[23] This visionary tradition had a decisive influence on the Jewish and Christian apocalyptic but did not exhaust the references to which first-century Jews could turn to explain their visions. God had communicated with the patriarchs and prophets through dreams and visions (Gen 15:1.12; Num 12:6), often at night (1 Sam 15:16; Isa 29:7; Job 4:13). Some figures, like Moses, had experienced God's vision in a different way (Exod 24). In the first century, the biblical tradition provided different models to construct the visionary experience. These different ways of constructing the visionary experience were part of the cultural grammar of people living in that society.

This cultural grammar played a crucial role in the visionary experiences of Jesus and his disciples narrated in the Gospels. However, to understand the visions properly, it is not enough to describe the elements of the cultural grammar that Jesus and his disciples used to describe their experiences. It is also necessary to know how elements of the cultural grammar were articulated and, above all, how individuals belonging to the culture used elements of the cultural grammar to construct their own visionary experiences. In this connection, Michael Lieb speaks of the "visionary mode" as the means to access that primordial experience that transcends human understanding.[24] By its very nature, this kind of experience cannot be explained with the categories of everyday experience. For that reason, it is usually accessed through the re-creation of the reported vision. This means that any interpretation of it implies a creative appropriation of that experience.[25]

---

23. Lieb, *Visionary Mode*, 15–41; Tiemeyer, *Zechariah and His Visions*, 37–44.

24. Lieb, *Visionary Mode*, 2–3, assumes a distinction proposed by psychologist Carl Jung, who, speaking of the modes of artistic creation, distinguishes between the *psychological mode* and the *visionary mode*. The first one uses elements of everyday consciousness, while the second refers to a primordial experience that transcends human understanding.

25. Lieb states: "These reformulations are the means by which the visionary is acculturated in a complex act of transmission. Underlying this act is a hermeneutics in which the propensity of the *Urerlebnis* to undergo transformation at every state is realized in the very act of implementing it in knowable form. Whether as a hermeneutics or as a poetics, that form is itself a re-enactment of the vision, one that says as much about how the re-enactment occurs as it does about the vision it seeks to elucidate" (Lieb, *Visionary Mode*, 7).

Christopher Rowland et al. have formulated more explicitly the consequences of the peculiar nature of the visionary experience. According to them, people of ancient Mediterranean cultures interpreted visions not by explaining them but by what may be called an *exegesis through imagination*. This kind of exegesis presupposed that to understand a vision, it is necessary to see what the visionary saw. This process implied a reenactment of the visionary experience, a re-creation of the experience described in the vision.[26] Similarly, Dan Merkur has identified in Jewish and Christian apocalyptic literature some exegetical practices that were intended to induce visions. The starting point of this kind of visionary exegesis was usually one or more passages of Scripture (not necessarily a vision) that were displayed in the form of mental images as a means to induce visions.[27] This exegesis was performative, because the act of interpreting implied having an experience of what was interpreted. For this kind of exegesis, it was not enough to enact the vision, because the vision is only the means to accessing a new reality; it was also necessary to enter it. In the model of altered states of consciousness outlined above, the procedure presupposed by this exegesis could be defined as a culturally structured process to access an altered state of consciousness.

Thus, we may conclude that Jesus and his disciples shared a cultural grammar that afforded them the motives and forms to configure their visions. Moreover, that culture provided them with clues to articulate this experience as a means of accessing an altered state of consciousness. These two conclusions help us to place the visions of Jesus and his disciples in their original cultural context.

The Visions of Jesus and His Disciples in the Gospel of Mark

In the tradition about Jesus, as in the rabbinic stories about holy men, the *ecstatic* side of his actions and teachings has been less valued than the *rational* one.[28] However, in the memories preserved by his disciples, there is

---

26. Rowland et al. explain that the text of Ezek 1–3 has been transmitted in so many different forms that it is almost impossible to reconstruct its original formulation. This seemingly erratic textual transmission reveals that this fundamental text of Jewish visionary tradition was reformulated by interpreters who accessed the vision through it ("Visionary Experience," 47–50). On the complexity of the textual transmission, see Lieb, *Visionary Mode*, 16–23.

27. Merkur, "Cultivating Visions."

28. Green, "Palestinian Holy Men," 646–47.

clear evidence of his frequent interaction with the spirits, a kind of activity that his contemporaries related to ecstatic experiences.[29]

Visions belong to this less rational side of Jesus' ministry. For this reason, it is noteworthy that the Gospel of Mark describes two of them in a very detailed form: the vision that takes place after Jesus' baptism (Mark 1:10–11) and the one he shares with some of his followers on the occasion of his transfiguration (Mark 9:4–7). In the story told by Mark, these two visions enjoy a place of preference because they are intentionally located at the beginning of Jesus' public activity and at the beginning of his way to Jerusalem.

These reports of Jesus' visions fit well into the culture of Mark's time. It is, therefore, entirely plausible that Jesus may have gone through such experiences and that he may have initiated his disciples into them. Therefore, the stories and sayings that portray these visions should not be interpreted as literary formulations of theological ideas but rather as testimonies of actual experiences. These experiences must be understood in the context of a polyphasic culture that valued dreams, visions, and other altered states of consciousness as sources of experience and knowledge.

We will consider, then, that the visions reported in the Gospel of Mark are literary elaborations of actual experiences, which were constructed using a specific cultural grammar. Identifying this cultural grammar is crucial to understand their meaning more accurately. Cultural clues may also reveal to what extent Jesus and his disciples were reenacting previous visions and if they were using them to induce an altered state of consciousness.

Jesus' Vision after His Baptism

Although in the Fourth Gospel John the Baptist claims to have witnessed Jesus' vision after his baptism (John 1:33–34: "I have seen"), in the Gospel of Mark, Jesus' baptism is reported to have been a private event to which only Jesus seems to have had access (Mark 1:10: "he [Jesus] saw"). Mark's portrayal of that event draws on a well-known cultural grammar: the heavens open, the Spirit of God descends, and a heavenly voice is heard. Traditional exegesis has accurately identified these allusions to Scripture and has established the precise meaning of the statement that the voice from heaven

---

29. On the relationship of Jesus with the spirits, see Miquel Pericás, *Jesús y los espíritus*. On the relationship between possession and ecstatic experience, see Neufeld, "Eating, Ecstasy, and Exorcism."

makes about Jesus. Here I would like to complement these explanations, showing that the narrative describes an altered state of consciousness.

The elements of the cultural grammar—namely, the heavens being torn, the Spirit of God descending in bodily form, and the voice that comes from the divine realm ("from the heavens")—call to mind Isaiah's oracle: "Oh that you would rend the heavens and come down" (Isa 63:19, according to the Hebrew text). However, first and foremost, these elements recall the visionary tradition of the *Merkabah*, which by Jesus' time, was quite developed. The critical element of this tradition was the interaction between the divine realm (the heavens) and the human one (the earth), primarily through the revelation of heavenly glory.[30] The basic movement was top-down, but the forms of this communication could differ: divine communication could come in the form of the celestial chariot, the Son of Man, or the Spirit of God. Such revelatory movement allowed humans to access the divine realm—to hear the heavenly voice, to ascend to heaven, and so forth.

The relationship of Jesus' vision after baptism with Ezekiel's (Ezek 1–3) is reinforced by the fact that within the Gospel story the function of the vision after baptism is very similar to the function of Ezekiel's vision through oracles and prophetic ministry. In both cases, the encounter with the divine takes place in a vision, and, as a result of this encounter, the seer is transformed and receives a mission.[31] Despite the apparent differences between the two stories, these structural connections suggest that the vision of Jesus could be the result of a reenactment of Ezekiel's vision, which Jesus may have used as a means to accessing an altered state of consciousness.[32]

The baptismal vision of Jesus has, in fact, some of the characteristic traits of altered states of consciousness, such as sensory excitement or alterations in the perception of the external world and of one's own identity.[33] However, this does not necessarily imply that the visions themselves

---

30. Lieb, *Visionary Mode*, 47, contends that "from the perspective of the Hebrew Bible, the visionary experience is one largely enacted by means of a revelation of deity that moves from the celestial region (the realm of God) to the terrestrial region (the human realm)."

31. On baptism as a visionary experience, see Rowland, *Open Heaven*, 358–63. On the symbolic ties with Ezekiel's vision, see Orlov, *Glory of the Invisible God*, 145–48.

32. As we have seen in the second chapter of this book (pp. 47–48), the baptismal vision of Jesus belongs to an initiation process that includes fasting, undergoing temptations, and other practices.

33. Tart, *States of Consciousness*, 12–13.

determined the quality of the altered state through which Jesus entered into his experience. As we have seen above, in the performative exegesis of the visionary tradition, the reenactment of such visions facilitated access to another realm of reality but did not determine the experience that the seer had in it.

Although the Gospel of Mark mentions only one such episode on the occasion of Jesus' baptism, this kind of experience was not unusual during his ministry. The widespread opinion that Jesus was "out of his mind" (Mark 3:21) is an apparent reference to ecstatic practices. In the Gospel of Luke, Jesus himself refers to another vision in the enigmatic saying of Luke 10:18: "I saw Satan fall like lightning from heaven," where the opening of the heavens is presupposed. The opening of the heavens is also a central motif in some visions of Jesus' followers, such as the one announced by Jesus in the Gospel of John (John 1:52: "you will see the heavens open"). In the books of the New Testament, other characters have similar experiences. In the Acts of the Apostles, Stephen and Peter are reported to have seen "the heavens open" (Acts 7:56; 10:11), and the seer in the book of Revelation sees "a gate opened in heaven," which, in turn, allows him to see the heavenly throne (Rev 4:1–2). The frequent mentions of the open-heavens motif recall Jewish experiences of the *Merkabah* and suggest that this tradition of visionary experiences may be part of the cultural grammar that shaped Jesus' vision. The allusion to the heavens opened also connects Jesus' baptismal vision to subsequent visions of his followers.

The Vision of Jesus and His Disciples during the Transfiguration

The other important vision of Jesus reported by Mark takes place during his transfiguration (Mark 9:4–8). This new vision is related to the previous one since in both we hear the divine voice name Jesus as the beloved Son: "You are my beloved Son; with you, I am well pleased" (Mark 1:11); "This is my beloved Son; listen to him" (Mark 9:7). However, both the circumstances in which the new vision occurs and the elements that compose it make it different from the vision after Jesus' baptism. To begin with, this new vision does not take place in the Jordan, but on a mountain, which Jesus has climbed with some of his disciples. In addition, Jesus is not the only beneficiary of this vision; those who are with him are also involved in it.[34]

---

34. Later tradition will picture them as those who heard the voice on the mountain (2 Pet 1:17–18).

Thirdly, in this case, two well-known figures from Israel's past (Moses and Elijah) appear in the vision. Finally, the voice that declares the identity of Jesus does not come from the open heavens but from a cloud that overshadows them.

The content of the second vision and the circumstances surrounding it are typical of the transition to an altered state of consciousness. In this case, the transition from the baseline state of consciousness to the altered one occurs in the context of an initiation process for the disciples who are with Jesus. Hiking up a "high mountain" (Mark 9:2) and witnessing the subsequent transformation of Jesus that takes place in the vision prepare this small group of disciples to access a different state of consciousness. Finally, the vision they experience happens in a state in which the perception of the self and the environment is changed.[35]

The cultural grammar accessed to describe this vision is different from the grammar called on to depict the baptism. Although the mention of the cloud that overshadows Jesus and those with him may imply that there is a movement from above, what is most relevant in this episode is the movement upwards, a movement that the narrative emphasizes by telling that Jesus climbed with his disciples a "high mountain" (Mark 9:2). The model of this vision is not, then, that of the *Merkabah*, but another one, which attentive readers can identify by paying attention to the characters who appear in the vision. The appearance of Elijah and Moses is not, in fact, a casual one: they play an essential role in the vision. Their task is to guide the participants because both of them were known to have benefited from a vision of God after having climbed a mountain (Exod 24:12–18; 1 Kgs 19:9–18).

Traditional exegesis has noticed that in the story of the transfiguration clear allusions to Moses's vision on Mount Sinai: "Like Moses, Jesus climbs the mountain, takes with him three companions whose names are mentioned (Exod 24:1, 9). On the seventh day, God's voice is addressed to Moses... The cloud (in the singular!) is, as in Exod 24:6, 16[ff], a sign of God's presence. There is also an important coincidence in the fact that God's voice resonates from the cloud."[36]

---

35. See Pilch, *Flights of the Soul*, 137–42, where some of the traits of the altered states of consciousness that appear in this passage are identified.

36. Gnilka, *Evangelium*, 2:32 (my translation). In an excursus about biblical parallels of the transfiguration story, Joel Marcus concludes that Exod 24 is the most evident cross-reference: Marcus, *Mark 8–16*, 1108–18. Orlov, *Glory of the Invisible God*, 108–43, has recently provided sound arguments in favor of the traditional view, showing the

The Visions of Jesus and His Disciples

The grammar of this vision is easy to identify. Still, the experience of Jesus and his disciples differs from that of Moses and those with him.[37] The reenactment of Moses's or Elijah's vision may have enabled access to an altered state of consciousness but did not determine what Jesus and his close disciples experienced in it. In this vision, Jesus has a central role because in addition to acting as the one who instructs his disciples, he himself, not the encounter with God, appears as the object of the vision.

The different cultural grammars presupposed in the vision after the baptism and the vision during the transfiguration reveal various ways of accessing the visionary experience. This fact is a partial confirmation of the thesis that Jesus had been party to more than one visionary experience. However, the most revealing aspect of the transfiguration story is that Jesus initiates his disciples into visionary experiences.[38] The transfiguration narrative highlights the stages of the initiation process. First, Jesus chooses a small group from among his disciples. Then, he climbs with them a high mountain. In the next step, before the vision occurs, Jesus is transfigured in their presence in order to show them how to access an altered state of consciousness. Only after these three steps have been completed are the disciples ready to experience the vision. In it, the appearance of Moses and Elijah offers them a clue to make sense of what is happening: they are having a vision like the one Moses and Elijah each had. Still, the content of their experience is not the vision of God but the revelation of Jesus' identity.

If this interpretation of the transfiguration story is correct, we may argue that Jesus initiated his disciples into such visionary practices. Moreover, the similarity between this vision and the Easter appearances suggests that this initiation of the disciples prepared them to experience the Easter visions.[39]

Mosaic features of the transfiguration story.

37. The differences between the two episodes allow an explanation of the relationship between them. Some think the episode of the transfiguration could have been created from Exod 24. Others, however, tend to think that the vision of Moses was recalled to interpret the experience of Jesus; see Focant, *Évangile selon Marc*, 333–34.

38. Destro and Pesce, "Continuity or Discontinuity," 60–61.

39. The structural similarity between the story of the transfiguration and the Easter visions has often been explained by postulating a relationship the other way around (i.e., from the Easter visions to the transfiguration). According to this explanation, the transfiguration story would have originally been an appearance story that Mark would have placed at the beginning of Jesus' journey to Jerusalem; see Weeden, *Mark. Traditions in Conflict*, 128–36. This interpretation, however, does not explain the differences between the two narratives, as noted by Marcus, *Mark 8-16*, 1118.

Conclusion

The inquiry carried out in this chapter shows how the use of a reading scenario elaborated with models from the social sciences can contribute to understanding better the pre-Easter visions reported in the Gospel of Mark.

In the first place, this reading scenario has revealed the complexities of visual perception. The process of seeing is not a simple or straight one but involves an elaborate construction in which the cultural background plays an important role. *To see* is a constructive process determined by the cultural grammar of the society in which the vision takes place.

Second, the distinction between monophasic and polyphasic cultures provides an essential clue to understanding the place and the role of visions in Western culture and in ancient Mediterranean cultures. To bridge the cultural gap between them, we adopted an eclectic approach that considers both understandings of visions. In this framework, the identification of visions as altered states of consciousness has helped us understand the visual experience as a means to access a different reality. Like most societies past and present, ancient Mediterranean societies recognized the existence of these states of consciousness and had culturally structured means of accessing them. Visions were one of such means that granted access to those states of consciousness

Finally, the hypothesis proposed in previous studies of visions about the existence of a performative exegesis facilitates a better understanding of the initiating function of the transfiguration story. In it, in fact, Jesus progressively introduces some of his closest disciples to the visionary experience, providing them with essential clues to accessing God's realm. In this connection, it is worth noting that Mark has placed this initiation of the disciples in the context of a narrative section in which Jesus instructs the Twelve on discipleship (Mark 8:31—10:52). This initiation to the visual experience will prepare them to experience and interpret the Easter visions.

CHAPTER 5

Healing Stories and Medical Anthropology

(Mark 10:46–52)

Introduction

IN THE INTRODUCTION TO this book, I stated that reading the Bible implies participating in an intercultural dialogue. We modern Western readers, socialized in a postindustrial, low-context, monophasic culture, find it difficult to understand some aspects of texts produced in an ancient Mediterranean culture, which was a preindustrial, high-context, polyphasic culture. In the previous chapter, we examined Mark's reports of visions, trying to bridge this cultural gap with the help of an adequate reading scenario. In this chapter, we turn to another foreign feature of Mark's narrative: Jesus' healings.

Persuaded that the biomedical model of modern Western medicine is not an adequate tool to explain the meaning of ancient healing stories, exegetes have concentrated on their literary and theological features.[1] These studies have significantly contributed to our understanding of healing narratives, but we cannot forget that the primary purpose of these narratives was reporting on Jesus' healings, and so we cannot avoid the task of interpreting them as such events.

To understand the meaning of these narratives in their original context, I will make use in this chapter of *medical anthropology*, a subdiscipline of cultural anthropology, whose object is the study of non-Western

---

1. Representative of this trend is Theissen, *Urchristliche Wundergeschichten* [ET = *Miracle Stories*]; see also Leon-Dufour, *Milagros de Jesús*; and Latourelle, *Milagros de Jesús*.

medical systems from a cross-cultural perspective.[2] Scholars in this branch of learning have elaborated some conceptual models that are appropriate for understanding illness and healing in the ancient world. Following the lead of studies that have applied these models to the study of Jesus' healings, I propose here a reading scenario to interpret the healing of the blind man from Jericho reported in Mark 10:46–52.[3]

Illness and Healing in Mark's Times and Today

Medical anthropologists have discovered that different cultures experience and understand illness differently, so culture determines how an individual or a group perceives, symbolizes, and reacts to it. Arthur Kleinman describes medicine as a cultural system that includes all the elements related to health in a given society. These elements comprise the perception of illness and its etiology, the individual and collective ways of reacting to it, the values that determine both, as well as the therapeutic strategies available, or the social institutions dedicated to healthcare. These elements are mutually connected and form an integrated system.[4] This means that illness and healing can be adequately understood only within the framework of a specific culture.

The ways of understanding and experiencing health and illness in the world of Mark show noteworthy similarities with so-called non-Western medicine, which is predominant in preindustrial societies. The medical systems of these societies have in common a series of traits such as the following:

---

2. For an overview, see Worsley, "Non-Western Medical Systems"; and Young, "Anthropologies of Illness."

3. Peder Borgen ("Miracles of Healing") took this approach in an insightful study years ago, but his suggestion was not followed by mainstream scholarship. At around the same time John Pilch began to publish a series of articles, in which he applied different models taken from medical anthropological studies to New Testament texts (Pilch, *Healing in the New Testament,*). By that time also, Hector Avalos produced two interesting studies on the role of the temple in the healthcare system of the ancient Near East, and on the import of the healthcare strategies for the rise of Christianity (Avalos, *Illness and Health Care*; Avalos, *Health Care*).

4. Kleinman, *Patients and Healers*, 24–25; on the relationship between the health system and culture, see Kleinman, *Patients and Healers*, 35–45, and the overview in Worsley, "Non-Western Medical Systems," 327–30.

1. The symptoms of illness are explained on the basis of the belief that there is interdependence between the natural, the supernatural, the society, and the person.
2. The healer has precise knowledge of the patient's social roles within the community and shares the values and social norms of the patient.
3. Participation in the healing process of other significant persons—mainly members of the extended family, relatives, and neighbors—is decisive in the overall process.

In contrast, Western biomedicine, which is the prevailing model in industrialized societies, is rooted in an empirical conception of disease, whose goal is the treatment of pathologies. As a result of those presuppositions, it does not pay much attention to the personal, social, and supernatural factors, which determine the perception and interpretation of illness in most cultures.[5]

To understand how illness and healing were perceived in the world of Mark and to identify the most relevant differences between that healthcare system and ours, I will draw on three conceptual models that allow a systematic comparison between various ways of understanding and experiencing health and illness. These will allow us to find out (a) in which sector of the healthcare system the healing reported by Mark should be located; (b) which understanding of the illness is transparent in this episode, and how this understanding of illness affects the status of the sick person; and (c) what therapeutic strategy was followed by Jesus.

The Healthcare System

The healthcare system is not an actual entity but rather a conceptual model elaborated on the basis of what the persons involved think and do vis-à-vis health and illness in a specific social context. This model includes perceptions, expectations, and value judgments that are not always conscious. It also considers the reactions and behavior patterns of those involved in the illness and the healing process. Both the perception of illness and the reactions to it are governed by cultural values and are subject to the influence of certain social factors such as institutions, roles, and relations in which the evaluation and treatment of the illness take place. The cross-cultural nature

---

5. Worsley, "Non-Western Medical Systems," 316–7; Good and Delvecchio-Good, "Meaning of Symptoms," 167–74.

of this model makes it especially appropriate for comparing different health systems.[6]

In its overall structure, a healthcare system consists of three interrelated sectors: the popular, the professional, and the folk sector. In the popular sector, the most important one, those belonging to the social networks of the sick person, notably family and relatives, carry out the treatment of the illness. In most cases, it is in this nonspecialized sector, deeply rooted in popular culture, where the treatment of illness is defined and initiated. The professional sector is governed by formal institutions and persons trained through a socially sanctioned process. Due to their specialization, personnel in this sector usually propose their version of clinical reality as the only acceptable one. Finally, the folk sector comprises another series of different treatments. Some of them are close to the professional sector, but most are related to the popular one. It is in this last sector that we find the traditional healers.[7]

These three sectors are defined differently within each culture and even within various social groups in the same culture. Furthermore, each culture establishes an implicit hierarchy that determines how a sick person will pass from one sector to another in the search of health. To understand the story of Bartimaeus's healing, we must place it in the adequate sector of the ancient Mediterranean healthcare system, and for that, we need to gain some knowledge of these three sectors.

In most cultures, the *popular sector* provides the first explanations and remedies to treat sickness. Considering the centrality of the family in ancient Mediterranean cultures, we may assume that the participants in this first sector were above all those related to the sick person by kinship or fictive kinship ties. Thus, the popular sector's network may have included family relations, neighbors, clients, and patrons. Usually, the sick person and the social networks to which he or she belongs make use of the values and beliefs of popular culture about specific illnesses in order to interpret them and react to them in a culturally meaningful way. The Gospel narratives provide some sporadic evidence of this sector. In them, we find relatives that look after the sick (Mark 1:30) or ask for healing on behalf of an ill person (Mark 7:25; 9:17–18). We also find neighbors or clients who help

---

6. According to Kleinman, *Patients and Healers*, 25–27, this model can be used to describe the variations and structural elements of distant cultures over time, which makes it especially suitable for our purposes.

7. For a more detailed description of these three sectors, see Kleinman, *Patients and Healers*, 49–60.

the sick person (Mark 2:3–4), and even patrons who intercede for their clients (Luke 7:7–8). Given the prevalence of this sector in non-Western healthcare systems, we ought to suppose that this was also the most crucial sector in the healthcare system of Mark's world. This presupposition is confirmed when we consider the healthcare functions performed by the family vis-à-vis its members, although not every family could perform those functions in the same way.[8]

The second sector was *professional medicine*. In ancient Palestine, this kind of medicine was practiced in groups under Greek influence from the Hellenistic period on. Ben Sira (Sir 38:1–15) praised physicians and their profession and reminded his readers that healing was always in God's hands.[9] In the same vein, the Jewish historian Josephus mentions several times the activity of physicians in first-century Palestine (*Life* 404; *Antiquities of the Jews* 19.157), pointing out their failures (*Jewish War* 1.598) and their inability to heal, as in the case of Herod the Great (*Antiquities of the Jews* 15.245–246). Even Jesus figuratively referred to himself as a physician (Mark 2:17; Gospel of Thomas 31). Despite these positive references, the traditional attitude towards physicians in Judean society was one of distrust. Israelite monotheism could only think of God as the source of health, and consequently, healing could only be acquired through his mediators, primarily through the prophets, who were the authorized consultants in the traditional healthcare system of Israelite society.[10] As in the rest of the Hellenistic-Roman world, professional physicians, following the teachings of Hippocrates, sought to find out the causes of illnesses and their remedies. These professionals had a global, philosophical perspective of the cosmos and an integrated idea of the human person.[11] Mark mentions only one case of recourse to this professional sector, that of the hemorrhaging woman, and he does not fail to mention that she had spent a considerable fortune on physicians (Mark 5:25–26). To this same sector of professional medicine can be ascribed most of the activities carried out in the sanctuaries of Asclepius and in the therapeutic baths.[12] Excavations

---

8. On the various types of family, their health functions, and their ability to perform them depending on their social level, see Guijarro, *Fidelidades en conflicto*, 59–61.

9. Noorda, "Illness and Sin."

10. Avalos, *Illness and Health Care*, 260–77.

11. Scholars often identify medicine with the professional sector of medicine: Scarborough, "Medicine"; Kee, *Medicine, Miracle and Magic*, 27–66; Seybold and Mueller, *Sickness and Healing*, 98–100.

12. In addition to the traditional methods of Hippocratic medicine, other methods

at the pool of Bethesda in Jerusalem suggest this place may have been a sanctuary devoted to Asclepius.[13] In any case, it seems that the site was a healing center, at least from the Hellenistic period on.[14] We also know that there were therapeutic baths. Josephus mentions the fountains of Callirhoe to which Herod was sent by his physicians (*Antiquities of the Jews* 17.171), and archaeologists have uncovered other similar facilities on both sides of the Jordan in the Hellenistic and Roman periods.[15]

Finally, *folk medicine*, the third sector, which reached beyond the circle of family, relatives, and neighbors, depended on specialists who did not practice professional medicine. An outstanding feature of this sector is its proximity to the popular sector, with which it shares a common understanding of sickness and its etiology. Folk medicine is the realm of magic and exorcism and the arena of popular healers who constitute its most representative figures. Popular healers share a set of traits in different cultures: they share their patients' worldview and understand health and illness very much the way their patients do; they accept the symptoms presented to them as coincident elements of a syndrome; they treat their patients outdoors; and they usually know the social situation of the sick person.[16]

In the Hellenistic-Roman world, this type of popular healer was quite common. In most cases, their healings were a means to confirm the authority of their doctrine and the basis of the claims they made about their person.[17] In the Israelite tradition, as we have seen, the most representative figure of this kind was the healing prophet. This type of healer was not uncommon in the time of Jesus, although Jesus was the most notable instance in first-century Palestine. Other contemporary healers, such as Honni and Hannina ben Dosa, share with him, among other traits, a close connection to the prophet Elijah.[18]

---

were used such as *incubatio* (sleeping in the sanctuary in order to be healed by the god, or in order to receive from the god a communication about the remedy to be applied) and medicinal baths; see Seybold and Mueller, *Sickness and Healing*, 101–2.

13. Since the appearance of Duprez, *Jésus et les dieux guerisseurs*, on Jesus and the healing gods, this site has been identified as the place where the healing of the paralytic narrated in John 5:2–9 took place, but this identification has been challenged by recent research: Devillers, "Piscine"; Boismard, "Betzata."

14. Pierre and Rousée, "Sainte Marie de la Probatique," 26–27.

15. Dvorjetski, "Medical Hot Springs"; Weber, "Thermal Springs."

16. Pilch, "Sickness and Healing," 198–200.

17. Anderson, *Sage, Saint, and Sophist*, 103–5; Seybold and Mueller, *Sickness and Healing*, 103–5.

18. Green, "Palestinian Holy Men"; Vermes, *Jesus the Jew*, 78–80; Meier, *Mentor,*

Different factors determined access to these three sectors of the healthcare system. We can suppose that popular medicine was always the first option. When healing could not be achieved through it, resourceful families would turn to professional medicine, but this was a luxury reserved to few. Moreover, it is very likely that, among the most traditional strata of Palestinian society, turning to this kind of medicine would stir up considerable distrust since, in some ways, turning to medical professionals could be seen as an affront to the sovereignty of God. Finally, the majority of the population would have had access to popular healers. This option would avoid conflict with traditional allegiance to Israel's God because, in the end, it was a type of religious healing. It is in this sector of folk medicine where Jesus' healings must be located.

The Explanatory Model

There is always an explanatory model, explicit or implicit, behind the various ways of understanding illness and coping with it. Explanatory models are simplified, abstract representations of some complex real-world interaction, consisting of a set of directives followed by those participating in them. Healthcare models offer an explanation of illness, guide the participants in choosing among the various available therapies, and assign meaning to the illness from the personal and social point of view. The explanatory model determines which symptoms are relevant and how they are to be interpreted and treated.[19]

Underlying explanatory models surface in various ways in the vocabulary used to name and explain illness and healing.[20] Therefore, to identify the explanatory model, we should pay close attention to the semantic field used to describe them. The vocabulary used in the story of the healing of the blind man of Jericho and in other New Testament healing stories may give us access to the explanatory model of illness and health shared by Mark and his audience.

Message, and Miracles, 581–88.

19. According to Kleinman, explanatory models for disease are critical to two of the five basic clinical functions he identifies: (a) establishing criteria to guide the health-seeking process, and (b) identifying and classifying specific cases of disease. There is a previous function, which I will discuss later, that determines the explanatory models: the cultural interpretation of the disease (Kleinman, *Patients and Healers*, 104–10).

20. Young, "Anthropologies of Illness," 266–68.

The explanatory models employed in the various sectors of the health-care system, especially in the popular and in the folk sectors, depend in no small measure on the cultural interpretation of sickness. Medical anthropologists usually distinguish between *disease* and *illness* to stress this difference. *Disease* refers to abnormalities in the structure or functioning of a bodily organ or system of organs, whereas *illness* refers to a person's perceptions and experiences of a condition.[21]

Understanding sickness as illness is, then, a cultural process. All cultures have patterns of perceiving, comprehending, explaining, assessing, and treating sickness symptoms. These patterns are influenced by personal and family perceptions, and through them by the cultural values of each society. The identification of sickness takes place by labeling symptoms and assessing their significance for the individual and the group to which he or she belongs. In this way, the sickness itself takes on a precise meaning and is shaped according to specific behavior patterns, being transformed into a specific cultural form. That cultural form is what we call illness.[22] As a result of this process, the cultural construction of sickness establishes (a) the way it is understood and explained; (b) how it affects the status of the sick person; and (c) how to treat it, depending on the therapeutic strategies available.[23] This last aspect will be considered later. Now I turn to the first and second, which are closely related to the explanatory model.

As noted above, the cultural understanding of sickness and its etiology in the ancient world is reflected in the vocabulary used to name and describe it. A review of literary and epigraphic evidence reveals the native perception of popular and folk sectors. A survey of the language of healing in the dedications and inscriptions of the major Asclepius shrines of the Hellenistic world and in the New Testament shows that the terminology used in these two contexts is the same and has an almost identical meaning. This conclusion reveals that explanatory models of sickness were broadly shared in the Hellenistic-Roman world.[24]

An analysis of the literary evidence of the Second Temple period reveals that sickness could be caused by God or God's agents such as angels, demons, and so forth. Sickness could also be caused by evil spirits, stars,

---

21. On the distinction between pathology and disease, see Young, "Anthropologies of Illness," 264–66.

22. On disease as a cultural elaboration of the pathology, see Kleinman, *Patients and Healers*, 72–80.

23. Avalos, *Health Care*, 23–27.

24. Wells, *Greek Language of Healing*, 100–101 and 219–29.

and, above all, sin. God was also the ultimate source of healing and health, but there were various means of restoring it. The main ones were faith and prayer, repentance, exorcisms, physicians, folk medicine, and magic. Not all these means had the same value, but they shared the same explanatory model, which did not separate the natural from the supernatural, the social from the personal.[25] In any case, these features provide us with a very general framework, which has to be filled out in each case, taking into consideration the terminology used.

All these issues on the nature of sickness, its etiology, and therapeutic strategies are a broad framework in which we must include the regional differences that shaped many aspects of the cultural understanding of sickness and healing. Thus, for example, the Israelite explanatory model was configured by the Levitical system of purity.[26] The explanatory model of a given social group is a blending of the general and the regional cultural perceptions.

A crucial aspect of every explanatory model is the way it affects the status of the sick person. In most cultures, sickness is perceived as a form of social deviance and attaches a stigma to the sick person. The degree of stigmatization and its precise meaning depends on how a specific sickness is perceived. In the Levitical healthcare system, for example, some chronic diseases, such as leprosy, attached to the sick person a stigma that prompted exclusion from the community (Lev 13–15). This exclusion was not for sanitary reasons but was related to the purity system. This same understanding of purity determined that those affected by some physical blemishes such as lameness, deafness, or blindness were not allowed to enter the temple. To understand the meaning of those stigmas in ancient Mediterranean societies, we need to bear in mind that the status of a person was perceived then in terms of honor and shame, which were the core values of that culture.

The Therapeutic Strategy

An essential aspect of every healthcare system is its therapeutic strategy. A therapeutic strategy is the procedure followed to treat an illness in order to obtain healing. The first step in this process is to establish a hierarchy among the therapeutic options available. Once this hierarchy has been established, each sector initiates its therapeutic strategy.

25. Hogan, *Healing in the Second Temple Period*, 306–10.
26. Avalos, *Health Care*, 34–58.

The therapeutic strategy is the most noticeable feature in the healing stories of the Gospels. Yet it is also the aspect most difficult to understand for Western readers. The reason is that the therapeutic strategies in the Gospel narratives presuppose a perception of sickness and healing that is foreign to us. This understanding is derived from the explanatory model of popular and folk medicine of the first-century Mediterranean world, whereas our therapeutic strategies derive from the biomedical model of Western professional medicine. Consequently, to understand these stories, we need to compare the process of healing in professional Western medicine and in first-century popular and folk medicine.

Medical anthropologists have developed a model that facilitates such comparison. It considers different steps in the interpretation and treatment of symptoms and makes parallel descriptions of the therapeutic strategies followed by the biomedical model and the cultural model.[27] The biomedical and cultural models are steered by different cultural assumptions and consequently employ different explanatory models of sickness and healing. The biomedical model proceeds from an empiricist conception of sickness based on organ malfunction. Accordingly, within this model, healing consists in treating this physical malfunction. In contrast, the cultural model considers sickness a complex reality involving different aspects of human experience. Consequently, the cultural model conceives healing as a hermeneutic process whose goal is to interpret the multifaceted reality of illness.

The following table summarizes the different steps and strategies followed by both models.[28]

	BIOMEDICAL MODEL (Empiricist)	CULTURAL MODEL (Hermeneutic)
Pathological entity	Somatic or psychophysiological lesion or dysfunction	Meaningful construct, illness, reality of the sufferer
Structure of relevance	Relevant data reveal somatic disorder.	Relevant data reveal the meaning of illness
Elicitation procedures	Review systems, laboratory tests	Evaluate explanatory models; decode semantic network
Interpretive goal	To diagnose and explain the dysfunction	To understand the illness

27. Good and Delvecchio-Good, "Meaning of Symptoms," 167–81.
28. Good and Delvecchio-Good, "Meaning of Symptoms," 179.

Healing Stories and Medical Anthropology

Interpretive strategy	To dialectically explore the relationship between symptoms and the somatic disorder	To dialectically explore the relationship between symptoms and the semantic network
Therapeutic goal	To intervene in the somatic disease process	To treat the patient's experience: to bring to understanding hidden aspects of the reality of illness and to transform that reality

The biomedical model is useful for understanding disease and its treatment in the professional sector of contemporary Western medicine but is inadequate for understanding how sickness is perceived and treated in the Gospel stories. For this purpose the cultural model is much more useful. As we shall soon see, this second model can explain many of the unfamiliar traits that appear in the healing stories in the Gospels.

The Healing of the Blind Man from Jericho

The healing of the blind man from Jericho is one of the most elaborate miracle stories in the whole New Testament. The presence of some theological accents characteristic of Mark's Gospel and the story's place at the end of a section centered on teaching about discipleship (Mark 8:31—10:52) reveal its catechetical character. This catechetical orientation is a characteristic trait of the last miracles reported by Mark.[29] Such theological adaptation may have removed some characteristic traits of the healing process from the stories—traits that are more evident in other healing stories (touching, laying hands, and using saliva). However, these stories are still useful to identify how sickness and healing were perceived and treated in Jesus' and Mark's context.

The Healthcare System

The first step to understanding the story of the blind man of Jericho reported by Mark is to locate it in the framework of the healthcare system of his time and to find out in which sector of that system it should be placed. The reference to Bartimaeus's family can indicate the treatment of illness in the *popular sector*. This reference is implicit in the man's name ("son of Timaeus"). The family was the most important social institution in the

---

29. Kertelge, *Wunder Jesu*, 182–84.

ancient world. For that reason, it was the first place where healing was looked for. Bartimaeus's family was unsuccessful in providing a remedy for his blindness. The mention of his father shows that the family was affected by his situation. Therefore, we can presuppose that Bartimaeus approached Jesus after having sought healing in the popular-medicine sector without success. There is no indication that he had resorted to the *professional medicine* of his time. No doubt there were physicians in Jericho and Jerusalem, but only the members of elite families had access to them. The only recourse available to Bartimaeus, as to most sick persons of his time, was a folk healer.

Most of the traits that characterize *folk healers* appear, in fact, in the encounter of Jesus with Bartimaeus. Jesus accepts the sick person's description of his illness and shares his understanding of it because he asks no questions about its nature or etiology. The vocabulary used by both Jesus and Bartimaeus reflects a system of shared beliefs, and the therapy occurs through dialogue. Both interpret the illness and its healing in religious terms. The compassion Bartimaeus asks for is an attribute of God, and his request presupposes that only God can bestow healing. Accordingly, Jesus responds to him by attributing the healing to his faith.

These traits of folk medicine were related in Israelite society with the healing prophet. The ideal type of the Israelite healer was the prophet Elijah (1 Kgs 17:17–24) and his disciple Elisha (2 Kgs 4:8–37; 5:1–19). (In Jesus' time, we know about two other folk healers: Honi and Hannina ben Dosa.[30] Like John the Baptist and Jesus himself [Mark 6:15 par.; 8:28 par.; Luke 4:26; John 1:21], Honi and Hannina were associated by their contemporaries with Elijah.) Setting this story in Jericho could be a way of relating Jesus to Elijah because Elijah and Elisha were also active in that region.

This initial consideration of the story from the perspective of the healthcare system reveals a perception of illness and healing that cannot be reduced to its biological aspects. The societal and religious implications of the story are equally evident. On the other hand, the sick person's itinerary in search of healing had probably begun before Bartimaeus met Jesus, as had been the case of the hemorrhaging woman (Mark 5:25–27) and for the paralytic at Bethesda (John 5:5–7). The mention of Bartimaeus's father points to the popular-medicine sector as the first step of this search. In any case, the context in which this healing episode must be understood is the context of Israelite folk medicine, whose most prominent figure was the

---

30. Green, "Palestinian Holy Men," 646–47.

prophet who heals in God's name. Jesus acts as a folk healer, following in the footsteps of Elijah, thus claiming to be a legitimate intermediary through whom God grants healing to the sick. Jesus' claim to act with God's healing power explains the centrality of faith in this and other healing stories.

The Explanatory Model

To grasp how Jesus and his contemporaries understood and experienced illness and healing, we need to identify the adequate explanatory model to interpret these experiences. To this end, we must explore the semantic field of sickness. This includes unfamiliar aspects, such as Bartimaeus's request for compassion, the titles with which he addresses Jesus, and Jesus' response ascribing the healing to his faith. These traits reveal that, for Jesus, as for Mark and his audience, God was the source of illness and healing (Exod 15:26). Although the causes of the blindness are not mentioned in the story, we know that first-century Israelites ascribed it to the influence of a demon (Matt 12:22) or perhaps to some personal or inherited sin (John 9:2). These beliefs shaped the general framework of the story. Still, to grasp its significance, we must be more specific about the meaning of blindness and the implications of this condition in first-century Mediterranean societies.

A brief consideration of the use of terms related to vision ("blind," "eye," and "to see") in the New Testament reveals a complex reality that goes beyond physical ability.[31] "The blind" was a symbolic representation of those who could not guide others (Matt 15:15; 23:16. 24; Luke 6:39; Rom 2:19). "The eye" could be a source of scandal (Matt 5:29; Mark 9:47), of desire (Matt 5:27–28; 1 John 2:16), and even an instrument to harm others (Matt 6:22–23; 20:5). Closed eyes expressed the inability to understand (Matt 13:15; Luke 24:16), while raised eyes were a means to communicate with God through prayer (Luke 16:23; 18.15; John 6:5; 17:1). In the ancient world, there was a very close relationship between the eyes and the heart (Eph 1:18) so that when the eyes were shut, the heart was unable to understand (Matt 13:15; John 12:40; Acts 28:27; 1 Cor 2:9). In Cicero we read that the eyes are the way to the heart (Cicero, *De legibus* 1:26–27; *De oratore* 3:221), a belief that can also be found in the Old Testament.[32]

This relationship between the eyes and the heart derives from an understanding of the human person in terms of three symbolic zones: one of

---

31. Michaelis, "ὁράω κτλ.," 340–6.
32. Jenni and Vetter, "'*Áyin*, Ojo."

emotion-fused thought, which functions through the eyes and the heart; one of self-revelation and speech, which operates through the mouth and the ears; and one of deliberate action which finds expression through the hands and feet.[33] This perception of the individual determined how a healing was understood in the ancient Mediterranean world.[34] Of these three zones that constitute the human being, the first was crucial for knowledge of the individual. For this reason, ancient physiognomists thought that the study of the eyes was a fundamental task to ascertain or describe a person's character.[35] The eyes were not only an instrument of vision but also a channel of communication between persons and a way of accessing the innermost self. A blind person's eyes could not serve any of these functions.

Anthropological studies have emphasized that this focus on eyes and vision, as well as on the visual dimensions of things, is a common element in Mediterranean societies; indeed the eye is "an instrument of knowledge, power, predation, dominance, and sexuality."[36] For this reason, public exposure to the gaze of others entails a violation against the body, and the fear of such exposure is an essential motivation for control (resulting in the seclusion of women, in veiling, in the existence of interior courts, and so forth). This centrality of the visual surfaces in the belief in the *evil eye*, which is one of the most characteristic traits of Mediterranean societies.[37] According to this belief, some persons have the power to injure other people by means of how they look at others, generally as a consequence of envy or greed. For this reason, in the scriptural writings "the evil eye" is sometimes a synonym for "envy" (Matt 20:5). This pervasive belief reveals the conviction that the eye is an instrument of power over others

This perception determines the understanding that Jesus and his contemporaries had about blindness. The blind person was, in a certain way, someone whose access to the center of the emotions and thought (the heart) was barred, whether from the inside (the seat of desires and emotions) to the outside, or from the outside (where the evil eye showed itself) to the inside. The lack of vision excluded the blind person from social interactions, which revolved around honor, because honor and shame were visual values. Consequently, one of the most noteworthy aspects of blindness was

---

33. Malina, *New Testament World* (rev. ed.), 73–77.
34. Pilch, "Sickness and Healing," 203–7.
35. Malina and Neyrey, "Honor and Shame," 26–27.
36. Gilmore, "Anthropology of the Mediterranean," 197.
37. Elliott, "Fear of the Leer"; Derrett, "Evil Eye."

the lack of power: they who could not see could not control others or influence their lives.

These cultural clues shaped the social conditions of the blind person. As we have seen, in most cultures, sickness assigns a deviant status to the sick person. In ancient Mediterranean cultures, this deviant status was understood and expressed in relation to its core values, namely honor and shame. When the ancient rhetorical treatises talk about the *enkōmion*, they refer to good health as one of the attributes of the honorable person, while illness was considered something shameful.[38] The dishonorable condition of Bartimaeus surfaces in various details of the story: he is a beggar, he is outside the city, and he is not allowed to address Jesus. The father's name (*timaios* = honorable) and the son's condition may provide subtle allusions to the dishonor (*atimos* = dishonorable) affecting the entire family.

The social condition of Bartimaeus is not understood in terms of physical deficiency but of social exclusion because blindness rendered him incapable of actively taking part in significant social interactions. This perception of blindness in terms of social exclusion appears in some passages of Scripture that presuppose the Levitical healthcare system. In 2 Sam 5:6–8, the author quotes a popular saying: "The blind and the lame will not enter the house of the LORD." In the same way, according to Levitical prescriptions, among the descendants of Aaron who were not allowed to present the offering were "the blind and the lame" (Lev 21:18). In Jesus' time, the exclusion of the blind was even more severe, at least in some religious groups in which purity was a central concern.[39]

Following this perception, healing was not defined in physical but rather in social terms. For this reason, the healing of the blind, the deaf, and the lame was a literary paradigm used in the prophetic writings to announce the restoration of the people of God.[40] This explains why in Mark's story, the result of the blind man's recovery of sight is the integration into

---

38. Malina and Neyrey, *Portraits of Paul*, 140–41.

39. In one of the halakhic documents found in the Qumran caves we read that the blind and the deaf are not pure: "And also concerning the blind who cannot see: they should keep themselves from all uncleanness, and they do not see the uncleanness of the sin-offering. And also concerning the deaf who do not hear the law or the regulations concerning purity and do not hear the laws of Israel; for whoever neither sees nor hears, does not know how to apply (them)" (4QMMT 52–57). And the Temple Scroll states, "No blind person shall enter it (the temple) throughout his whole life; he shall not defile the city in the centre of which I dwell" (11QT^a 45:12–14).

40. Clements, "Patterns in the Prophetic Canon."

the group of Jesus' disciples. This integration is, in fact, the last step in the process of social reintegration that runs through the entire story. The first step is to address Jesus without paying attention to those who command him to be silent. Then, Bartimaeus leaves behind the signs of his exclusion: his place beside the road and the beggar's mantle. Finally, he asks Jesus to heal him. In Mark's view, this process describes the ideal itinerary of the disciple, who must recover sight in order to be able to follow Jesus on the way to the cross (Mark 10:51).

The Therapeutic Strategy

The therapeutic strategy that surfaces in this story is a strategy from the folk sector of the healthcare system in Mark's time and reflects the social connotations of blindness at that time. The first step in the healing process is the identification of the sickness. Cultural patterns would orient the sick person and those related to him (family, relatives, neighbors, and the like) to perceive the condition in social terms. For them, blindness was not primarily a physiological pathology but rather an illness with social implications.

The second step is the search for relevant data about the sickness. In this step, Western medicine looks for symptoms that reveal the existence of a physical pathology. This interest is completely lacking in the story of Bartimaeus. Instead, we are told about signs revealing the meaning of the illness. The place where Bartimaeus is situated, his condition as a beggar, and the fact that he is not permitted to speak to Jesus—all these features indicate which symptoms were relevant for them.

The third stage is the interpretation of the sickness. Here the explanatory model shared by Mark and his contemporaries can be identified by looking at the semantic field employed. This semantic field includes references to the origin of the sickness (perhaps sin) and healing (God). This semantic field reveals an *emic* understanding of blindness, which stresses the importance of the visual in ancient Mediterranean culture. Unlike the biomedical model, which focuses primarily on the physical examination of the patient, the cultural model considers various dimensions of human experience: the natural (physical blindness), the divine (only God and faith can heal), the personal (the inability to see) and the social (exclusion and dishonor). All these dimensions appear in the story, but the divine and social ones are the most relevant to identify the significance of blindness.

The interpretive goal of this process is not, as in the biomedical model, diagnosing and explaining physical symptoms but rather understanding the meaning that the illness has for the patient. Consequently, the interpretive strategy does not rest on exploring the relationship between the physical symptoms and dysfunctions but instead on exploring the relationship between the symptoms and the semantic field of the illness. This is what we find in the story, mainly in the brief dialogue between Jesus and Bartimaeus. Bartiimaeus asks Jesus to have compassion on him, but Jesus makes him articulate his request in a more specific way: "What do you want me to do for you?" (Mark 10:51) Readers get the impression that the blind man does not want to mention his blindness because of its social connotations, but Jesus compels him to identify the source of his situation.

Finally, the healing process is not about intervening in the physical process of the pathology but about treating the patient's experience by establishing a new frame of reference for the patient. Jesus pays no attention to the physical dimensions of the sickness. (He does not lay hands on him; neither does Jesus apply dust or saliva.) Instead, Jesus concentrates on the meaning of the sickness (i.e., the illness). The healing is interpreted in terms of salvation, which occurs thanks to faith in God. The first consequence of the man's recovering his sight is his incorporation into Jesus' group of disciples. This creates a new significant social framework that erases all the signs of the social exclusion caused by the stigma attached to the sickness: he is not beside the road, but on it; he has thrown away the beggar's mantle and becomes part of a new social group.

Conclusion

In this chapter, I have tried to show the usefulness of medical anthropology for an adequate understanding of healing stories in Mark's Gospel and the gospel traditions in general. Combining relevant aspects of different cultural models, I have proposed a reading scenario that has heuristic and explanatory potential because it permits us to discover some features implicit in the story and to interpret them in the appropriate context.

Reading Mark 10:46–52 in that scenario has shown that the healing of Bar Timaeus makes sense in the healthcare system of first-century Palestine. The healing takes place in the folk sector of that system, although the sickness was treated first in the popular sector. As we have seen, the folk sector of the Israelite healthcare system was closely related to the tradition of the healing prophet. This relationship points to the Israelite roots of Jesus' healing activity reflected in the story.

The explanatory model presupposed by the story helps us to perceive how blindness was understood and experienced by Mark's audience. For Jesus as for Mark, it was not only a disease but also an illness that had religious, social, and cultural implications. According to the Levitical purity system, blindness implied exclusion from the political-religious system. This exclusion was symbolized in the prohibition to enter the temple. Furthermore, in a society whose core value was honor, blindness entailed social segregation because those who could not see could not participate in the main social interactions.

On the other hand, understanding the story from the perspective of the cultural model of the healing process allows us to unveil the purpose of the healing reported by Mark. In it, the miraculous dimension emphasized in traditional apologetics was really of little importance. What was important was the social and political-religious nature of the process. The healing of the blind man affected the roots of sin, validated the man's faith in the God of Israel (the healing's political-religious dimension), and produced a social reintegration that entailed the removal of all the signs of his exclusion (the healing's social dimension).

Finally, a better knowledge of how sickness and healing were perceived in that social context can help to elucidate the specific traits of Jesus' activity as a healer. Perhaps the most relevant quality of Jesus' healings was that his therapeutic strategy was completely different from the therapeutic strategy promoted by the Levitical healthcare system. These two strategies rested on different understandings of purity: While the Levitical system promoted the exclusion of the sick, the strategy followed by Jesus strove for inclusion of the sick.

CHAPTER 6

The Messianic Anointing: Cultural Memory and Jesus' Identity

(Mark 14:3–9)

Introduction

THE MARKAN PASSION STORY begins with a literary sandwich whose central scene is the anointing of Jesus in Bethany (Mark 14:1–11). At the outset of the decisive and dramatic events that will put an end to Jesus' life, the narrator expressly directs the attention of readers to the modest act of a woman that takes place in a house. The event's relevance is underlined by the solemn declaration of Jesus, who commands that the woman's action should be remembered wherever the gospel would be preached. This mandate confers a unique status to this scene because this is the only explicit exhortation to remember reported in the Gospel of Mark. Nonetheless, it is not easy to appreciate why an act such as this should be remembered time and again in the proclamation of the good news. The mandate to remember what the woman did for Jesus invites readers to discover the message hidden in her gesture.

Likely for this reason, the scene in Bethany has awakened considerable interest among scholars. Its origin and composition have been widely discussed.[1] On the other hand, its message has been exposed, emphasizing

---

1. This concern already appears in form-critical studies such as Bultmann, *History of the Synoptic Tradition*, 263; Dibelius, *From Tradition to Gospel*, 43; Legault, "Application of the Form-Critique"; Elliott, "Anointing of Jesus"; Holst, "One Anointing of Jesus." It

how this anonymous woman becomes a model for those who accept the gospel.[2] However, these studies have not disclosed adequately the significance and the symbolic implication of the woman's act (the anointing of Jesus' head), which differs from that described in the parallel versions of Luke 7:36–50 and John 12:1–8 (the anointing of Jesus' feet). Conventional readings of this episode have concentrated on the solemn command to remember found only in Mark (and in Matthew, which depends on Mark), wondering whether it is only a means to reinforce the meaning of the passage, or a clue for interpreting the whole Gospel.

The unique character of this mandate reveals that this episode was relevant for the group or groups to whom Mark's Life of Jesus was addressed. The fact that the exhortation to remember is a peculiar trait of this gospel suggests that his author could have modified a story received from the tradition to assign it a more precise meaning. Hence, before exploring the significance and implication of this mandate in more detail, we will try to find out how the author of the Gospel of Mark reworked the traditional story of Jesus' anointing.

The Markan Version of Jesus' Anointing

The four versions of this event transmitted by the canonical Gospels (Matt 26:6–13; Mark 14:3–9; Luke 7:36–50; John 12:1–8) occasionally agree in some details, but they also display marked differences, including the transposition of some of the story's most significant elements. These similarities and differences suggest that the independent accounts of Mark, Luke, and John are elaborations of the same story, which in the course of oral transmission was amplified in two different ways, resulting in the two versions that lie beneath the three accounts: one transmitted by Luke, and the other one by Mark and John.[3]

The original anecdote may have contained these three basic elements:

1. In the course of a meal, a woman anointed Jesus' feet with perfume.

---

continues in more recent studies: Malzoni, "Da cabeça aos pés"; Coakley, "Anointing at Bethany"; and Breytenbach, "MNHMONEYEIN."

2. Graham, "Silent Voices," 153; Grassi, "Secret Heroine," 11–13; Miller, *Women in Mark's Gospel*, 128–44; Malbon, "Fallible Followers," 39–40; van Iersel, *Mark*, 418; Navarro, *Ungido para la vida*, 101–30; and Swartley, "Role of Women," 20.

3. Mack, "Anointing of Jesus," 89–104; Lücking, *Mimesis der Verachteten*, 73–75.

The Messianic Anointing: Cultural Memory and Jesus' Identity

2. This action provoked shock or surprise among the guests.
3. Jesus responded to their reaction by approving of the woman's act.

The embarrassment caused by this story, in which Jesus seems to accept the woman's inappropriate advance, would have occasioned two apologetic elaborations of the story. One of them, preserved in Luke's version, identified the woman clearly as a sinner and interpreted her gesture as an act of repentance, and Jesus' approval as an act of pardon or forgiveness. The other one, preserved by Mark and John, centered on the waste of expensive perfume and construed the woman's gesture as an anticipation of the anointing of Jesus' body for burial.[4] These two amplified versions might have circulated in the oral tradition. Although Luke probably knew Mark's account, nevertheless he chose the other version because it was more appropriate for his purposes. According to this explanation, the history of the tradition could be represented with the following diagram (with the dotted arrows suggesting that Luke and John probably knew the Markan version):

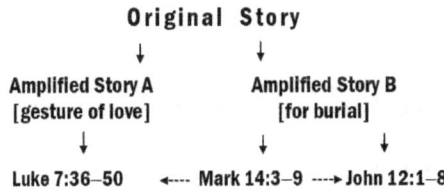

According to this proposal, the Markan version was a further elaboration of the amplified story in which the woman's action was related to funeral rites. The inconsistency between the woman's act, which affects only one part of Jesus' body (the head or the feet), and its interpretation, which refers to the body in its entirety (in preparation for Jesus' burial), reveals that this interpretation, which Mark and John share, is a development of the original story. At the same time, this elaboration includes an argument that is alien to the original anecdote insofar as it introduces a typical rabbinic discussion concerning the precedence of the works of love over alms.[5] This change leaves the woman's gesture in the background, stressing its significance for the impending burial of Jesus.

Assuming this reconstruction of the history of the tradition, we must consider now whether the evangelist introduced the two features

---

4. Miquel Pericás, *Amigos de esclavos*, 308–29.
5. Jeremias, "Salbungsgeschichte."

characteristic of the Markan version. We consider, first, the peculiar description of the woman's act, the pouring of the perfume over Jesus' head. This is a striking feature, for in the Lukan and Johannine versions, the woman anoints Jesus' feet. The coincidence of Luke and John shows that in the two amplified stories, as in the original, the woman's gesture consisted in anointing Jesus' feet. Although John may have known the Lukan version of this episode, it is not likely that he would have taken from it only this detail. It is much more plausible that John's version of the scene reproduces the second amplified story (namely the one that related the anointing with the burial of Jesus), which is the same version that Mark appears to have known. Consequently, if we compare how Mark and John describe the woman's action, we will be able to identify more easily the various modifications that each of them introduced—especially if we compare both versions with the parallel (and presumably independent) version of Luke:

Luke 7:37–38	John 12:3	Mark 14:3
a woman … sinner … … an alabaster jar of ointment …	*Mary took a pound* of costly ointment *made of pure nard,*	A woman came with an alabaster jar of very costly ointment of pure nard
began to bathe his (Jesus') feet with her tears and she dried them with her hair, and she kissed his feet, and she anointed them with the ointment …	anointed the feet of Jesus and dried them with her hair	*and she broke open the jar and* poured the ointment *over his head*

If Mark and John knew a version of the story different from the one reported by Luke, then their agreements with Luke, when they do not agree with each other, may reveal the formulation of the original anecdote. By contrast, the points at which one of them diverges from the other when the other agrees with Luke serve to identify the modifications introduced by Luke. In the above synopsis, these modifications appear in italics. In the Markan story, in addition to the change already mentioned (namely, the anointing of the head instead of the feet), we also notice that the woman breaks the alabaster flask that contains the perfume.

Having thus clarified the origin of the first feature peculiar to Mark, we turn now to consider whether the mandate to remember the woman's action is also the evangelist's work. The fact that it is peculiar to Mark and Matthew, as well as the presence of Markan vocabulary ("to preach" … "good news"), suggests that this may be the case. This suggestion is confirmed by the lack of connection between the mandate (Mark 14:9) and the previous verses. The scene (Mark 14:2–8) exhibits traits of a prophetic sign by which something is partially accomplished that God will realize in the future.[6] The conclusion, introduced by the solemn formula "Truly I say you," appears as an addition because it is alien to the literary genre.[7] Narrative analysis suggests the same conclusion, insofar as Jesus' words are attached to the preceding discourse as a paratext that interprets the text to which it has been added. Actually, the verb in the future tense ("will be told"), and the reference to the spreading of the gospel throughout the whole world effectively situates the account unambiguously after Jesus' death.

We can conclude then that the author of the Gospel of Mark introduced both the anointing of Jesus' head and the mandate to remember. These changes reveal an interest to reformulate the amplified story received from the oral tradition. These features proper to Mark emphasize in many ways the symbolic nature of the scene and its concentration on Jesus' identity. First, by situating the scene at the beginning of the passion account, the evangelist underlines the episode's relation to Jesus' death. Second, by shifting the anointing to the head, he gives new significance to the woman's action. Last, by adding a mandate to remember, the redactor presents the final saying of Jesus as the episode's interpretive key. With these modifications, Mark intended to make the woman's gesture both more precise and more recognizable. Most probably, Mark has her pour the perfume over Jesus' head to evoke a gesture that was well-known to his audience. In Jewish literature, the anointing of feet finds hardly a significant parallel, but the same cannot be said of the anointing of the head. In the Scriptures of Israel, this act was closely related to the anointing of a king. Although Mark does not use the verb "to anoint" (*aleiphō*), he does describe the act of anointing, which involved pouring perfumed oil over the head of the future king.

This interpretation of the woman's gesture against the background of the messianic ritual is not the majority view, although some scholars have proposed it with good arguments.[8] Others have entertained the possibility but find a serious difficulty in the fact that the anointing is performed by a woman, not by a priest.[9] Nonetheless, the ritual character of the act, rein-

---

6. Fander, "Frauen in der Nachfolge," 424.

7. Neirynck, "Redactional Text of Mark," 16.

8. Fander, *Stellung der Frau*, 120–34; Lücking, *Mimesis der Verachteten*, 110–11; Sawicki, *Seeing the Lord*, 149–59.

9. Fander, "Frauen in der Nachfolge," 427.

forced by Jesus' mandate to remember what the woman has done, invites us to consider this possibility. The modifications introduced by Mark give the account an ambiguity that is lacking in the versions in Luke and John. The clear allusion to the royal anointing, in particular, shifted the significance of the gesture. This symbolic opening situated the woman's action within a new horizon,[10] inviting the conclusion that through this modification Mark has intended to give the woman's action a new meaning. The two details proper to the Markan version of the scene—the anointing of the head and the mandate to remember—are key to an adequate understanding of such meaning. For this reason, before determining the function of the episode within Mark's narrative, it is necessary to clarify the purpose of the mandate to remember and the significance of the anointing of the head.

The Anointing of Jesus in the Memory of the Group

The mandate to remember ties the episode in Bethany with the proclamation of the gospel throughout the world (Mark 14:9). This connection associates an event in the ministry of Jesus with an activity of his disciples after Easter,[11] stressing that the exemplary character of the woman's act is likewise underlined. The evangelist describes the woman's action in contrast with the disciples' attitude, presenting her as a model for his audience. On the other hand, Jesus insists that this event should not be forgotten. The relationship between exemplarity and memory is a crucial feature of Mark's story of Jesus' anointing, for it encapsulates a living memory intended both to re-create the identity of the community and to remind it of its mission.

To understand the meaning of this scene, it is necessary to ascertain the function played by memory in groups that share similar situations. This seems a possible and even promising discussion because the passage offers several indications that allow us to situate it within a rather precise theoretical frame. In the first place, the oral context in which this memory was transmitted and in which the Gospel was composed is characteristic of memory practices. Second, the appearance of the word "remembrance" (*mnēmosynon*) transforms the woman's act into a crucial element of group memory. Finally, the ritual character of the anointing makes this a memory likely to be remembered.

---

10. Hearon, "Story of the Woman," 112.
11. Maunder, "*Sitz im Leben* for Mark 14:9," 80.

The Messianic Anointing: Cultural Memory and Jesus' Identity

These traits suggest that Jesus' exhortation to remember the woman's action is significant for the memory of the group of disciples to whom the Gospel of Mark was addressed. Consequently, it might be useful to interpret it within the framework of studies on social memory. These studies have attempted to articulate the internal structure of collective memories—how these are transmitted, how cultural bias plays a role in the selection of images of the past, and how these memories serve to configure and nourish group identity.[12]

In his studies about the role of memory in societies of the ancient world, Jan Assmann has elaborated a model that distinguishes between collective memory and cultural memory. Cultural memory can be defined as "a body of reusable texts, images, and rituals specific to each society in each epoch, whose cultivation serves to stabilize and convey that society's self-image."[13] Cultural memory is the result of a long process in which foundational memories are interpreted and expressed in different ways. This type of memory is elaborated over a lengthy period of time during which shared knowledge creates accounts, symbols, rituals, or monuments which, by transmitting and updating it, confers on the group a sense of stability and strength.

When the Gospels were written, there was not a *Christian* cultural memory. The Gospels themselves represent an initial phase in the formation of such collective memory, for in them the memories about Jesus were selected, transmitted, and elaborated.[14] This process took place in the framework of the cultural memory of Israel, which permeates the memories evoked in the Gospels. This means that the identity of the first Christian groups was shaped by values and identities embedded in the cultural memory of Israel. These groups related to that shared memory in terms of continuity and rupture. As these groups were emerging in a society with a robust shared memory, part of their identity formation consisted in assuming some aspects of that memory and adapting them to their new experiences. This process triggered a conflict with other interpretations and appropriations of the same collective memory. After Jesus' death, his

---

12. The groundbreaking study of Halbwachs, *Mémoire collective*, has been developed in different directions. See Connerton, *How Societies Remember*; Fentress and Wickham, *Social Memory*; Olick and Robbins, "Social Memory Studies"; and Kirk, "Social and Cultural Memory."

13. Assmann, "Collective Memory," 130.

14. Mendels, *Memory in Jewish, Pagan and Christian Societies*, 33; Kirk and Thatcher, "Jesus Tradition," 34.

followers began to preserve their memories about him, thus creating their own traditions and a collective memory distinct from those of other groups and society at large. Still, for this new collective memory to be significant, it had to fit plausibly in the cultural memory of Israel.

Another important aspect of cultural memory in the ancient world is that memory about *the beginnings* was almost always sacralized or ritualized. Given its strong association with group identity, ritual was an ideal instrument for transmitting the significant past of a group.[15] Ritual memory was often elaborated through ceremonies that united word and deed in order to preserve the identity of the group. The critical events of the past were then remembered in a ritual context in which those events had a performative character and an exemplary value. By transmitting this past in commemorative activities, memory was transformed into action and acquired the power to legitimate the group's significance and function in the present.[16]

The relationship between collective memory and cultural memory and the function that each of them serves in the construction of group identity provides a framework in which to interpret several aspects of Jesus' anointing in Mark. In this story, the interest in memory is explicitly underlined. At the same time, the scene refers to memory practices related to a ritual action by which a normative behavior is proposed for the group. The combination of these elements is significant because, as we have seen, memory tied to a rite is a powerful means of defining and preserving group identity.[17]

We can sum up the preceding observations by saying that the anointing scene recalls an anecdote in the life of Jesus that was carefully re-elaborated in order to underline the ritual character of the woman's action. This memory was advanced as a fundamental aspect of the group memory for Mark's audience. This group memory was defined against the background of the cultural memory of Israel, in which the rite of royal anointing played an important role. Mark's account of Jesus' anointing presupposes an audience sufficiently attuned to this memory so as to recognize the rite of a king's messianic anointing. In fact, the rhetorical organization of the narrative around this element creates a density without which the scene becomes

---

15. Mendels, "Societies of Memory."
16. Poole, "Memory, History and the Claims of the Past," 162.
17. Connerton, *How Societies Remember*, 48–53.

abstract or incomplete.[18] The allusion to a well-known rite, which possessed an enormous symbolic meaning, situates this scene in an evocative setting. Nevertheless, the way the rite is evoked and the meaning attached to it are very different from those ascribed to the ancient rite.[19]

The Ritual Character of Jesus' Anointing

At the beginning of the scene, Jesus is reclining at the table in the house of Simon the leper. Without a word, a woman performs an ambiguous gesture. Norms of hospitality included washing a guest's feet as a sign of welcome,[20] but this is not what the woman does. The anointing of the head is also attested as a gesture of hospitality, but the examples known to us show that the gesture tended to be performed by the owner of the house and that oil, not perfume, was used in it (Luke 7:46; cf. Ps 22:5). The woman's gesture, at least as Mark relates it, is not consistent with this practice.

Actually, the way the narrative develops in Mark does not imply that hospitality is present in the immediate context in any other way; this contrasts with the Lukan parallel, where hospitality is implied in the woman's anointing of Jesus: the anonymous woman (rather than Simon the Pharisee, who is hosting the meal in Luke) demonstrates hospitality (Luke 7:36–50). The contrast between the episode in Mark and the parallel episode in Luke confers a certain ambiguity to the scene in Mark, so that its meaning is not immediately apparent. Hence, it seems reasonable to suggest that Mark's scene may be evoking the less-than-ordinary ritual of royal anointing. This rite belonged to the cultural memory of Israel and is well attested in the ancient Near East.[21] However, to establish this relationship (namely, that the anointing of the head can be understood as a direct reference to the royal anointing), we will need to explore the parallels between the woman's action and the royal ritual in more detail.

---

18. Le Donne, "Theological Memory Distortion," 164.

19. Monika Fander has insisted that this scene should be read against the background of the rite of the royal anointing; see Fander, *Stellung der Frau*, 131–34; and Fander, "Frauen in der Nachfolge," 423–27.

20. Plato, *Symposium* 175a; Plutarch, *Mulierum virtutes* 242e–263c; Quintus Curtius Rufus, *Historiae Alexandri Magni* 8.9.27; On the meaning and background of this gesture, see Malina and Rohrbaugh. *Commentary on the Gospel of John*, 223; González Echegaray, *Arqueología y evangelios*, 201–4.

21. Kutsch, *Salbung als Rechtsakt*.

The passages in the Scriptures that describe the ritual of anointing refer to a sacred act that takes place at the king's enthronement (1 Kgs 1:32–48; 2 Kgs 11:12–20). Relying on the texts that give some indication of the location, officiating figures, gestures, and/or effects of royal anointing (1 Sam 9:16; 10:1; 2 Sam 16:13; 1 Kgs 1:39; 2 Kgs 9:3, 6; 11:12), we can define the rite as one of status transformation by which the person anointed acquires a new social role.[22] The pivotal moment of this ritual is the act of pouring perfumed oil over the head of the future king. Through this rite, the new king is invested in heavenly power. From this moment on, he could be called "the Anointed of Yahweh" (1 Sam 24:7; 26:16; 2 Sam 1:14, 16; 19:22; Lam 4:20). He answered directly to God and received the charge of governance.

With the decline of the monarchy, this rite was no longer practiced. However, interest in the figure of the Anointed remained alive throughout the Second Temple period, becoming increasingly popular at the beginning of the second half of the second century BCE.[23] The end of the Hasmonean dynasty and the Roman occupation (68 BCE) triggered a renewed hope in the coming of the Anointed (Messiah), who would occupy the throne of David. This renewed hope appears in the Psalms of Solomon (17:32; 18:5, 7), where Yahweh is asked to raise his Anointed to liberate the people. Other writings of the same period acclaim this figure (1 Enoch 48:8–10; 2 Baruch 29:3; 30:1; 4 Ezra 12:32; 4QCommGen A [4Q252]), thus confirming that the hope of the Davidic messiah and the symbolism associated with him was present during the first century CE. This hope also played an active role in the Jewish uprisings before and after the year 70 CE.[24] Although the figure of the messiah was not conceived always in Davidic categories, the complex of ideas that surrounded the traditions of the monarchy were present in the various messianic images.[25] The majority of Judeans in the first century who conceived of a messiah in priestly categories or with eschatological overtones, including those belonging to marginal groups, thought of a Davidic figure when they used the title Anointed. The Psalms bear witness to this widespread perception because in them the term "anointed"

---

22. McVann, "Rituals of Status Transformation," 335–41. See also Chapter 2, above.

23. Horbury, "Messianism in the Old Testament Apocrypha and Pseudepigrapha," 406–19.

24. Collins, *Scepter and the Star*, 199–204.

25. Horbury, "Messianism in the Old Testament Apocrypha and Pseudepigrapha," 423–32.

refers explicitly to the king (LXX Pss 2:2–6; 17:50–51; 44:8; 88:21; 131:10, 17).

The frequent mention of the ritual of royal anointing in these texts and the centrality of Messiah-King in later literature underwrites the suggestion that this ritual belonged to the cultural memory of Israel and was part of its symbolic heritage in the first century CE. This suggestion is confirmed by the lengthy discussion in the Babylonian Talmud concerning the specific composition and use of the anointing oil (*b. Keritot* 5a–6a).[26] This discussion draws on various oral traditions transmitted by Jewish scribes that were active shortly after the composition of the Gospel of Mark. The specific details of this discussion allude to aspects that also appear in the Markan story of the anointing. The oil is said to contain various aromatic ointments, including myrrh (5a). The discussion focuses on the anointing of kings (5b), although it also mentions the anointing of the tabernacle and the high priest. There is also an interesting discussion about the order of the ritual: the pouring of the oil over the head and the anointing of the forehead (6a). The Markan account of the anointing accords well with the ritual of royal anointing presupposed in this discussion, where the use of perfume, the close connection of the rite with the enthronement of the king, and the description of the act of pouring perfume over the head are essential parts of the rite.

We can presume that the audience of Mark's Gospel might have been sensitive to these echoes, but if the woman's gesture reproduces the rite of royal anointing, it does so in such a new way that the ancient rite is in it wholly redefined.

The Meaning of Jesus' Messianic Anointing

Read against the background of the cultural memory of Israel, the scene as narrated by Mark is at once an evocation of the rite of anointing and a completely new interpretation of it. By including some dissonant elements, the evangelist has produced a careful redefinition of the messianic identity of Jesus. He has done it through a process of appropriation and reinterpretation of the cultural memory of Israel.

Both the common elements and the radical novelty of the woman's gesture can be observed by comparing the ancient ritual of royal anointing with the scene at Bethany.

26. Epstein, ed., *Babylonian Talmud*, 31–38.

	ANCIENT ACCOUNTS OF ROYAL ANOINTING	**ANOINTING AT BETHANY**
Location	House of Jesse (David: 1 Sam 16:13); Sanctuary of Gihon (Solomon: 1 Kgs 1:33–34); Temple (Jehoash and the kings of Judah beginning with Solomon).	House of Simon the Leper (Mark 14:3)
Officiant	Prophet (Saul and David are anointed by Samuel: 1 Sam 10:1; 16:13; Jehu is anointed by Elisha: 2 Kgs 9:3, 6); Priest (Solomon is anointed by Zadok: 1 Kgs 1:39 and Jehoash by Jehoiada: 2 Kgs 11:12).	Anonymous woman (Mark 14:3)
Subject	Candidate for the throne (1 Sam 9:16; 2 Sam 2:4; 5:3; 2 Kgs 23:30; 2 Kgs 6:3).	Jesus (Mark 14:3)
Rite	To take a particular container (1 Sam 16:13) that has olive oil with various additives (1 Sam 10:1; 1 Sam 16:13; 2 Kgs 9:3, 6) and pour it over the head of the candidate for the throne.	Break a jar of perfume (and pour it over the head of Jesus) (Mark 14:3)
Witnesses	People (1 Sam 16:13; 2 Sam 2:4; 1 Kgs 1:39; 2 Kgs 11:12).	Guests (Mark 14:4)
Effect	Symbolically, the candidate receives the Spirit of God (1 Sam 16:13). The effect is charismatic; it bestows new status as leader of the people with political, social, and military power (2 Kgs 9:6–9).	New status: Jesus is Messiah through his passion and death (Mark 14:8).

In the new ritual, the spatial location has been changed, denoting a polemical attitude towards the temple. The scene is closely related to other Markan episodes in which Jesus questions the temple's validity more explicitly (Mark 11:15–17) and challenges the teaching of the scribes concerning the expected messiah (Mark 12:35–37). The same can be said about the scenes of betrayal (Mark 14:1–2, 10–11) between which the anointing in Bethany is intercalated. By contrast, the new rite occurs in a distant and unofficial place—the interior of a house—which becomes an adequate space to reveal the new messianic identity of Jesus.

In the Markan story, a second change reflects an inversion of social and religious roles. The celebrant of the rite is not a prophet but a woman who performs a function all but unthinkable in first-century Judaism. This

The Messianic Anointing: Cultural Memory and Jesus' Identity

new rite stands in direct contrast with the typical values of society and the dominant religious group. This is, perhaps, the most notable characteristic of the redefinition of the rite of messianic anointing, and it is so radical as to make this interpretation too challenging to accept.[27] The eccentricity of the woman's gesture prompts the adverse reaction of the guests. Nonetheless, Jesus' response praising her is an invitation to consider her action's meaning and to discover its relationship with his own death. The ritual action is directed to the body of Jesus. He occupies the center of the symbolic interpretation. In this way, the woman's action points to the revelation of Jesus' identity.

Thirdly, a new interpretation of the ritual corresponds to this transformation. Here the messianic expectation is redefined most radically. The evangelist has placed this episode at the beginning of the passion account to reinforce his understanding of Jesus' messianic identity. The anointing reinforces Jesus' messianic identity not by words or abstract concepts but by redefining a known rite. To be sure, this new definition of the messianic identity of Jesus is not reflected solely in the ruptures or changes perceived in the new rite. In the final verse (Mark 14:9), Jesus' words identify the woman as a model, and place her at the heart of the memory for the Markan audience. In this way, the meaning of her action becomes more evident. It is not a rite that must be repeated, but is rather an action that must be remembered and recounted "in memory of her." The gesture not only discloses Jesus' identity; it also carries implications for this group of disciples and their mission to the world. In other words, the Markan story reflects a high degree of interest in defining the identity of Jesus of this group of followers.

The fact that this mandate to remember appears at the beginning of the passion narrative reveals that the scene has a foundational character. The present situation of the community is projected onto the life of Jesus.[28] This suggests that the woman's ritual action is highly relevant for the group's identity; this is why it cannot be forgotten. The mandate refers to the proclamation of the gospel in the whole world, but the focus is on the woman herself and her act—those who announce the good news should remember her action and its significance. Her action encapsulates what needs to be proclaimed about Jesus according to Mark: that he is a suffering Messiah, God's obedient Son (Mark 14:32–42). This is the memory of Jesus that must be maintained and proclaimed as good news.

---

27. Fander, "Frauen in der Nachfolge," 427.
28. On the foundational character of the passion narrative, see Chapter 7, below.

We can sum up the preceding discussion saying that the Markan scene of Jesus' anointing presents a ritual action in which the perceptions, symbols, and images that give new significance to the messianic character of Jesus are brought to the fore. At the root of the scene there is a traditional rite of Israel, which has been radically transformed to express the Markan vision of Jesus as the Messiah Son of God. Mark has modified one of the versions of the story that circulated in the oral tradition to show that Jesus is not Messiah in power but in suffering, thus encouraging his audience to redefine their own messianic expectations and their own group identity.[29] As we will see, the relevance of this episode for Mark's addressees is reinforced by the place it occupies in the literary plot of the Gospel.

The Messianic Identity of Jesus in the Gospel of Mark

The question of Jesus' identity plays a central role in the Gospel of Mark. It is an open question, which does not find a complete answer until Mark's final episodes. The emphatic and categorical affirmations about Jesus' identity—the title of Messiah (Mark 1:1) and the title Son of God (Mark 1:11) in particular—are in this regard only a point of departure for a process of clarification and refinement.[30] To be sure, the narrator assumes these two affirmations initially. Nevertheless, by the end of the narrative, it will be apparent that an adequate understanding of their significance is easy to come by neither for the characters in the story nor for the readers of the Gospel, because Jesus' actions and teachings reveal a profound departure from the images these titles traditionally evoke. The uncertainty around the person of Jesus only grows as the narrative progresses. This fact leaves readers always more interested in the search, which so evidently occupies the characters in the story.

---

29. We should keep in mind that Jewish messianism was not a uniform reality. John Collins, for example, identifies four basic messianic paradigms: royal, prophetic, priestly and heavenly, but he recognizes that not all were equally widespread (see Collins, *Scepter and the Star*). However, this is such a varied and complex reality that it would be better to speak, as Matthew Novenson does, of a *grammar of messianism*, that is, a set of features that the various forms of messianism developed; see Novenson, *Grammar of Messianism*, 11–26.

30. Some manuscripts add the title Son of God in Mark 1:1, but textual critics are divided over whether or not it belongs to Mark's original text; see Vironda, *Gesù nel Vangelo di Marco*, 40–41.

The Messianic Anointing: Cultural Memory and Jesus' Identity

The two basic affirmations concerning the identity of Jesus that appear in Mark's initial presentation of him (Mark 1:1–13) are present implicitly throughout the entire narrative. Through this presentation, the narrator has placed the readers in an advantageous position vis-a-vis the characters in the story, who know nothing of this initial revelation. In these opening scenes, the affirmation that Jesus is Messiah (Mark 1:1) is subordinated to the heavenly revelation of his identity as Son of God (Mark 1:11). Indeed, it is possible to trace the trajectory of these two titles and their relationship in order to discover how the narrator values them. This evaluation presents a normative point of view by which it is possible to articulate the rhetorical intention of the account and to know the true identity of Jesus.

From the outset, it is apparent that to discover this identity readers should recognize Jesus as the Son of God (Mark 1:11). Subsequently, this title appears at critical points in the Markan narrative (Mark 9:7; 14:62–63; 15:39), but it is also present implicitly in the way Jesus acts and in his words (Mark 2:5–7, 28). The narrator's point of view concerning this title is always positive, even though in almost every case the revelation involved is veiled.[31] The same is not the case with the characterization of Jesus as Messiah, for when this title appears and is applied to Jesus, it is necessary to articulate its meaning as precisely as possible. The narrator seems to suggest in this way that an inadequate understanding of this title can lead to an inaccurate vision of Jesus.

In the chapters that narrate the first phase of Jesus' public ministry (Mark 1:14—8:26), his words and actions raise different questions concerning his identity (Mark 1:27; 2:7; 4:41; 6:3). His fame precedes him, but nobody knows, precisely, who he is. The suspense that this creates about his person is only heightened by the prohibition to speak about him (Mark 1:25; 3:12; 5:8; 8:30). The question regarding the identity of Jesus finds its first explicit answer in the opinions of the people and Herod (Mark 6:14–16). However, the narrator considers these opinions insufficient and inadequate.

For this reason, after the first phase of his public ministry, Jesus himself asks the disciples about the people's assessment (Mark 8:27–28) and their own (Mark 8:29–30). Peter's response, "You are the Messiah (Anointed)" (Mark 8:29), would seem to indicate that the disciples have discovered Jesus' true identity. Actually, this affirmation coincides with the information provided by the narrator at the outset (Mark 1:1). Noticing this agreement,

---

31. Chronis, "To Reveal and to Conceal."

readers might suspect that Peter and the other disciples have interpreted the ministry of Jesus correctly, for their point of view now matches that of the narrator. But Jesus' reaction shows immediately that this is also an insufficient answer, for the command of silence refers expressly to his own identity: "he charged them to tell no one about him" (Mark 8:30). The passion prediction and the teaching that follows it reveal that Peter's affirmation must also include Jesus' suffering and his death on the cross. Granted, the narrator approves his confession; but both Peter and the other disciples are instructed not to speak further about Jesus, at least for the moment, in the hope that the teaching that follows will help them to understand in what sense it is right to say that Jesus is the Anointed One.[32]

In the teaching that follows (Mark 8:31—9:1), Jesus' identity is even more effectively linked to his death. As long as the disciples do not understand that suffering and death are an essential part of the Messiah's fate, they will be unable to understand who he is. Even though Jesus speaks in all clarity (Mark 8:38) and the prediction of his passion is subsequently repeated twice more (Mark 9:30–32; 10:32–34), the reaction of the disciples repeatedly reveals their inability to understand (Mark 9:35; 10:37). Thus, it is no surprise that when the moment of the passion arrives, all abandon him (Mark 14:50) and Peter denies him (Mark 14:66–68). In particular, Peter's trajectory invites readers to reflect on their understanding of Jesus' messianic identity.[33]

This invitation to the Gospel's audience continues in the following chapters, which record the activities of Jesus in Jerusalem (Mark 11–13). On the road to the holy city and, indeed, at the moment he enters it, Jesus is acclaimed Son of David first by a blind man (Mark 10:47–48) and later by those who accompany him (Mark 11:9–10). This affirmation evokes the earlier response of Peter, but it is now a much broader group that echoes this understanding of the messianic character of Jesus. Further on, in the context of his public teaching in the temple, Jesus will reveal that this vision of the Messiah reflects the scribes' opinion and teaching (Mark 12:35). Jesus is quick to distance himself from this sort of dynastic messianism using an argument from Scripture (Mark 12:35–37). At this point, readers discover that the title Son of David does not express the messianic identity

---

32. Vironda, *Gesù nel Vangelo di Marco*, 143–46.

33. Peter's attitude toward Jesus is very positive in the beginning, for he leaves everything to follow him (Mark 1:16–18), but negative in the end because he denies knowing Jesus (Mark 14:66–69). On this puzzling presentation of the disciples in Mark, see Guijarro, *Camino del discípulo*, 37–83.

The Messianic Anointing: Cultural Memory and Jesus' Identity

of Jesus adequately and, at the same time, that the confession "Jesus is the Messiah" needs to be correctly understood.[34]

After these critical observations about the meaning of the title Messiah, in one of the most notable and surprising scenes in the Markan story, the narrator presents Jesus himself acknowledging his identity as Messiah before the Sanhedrin (Mark 14:61–62). When the high priest asks if he is "the Messiah Son of the Blessed," Jesus responds in the affirmative, "I am," provoking in this way his condemnation (Mark 14:64). This plain answer, which echoes the revelation of the name of God at Sinai (Exod 3:6), is followed immediately by a clarification that announces Jesus' enthronement at the right hand of God and his future manifestation in glory. In this declaration, placed almost at the end of the Markan account, the two titles that appear in Jesus' initial presentation (Mark 1:1, 11) are fussed in a single one that finally reveals Jesus' identity: He is not the Messiah Son of David, but the Messiah Son of God.[35] In this scene, the narrator brings to an end the ambiguity running through the entire gospel about Jesus' identity.

The radical redefinition of the title Messiah, which the narrator has been preparing throughout the second part of Jesus' public activity, may explain the surprising change in attitude implied in Jesus' confession before the high priest, for there is a discontinuity between Jesus' critical attitude toward those who acknowledged him as Messiah during his public ministry and his positive answer before the Sanhedrin. However, this apparent contradiction disappears when we realize that in Bethany he had been anointed Messiah with a new rite, which embodies in itself the novelty of his messianic identity.

As noted above, Mark has situated the scene of the anointing quite intentionally at the beginning of the passion. It belongs to an intercalation composed by the evangelist in order to relate the anointing to the plot that sets the passion in motion.[36] In the Markan narrative, the passion account plays a very precise role, which in ancient rhetoric is known by the name *anagnōrisis* (recognition). This consists in the discovery of the hidden truth

---

34. Marcus, "Jewish War," 456–60; Vironda, *Gesù nel Vangelo di Marco*, 149–54.

35. As Joel Marcus observes, the two titles are here in restrictive apposition, so that the second member specifies the first by indicating to which class it belongs. The high priest's question should, then, be understood this way: "Are you the Messiah Son of the Blessed?" (and not: "Are you the Messiah, i.e., the Son of the Blessed?"); see Marcus, "Mark 14:61."

36. On this typically Markan resource, see Edwards, "Markan Sandwiches," 208–9; see also Broadhead, *Prophet, Son, Messiah*, 35–36.

concerning the characters, usually the protagonist, occasioned by an essential change in the course of the action (Aristotle, *Poetics* 1452b). In Mark, the discovery of Jesus' identity, his *anagnōrisis*, takes place in the passion narrative. In this sense, the climax of the Markan narrative is not actually Peter's response to Jesus' question (Mark 8:29), but rather the response of Jesus to the question put to him by the high priest (Mark 14:61–62). It is in this answer that the true identity of Jesus is finally revealed.[37]

Conclusion

Placed at the beginning of the passion account, the scene of Jesus' anointing introduces readers to the mystery of Jesus' identity. It is the key required to adequately understand the subsequent account, for from the start it is clear that the woman who anoints Jesus is the only one to have understood the meaning of what is about to happen to him. That meaning is revealed in what she does, particularly in the act of anointing Jesus' head, a gesture that, as we have seen, would have evoked the ritual of messianic anointing, which is redefined here. In this new understanding of the rite, the anointing no longer has to do with glory and power, but rather with giving one's own life (Mark 10:45) in obedience to the will of God (Mark 14:32–42). The anticipated anointing announces that Jesus' messianism will be disclosed in his death, where he will reveal himself as the obedient Son of God.

The mandate to remember what the woman has done confirms that this ritual gesture encapsulates Jesus' identity. The ritual character of the woman's act makes this memory much more eloquent than mere words or teaching. At the same time, the close connection of this gesture with the revelation of Jesus' messianic identity explains why it should be remembered wherever the gospel is announced. For the narrator, the foundational conviction of the gospel is the confession that Jesus is Messiah (Mark 1:1), but the meaning of this statement can only be understood after the identity of Jesus is fully revealed in his passion. The woman's gesture must be remembered because in it this new identity is expressed as nowhere else.

---

37. Lücking, *Mimesis der Verachteten*, 108–11.

CHAPTER 7

The Gospel of Mark as Progressive Narrative: Cultural Trauma, Collective Memory, and Social Identity

(Mark 11–16)

Introduction

THE GOSPEL ACCORDING TO Mark has been defined as a "text of trauma."[1] The trauma to which this statement refers was the outcome of the social disruption caused by the Jewish War—an event that had a significant impact on the land of Israel, the region of Syria, and the Judaism of the diaspora. To read Mark's Gospel as a text of trauma would be to understand the Gospel as an answer to the traumatic experience lived by the followers of Jesus to whom this text was addressed. Although there is not yet a widespread consensus about the historical setting of the Gospel of Mark, the arguments for locating it in the Syro-Palestinian region in the aftermath of the Jewish War (71 CE) are compelling enough to take that historical situation as a starting point for this inquiry.[2]

The purpose of the following pages is to find out to what extent this traumatic experience shaped the rhetoric of the final chapters of Mark's

---

1. Vaage, "Violence as Religious Experience," 125: "I read the Gospel of Mark as a text of trauma that reflects and articulates the social disruption occasioned by the First Jewish War against Rome (66–73 C.E.)."

2. See Chapter 1, above.

Gospel. I will turn to studies on cultural trauma developed in the social sciences to elaborate a reading scenario that helps unearth some elements of the Gospel that reflect the trauma of living through the Jewish War. As will become apparent, these studies provide an adequate framework for the analysis of collective practices in which the elaboration of the experience of trauma contributes to creating a new collective identity. I contend that Mark's account of the last days of Jesus reflects such a process. Yet, before approaching the main subject of this chapter, it might be helpful to review how the Jewish War affected the early groups of Jesus believers.

The Impact of the Jewish War on Jesus' Followers

We do not have explicit evidence about how the Jewish War affected Jesus' followers. To clarify this issue and situate the Gospel of Mark historically, we need to resort to external information, specifically that provided by Flavius Josephus and other Jewish authors on the impact of the war in general. We should also check the data of the Gospel itself in which we have identified the effects of that situation.[3]

According to Josephus, in the wake of the revolt, the different Jewish groups were divided on the issue of the sacrifices offered by pagans and on behalf of them:

> Eleazar, son of Ananias the high-priest, a very daring youth, then holding the position of captain, persuaded those who officiated in the Temple services to accept no gift or sacrifice from a foreigner. This action laid the foundation of the War with the Romans; for the sacrifices offered on behalf of that nation and the emperor were in consequence rejected. The chief priests and the notables earnestly besought them not to abandon the customary offering for their rulers, but the priests remained obdurate (*Jewish War* 2.409–10).

This ethnic tension was present in the different phases of the conflict. On the one hand, the rebels held fast to their nationalist claims in order to achieve the reestablishment of the ancient monarchy.[4] On the other hand, pagans (i.e., non-Jews) reacted to this claim in many cases in a violent

---

3. Lücking, "Zerstörung des Tempels," 144–46, describes a general framework by using a similar methodology.

4. Flavius Josephus explains in detail the case of Manahem, who "came to Jerusalem as a king" (*Jewish War* 2.434), and who entered in the temple "with an arrogant attitude and with royal clothing" (*Jewish War* 2.434).

way, as happened in Caesarea Maritima, where the nationalist claims were answered fiercely by the non-Jewish inhabitants of the city (*Jewish War* 2.266–70). This answer, in turn, provoked a reaction from the Jews:

> The same day and at the same hour, as it were by the hand of Providence, the inhabitants of Caesarea massacred the Jews who resided in their city; within one hour, more than twenty thousand were slaughtered, and Caesarea was completely emptied of Jews, for the fugitives were arrested by orders of Florus and conducted, in chains, to the dockyards. The news of the disaster at Caesarea infuriated the whole nation; and parties of Jews sacked the Syrian villages and the neighboring cities, Philadelphia, Heshbon and its district, Gerasa, Pella, and Scythopolis. Next, they fell upon Gadara, Hippos, and Gaulanitis, destroying or setting fire to all in their path. (*Jewish War* 2.457–59).

Mark's story not only questions the ambitions of an exclusivist and nationalistic messianism but also openly supports those who accepted the offerings of the pagans in the temple: "My house will be called a house of prayer *for all the nations*" (Mark 11:17). In all probability, those who accepted sacrifices for the "nations" had to endure the harsh reaction of the rebels. The same can be said of those groups who welcomed pagans.[5] Both the attitude of Jesus towards non-Jews and his teachings suggest that Mark's audience was composed of mixed communities, in which the acceptance of non-Jews was encouraged. If the Gospel of Mark was addressed to groups of Jesus followers who lived in or near Palestine, probably in Phoenicia or the Decapolis, then they were likely affected by the conflict.[6]

Those mixed communities may have aroused the suspicion of the two opposing factions in the conflict. On the one hand, non-Jews, including those who had joined the community of believers in Jesus, were suspected by Jews as potential enemies. On the other hand, non-Jews would not distinguish between Jews by birth and Gentiles converted to Judaism. Flavius

---

5. Marcus, "Jewish War," 453. This situation fits the invitation made by the gospel to those who were in Judea to flee to the mountains (Mark 13:14), a recommendation that could be related to the tradition of the flight to Pella mentioned by Jerome, and later by Epiphanius (Marcus, "Jewish War," 461–62).

6. In Mark 6:6b—8:26, after the first multiplication of the bread, Jesus says to his disciples that all food is pure, so there is no reason for not eating with non-Jews. Later, during the second multiplication he says that many of those who participate "came from far away" (Mark 8:3), thus alluding to the pagans (Acts 2:39; 22:21; Eph 2:13, 17).

Josephus explains how the retaliation of non-Jews in the cities that Jews attacked included those who lived as Jews:

> The Syrians on their side killed no less a number of Jews; they, too, slaughtered those whom they caught in the towns, not merely now, as before, from hatred, but to forestall the peril which menaced themselves. The whole of Syria was a scene of frightful disorder; every city was divided into two camps, and the safety of one party lay in their anticipating the other. They passed their days in blood, their nights, yet more dreadful, in terror. For, though believing that they had rid themselves of the Jews, still each city had its Judaizers, who aroused suspicion; and while they shrunk from killing offhand this equivocal element in their midst, they feared these neutrals as much as pronounced aliens. Even those who had long been reputed the very mildest of men were instigated by avarice to murder their adversaries. (*Jewish War* 2.461–63)

This passage mentions a group of people who were not Jews but who lived as Jews. Non-Jews suspected them because they were an ambiguous and mixed group that belonged to another bloodline. It is tempting to find in this description an allusion to the groups of Jesus believers who lived in the Syrophoenician region.[7] Even if Josephus does not explicitly refer to them, the situation he describes is very similar to the one those groups may have lived in.

The atmosphere experienced in the region of Syria during the war and after it was dramatic. On the one hand, the destruction of the temple and the interruption of worship compelled Jews to reassess their religious practices. On the other hand, the disappearance of the local ruling class, who had cooperated in the revolt, put the region under Roman control. However, it was above all famine and starvation, revenge, and unanswered offenses that provoked in the region a climate of instability and violence that affected all the inhabitants.[8] Because of the war, the world they once knew had disappeared, and now they had to face a new situation.

---

7. Theissen, *Lokalkolorit und Zeitgeschichte*, 281–83 [ET= *Gospels in Context*], already discusses this possibility. Schenke sees in this passage a clear reference to the situation of the group of believers in Jesus: "In the Hellenistic cities of Palestine and Syria, they formed their own communities, separated from Jewish synagogues, to which Gentile Christians also belonged as full members. Greeks and Syrians, however, considered them a special group within Judaism. Thus they were treated like Jews during riots and pogroms against them. The Syrian or Greek descent of Christians did not protect them from persecution. As 'friends of the Jews' they were suspicious" (Schenke, *Markusevangelium*, 23).

8. On the consequences of war see Goodman, *Ruling Class of Judaea*.

Not only was the region of Syria affected by the war, but also this event had a profound impact on the Jewish communities in the diaspora. Although these communities did not initially feel involved in the conflict, the destruction of the temple, which was their primary religious and ethnic reference, had significant social and economic consequences. As Jews, they were forced to pay a burdensome and humiliating tax, the *fiscus iudaicus*.[9] An eloquent indication of the impact of these events on Judaism is evident in several Jewish writings composed by the end of the first century. These writings witness different reactions to the crisis that led to the destruction of Jerusalem and its temple (2 Baruch; 3 Baruch; 4 Baruch; 4 Esdras; Sibylline Oracles 4–5; Apocalypse of Abraham). They confirm that the war had a high impact not only on Judaism but also on the groups of Jesus followers—an impact that caused them to question their own identity and that provoked collective reflection.[10]

Cultural Trauma, Social Identity, and Collective Memory

The situation created by the Jewish War had a tremendous impact on the entire Jewish diaspora.[11] Groups of Jesus followers, especially those who lived in the region of Syria, suffered through this situation. My thesis is that the Gospel of Mark reacts to this situation by redefining the group identity of the believers in Jesus through a creative recovery of the trauma of his passion. In order to understand how this process works, I will bring into play the notion of cultural trauma elaborated by the social sciences.[12]

First, it is necessary to clarify the very concept of *cultural trauma*. The frequent use of vocabulary related to the word *trauma* reveals that it is a widespread experience. In common parlance, this word describes the

---

9. According to Goodman, this tax had to be paid by all Jews of the diaspora, owing to the inherent ambiguity of the name with which they were labeled (*iudaeos* or *iudaioi*), as this was the same name used to refer to the inhabitants of Judea (Goodman, "Diaspora Reactions"). On the *fiscus iudaicus*, see Heemstra, *Fiscus Iudaicus*, 7–102.

10. In these writings, the Jews are encouraged to maintain their faith and the way of life of their ancestors, emphasizing the distinctive features that distinguish them from the Romans. See Jones, *Jewish Reactions*, 278.

11. War and postwar periods are the most frequent settings of cultural trauma, and, therefore most of the studies on this issue are related to these circumstances; see, for example: Eyerman et al., *Narrating Trauma*.

12. Biblical studies, although reluctantly, have started to apply the theory of trauma; see Garber, "Trauma Theory."

destabilizing effect that some situations cause in persons or groups. However, the enlightened understanding of this phenomenon does not insist on the event, but on the way it is lived, and defines *trauma* as a rational response to a sudden change. There is also a psychoanalytic approach to the phenomenon, characterized by placing the unconscious (fears, defense mechanisms, and so forth) between the external situation that causes the trauma and the response to it. The enlightened understanding (trauma as a rational response to a sudden change) and the psychoanalytic study of trauma (related to trauma and the unconscious) have transformed it into a scientific concept. Nevertheless, the enlightened approach and the psychoanaltyic approach both participate in the so-called *naturalistic fallacy*, which presupposes that events cause trauma. From a social perspective, however, trauma is not the direct outcome of severe or traumatic events, but the result of humans defining some experiences as such. Cultural trauma is the product of a collective process of interpretation and assimilation. Jeffrey Alexander, one of the pioneers in the study of cultural trauma, proposes the following definition:

> Cultural trauma occurs when members of a collectivity feel they have been subjected to a horrendous event that leaves indelible marks upon their group consciousness, marking their memories forever and changing their future identity in fundamental and irrevocable ways.[13]

This definition mentions three characteristics of cultural trauma. In the first place, cultural trauma only exists if the group members feel themselves affected by the event. This does not always happen with a disturbing event. In fact, many of the upsetting situations suffered by a group do not produce trauma, in the same way that many noteworthy events do not turn into news spread by the media. For that reason, cultural trauma "is not the result of a group experiencing pain. It is the result of this acute discomfort entering into the core of the collectivity's sense of its own identity."[14]

The second aspect mentioned in Alexander's definition is that the circumstances in which the distressing event is perceived leave indelible marks on the group's consciousness and transform the group's identity. According to the already classic definition proposed by Henry Tajfel, collective identity is "that part of an individual's self-concept which derives from his

---

13. Alexander, "Towards a Theory of Cultural Trauma," 1; see also 2–10.
14. Alexander, "Towards a Theory of Cultural Trauma," 10.

knowledge of his/her membership in a social group together with the value and emotional significance attached to that membership."[15] Social identity has, therefore, three dimensions. It has a cognitive dimension, by which the individual knows he or she is a member of the group. It also has an evaluative dimension, which is perceived by the comparison with other groups in which differences are emphasized. Lastly, it has an affective dimension, which involves emotional attachment to the group. All these elements are altered when the experience of trauma changes the identity of the group.[16]

Finally, in his definition of cultural trauma, Alexander mentions the impact of trauma on the group's memory, explaining that the group is marked by the experienced event. This is because the memory of a group and its identity are mutually interdependent.[17] For that reason, when a group's identity is challenged, a new search for collective memory begins, in order to secure a new identity.[18]

This relationship between cultural trauma, collective memory, and social identity provides an initial theoretical framework to interpret Mark's story. The Jewish War was a traumatic event that triggered the recovery of another traumatic event, the passion and death of Jesus, which already had been elaborated by early Christian groups as a cultural trauma. For the sake of clarity, I would like to emphasize that the two traumatic events implied in the process were not of the same kind, for the second one—namely, the shameful death of Jesus—was already elaborated as a cultural trauma by Mark's time.[19] The result of this process was the creation of a social identity.

To understand the relationship between the traumatic events behind Mark's Gospel and the cultural trauma of Jesus' death already elaborated by different Christian groups, it might be helpful to incorporate the concept of *chosen trauma* set forth by Vadmik Volkan. A chosen trauma is a shared representation of a historical event in which a group suffers a catastrophic

---

15. Tajfel, *Human Groups and Social Categories*, 63.

16. Alexander states, "Insofar as traumas are so experienced, and thus imagined and represented, the collective identity will become significantly revised" (Alexander, "Theory of Cultural Trauma," 22).

17. Assmann, "Cultural Memory," 162–69.

18. In the words of Alexander: "This identity revision means that there will be a searching re-remembering of the collective past, for memory is not only social and fluid but deeply connected to the contemporary sense of the self. Identities are continuously constructed and secured not only by facing the present and future but also by reconstructing the collectivity's life" ("Theory of Cultural Trauma," 22).

19. Dube, "Jesus' Death."

defeat, loss, or humiliation. Together with chosen glories, chosen traumas constitute the major events remembered and commemorated by a group because they configure the collective memory that shapes its identity.[20] A critical fact about chosen traumas is that they are often used to conceptualize new conflicts different from the conflict that resulted in the chosen trauma.

> [Chosen traumas] may lie dormant for a long period of time, yet can be reactivated and exert a powerful psychological force. Leaders intuitively seem to know how to reactivate a chosen trauma, especially when their large group is in conflict or has gone through a drastic change and needs to reconfirm or enhance its identity.[21]

My contention is that Mark reactivated the trauma of Jesus' death as a means of interpreting the situation created by the Jewish War.[22]

Finally, in order to understand the role of Mark's story in the redefinition of its audience's identity, I will use the category of *progressive narrative* elaborated by Ron Eyerman and others. In literary terms, a progressive narrative is a story in which the plot advances decisively to its denouement. In the process of identity construction, a progressive narrative is a story in which the events or experiences of the past are preserved and recovered because they are considered valuable in enabling the group to move forward in the present.[23] This kind of narrative takes events frequently treasured in people's memory as a starting point for further development in order to interpret a new social situation. This process involves selecting and interpreting events and memories.[24] In what follows, I will try to show that the Gospel of Mark is a progressive narrative that uses memories about

---

20. Bar-Tal, *Intractable Conflicts*, 145–48.

21. Volkan, "Transgenerational Transmissions," 88.

22. This would explain why the passion narrative played such an important role in the composition of the gospel; see Chapter 1, above.

23. Eyerman, "Cultural Trauma," 92.

24. In his studies of how the cultural trauma of slavery gave rise to the Afro-American identity, Ron Eyerman draws a distinction between two types of narratives: a progressive one and a redemptive one. The first "takes slavery as a starting-point for progressive development and eventual inclusion in modern society," while the second "sought to restore pride and glory to blacks through redemption in the home country [Africa]" (Eyerman, "The Past in the Present," 165). It is interesting to note that these two types of narratives began to emerge in the second generation after the civil war because only then did the necessary distance to assume the trauma in a creative way exist.

Jesus—especially the traumatic memory of his death—and reinterprets them in light of a new situation.

It is worth noting that this redefinition of group identity is carried out through narrative because although the past can be preserved in objects or rites, its significance is better explained, understood, and transmitted through language. This process of explaining, understanding, and transmitting the past results in narratives that strengthen a group's identity. In this sense, collective narratives, mainly those with a foundational character, are the perfect tools for elaborating alternative accounts of events. These stories oppose the official discourse—that is, the discourse that selects, unifies, and imposes an interpretation of the reality rooted in established power. For this reason, progressive narratives are typical of minority and oppressed groups. They often include a traumatic event from which the group emerged, and have enormous emotional power.[25] The Gospel according to Mark is this kind of narrative, as it not only focuses on the traumatic situation of Jesus' death, but also creates a new social identity and a new collective project.

The Gospel of Mark as Progressive Narrative

The Gospel of Mark includes several memories of Jesus transmitted among his disciples after his death.[26] Some of them, like his miracles, refer to glorious moments of his life, while others recall situations of crisis and confusion. Both result from a selection process and comprise the chosen glories and traumas that constituted the group memory of his followers. However, although Mark's story includes both types of memories, it is evident that from the narrative perspective, the traumas are more important than the glories. In fact, the entire narrative is oriented to Jesus' passion, which thus becomes its hermeneutical clue.

The traumatic events of the Jewish War triggered the creative recovery of the trauma of the passion and death of Jesus transmitted by the first generation of disciples. However, in Mark's narrative, the memory of that first trauma was integrated into a new story that tried to face the identity crisis that those events had caused among early Christian groups to which

---

25. Eyerman, "The Past in the Present," 162–63.
26. Not only single memories but also more elaborated compositions: See Kuhn, *Ältere Sammlungen*.

this Gospel was addressed.²⁷ In this sense, we may say that Mark's story is a progressive narrative.

The trauma of the death of Jesus pervades the entire narrative. The shadow of the cross reaches the very beginning of his activity, which the narrator associates with the "handing over" of John the Baptist (Mark 1:14).²⁸ In the same way, the beginning of Jesus' activity in Capernaum leads to a conspiracy and plot to kill him, which will reappear in the story (Mark 3:6; 11:18; 14:1). Therefore, despite Jesus' numerous achievements and the positive response of many people, his activity takes place in a threatening atmosphere, which becomes more and more explicit as the narrative unfolds. The passion predictions, which according to Mark were pronounced by Jesus during his journey from Galilee to Jerusalem, have in this context a crucial function because in them Jesus himself confirms that the threat will be fulfilled (Mark 8:31-33; 9:31; 10:32-34) and explains that it is the result of a divine plan.²⁹

However, it is at the end of the story (Mark 11–16) where we most clearly perceive how the situation created by the war led to a new interpretation of Jesus' death. This section, which is thoroughly elaborated, is located in Jerusalem, where the most tragic and significant events of the war took place. Jerusalem is the setting for this last part of the narrative because Jesus spent his last days there. Nevertheless, the rigid temporal structure of the Markan story, which situates Jesus in the holy city only at the end of his life and in close relationship with his passion, likely intends to recall the events that preceded the destruction of the city and its temple.

This last part of Mark's story (Mark 11–16) transpires with a realism lacking in the previous chapters. The sense of reality is evident in the indications of space and time, which are more precise and coherent. In the first part of Mark's Gospel, whose main setting is the region of Galilee, the indications of time are practically nonexistent, to the point that it is impossible to define the duration of Jesus' ministry there. Something similar happens

---

27. Lücking states: "The experience of the Jewish War and the destruction of the Jerusalem Temple is dealt with in the Gospel of Mark through the updated retelling of Jesus' suffering and death" (Lücking, "Zerstörung des Tempels," 61).

28. He does this by using the verb "to hand over" (*paradidōmi*), which will be used afterward to refer to the passion of Jesus (Mark 9:31; 10:33; 14:10, 11, 18 . . .) and his disciples (Mark 13:9, 11, 12).

29. The divine nature of this plan about Jesus is expressed in the first announcement through the impersonal *dei* (Mark 8:31), and in the third one through the use of the divine passive: *paradothēsetai* (Mark 10:33).

with the spatial references, which do not allow a precise reconstruction of the itinerary of his public activity. However, from the very moment Jesus enters Jerusalem, both the indications of time and the spatial references are concrete and precise. This concretization of narrated space and time gives the last part of Mark's narrative a consistency that makes readers perceive it as more real and close to their own experience.[30]

In this last part of the story, we discover an extended interlude that interrupts the narrative and shifts the attention of readers away from it. The narrator introduces here a didactic dialogue between Jesus and a small group of disciples about events that will happen in the future (Mark 13:4). From the perspective of the story, this dialogue introduces distance between Jesus' present life narrated in the Gospel and the future situation of the disciples that Jesus announces. However, from readers' perspective, the time relationship is precisely the opposite, for what Jesus announces in the story is happening in the addressees' own time (Mark 13:30).[31]

Thus, seen from the perspective of the author and his audience, the narrative of Jesus' activity in Jerusalem starts with a glance to the past in order to remember some of his deeds in the temple (Mark 11–12), then shifts to the present to describe the situation they are going through (Mark 13), and finally turns back to the past to recall the trauma of the passion and the death of Jesus from the point of view of that situation (Mark 14–16).

Jesus and the War (Mark 11–12)

In Mark's story, Jerusalem is the place of the passion and death of Jesus (Mark 10:33, my translation: "We are going up to Jerusalem, and the Son of Man will be handed over"). Jesus' activity in the city soon initiates the plot to kill him (Mark 11:18: "the chief priests and the scribes kept looking for a way to kill him"). For Jesus, as well as for the addressees of the Gospel, who suffer the consequences of the war, Jerusalem is a place of conflict and violence. Actually, the way the gospel narrates Jesus' activity in the city suggests that some of the events that triggered the war are evoked in the narrative.

30. Fander, "Mein Gott," 122–24, adds the interesting observation that the break between the concepts of place and time that characterizes the Gospel of Mark is a reflection of the break with the real world experienced by people who have suffered a trauma.

31. Fritzen, *Von Gott verlassen?*, 135–38, shows that the predictions, warnings, and menaces of this chapter refer to the time of the implied reader.

Jesus' entrance into the city (Mark 11:1–11) calls to mind the arrival of some of the messianic pretenders in the years preceding its destruction. Like them, Jesus goes to Jerusalem, but the way he enters the city and its temple shows that the narrator wants to detach him from those false messiahs. Therefore, although the actions and the attitude of those who acclaim Jesus give the scene a solemn tone, the fact that he arrives at the city riding a donkey reveals that he is not like those leaders who appeared with signs of power.[32] Similarly, the acclamation of the people (quoting Ps 118, which imagines Jerusalem surrounded by its enemies and liberated by the descendant of David) contrasts with the passivity of Jesus, who, after a brief visit to the temple, leaves the city and goes to Bethany (Mark 11:11).[33]

The events of the Jewish War are also evoked in the scene when Jesus expels the merchants from the temple (Mark 11:15–17). The words Jesus utters in this scene combine two scriptural quotations. The first (Isa 56:7: "My house shall be called a house of prayer for all the nations") defines a clear position on the question that triggered the war, according to Josephus: the prohibition to offer sacrifices for (and on behalf of) the Gentiles (*Jewish War* 2.409). The second of Jesus' scriptural citations (Jer 7:11: "you have made it a den of robbers") probably alludes to the desecration of the temple by revolutionaries.[34] In Mark's narrative, this scene is related to the preceding and the following ones. In the preceding scene, Jesus curses a fig tree for not bearing fruit (Mark 11:12–14), and in the following one he and his disciples verify that the curse has been fulfilled (Mark 11:20–24). The whole seems to be a reflection on the destruction of the temple—on its motives, its meaning, and its effect.[35]

The performance of Jesus in the temple raises a question that the leaders of the nation voice: "By what authority are you doing these things?" (Mark 11:28). This was a pressing question in the years before the war when

---

32. According to Flavius Josephus, one of those leaders, Menahem, "reached Jerusalem as a King" and he went to the temple "with a haughty attitude and with royal clothing" (*Jewish War* 2.344, 444). Matthew understood well the meaning of the gesture of Jesus and he related it to Zech 9:9, which talks about a different kind of messiah.

33. Marcus, *Mark 8-16*, 780, observes that this text recalls the promise of 2 Sam 7, where the kingdom of the Son of David is linked to the victory over Israel's enemies.

34. Josephus, *Jewish War* 2.135–57. See also the end of Chapter 1 of this book (pp. 26–29).

35. Miquel Pericás, "Impatient Jesus," discovers in this passage a masked language of resistance that reveals a context in whichd the destruction of the temple has made an important impact.

the leaders of the various factions claimed control over the temple and the city. In the Gospel of Mark, Jesus could have vindicated his authority by invoking his Davidic descent. This was what the people had reminded him of when he entered the city. However, instead of doing that, he tells them a parable in which, in a context of violence, he identifies himself as "the beloved Son" killed by the winegrowers and thrown outside the vineyard (Mark 12:1–12).[36] The scene concludes with a new quotation from Ps 118. However, the verses Jesus quotes this time are not about the triumphant arrival of the Davidic kingdom but about his rejection. This quotation also announces a change that will be God's work: "the stone that the builders rejected has become the cornerstone; this was the Lord's doing, and it is amazing in our eyes" (Mark 12:10–11, quoting Ps 118:22–23).[37] Once again, by speaking and acting this way, Jesus distances himself from the behavior that would later cause the Jewish War.

Accordingly, the controversies that follow this statement of Jesus' raise some questions about the situation created during and after the war. The payment of taxes to the oppressive authority (Mark 12:13–17) was an issue of intense debate among the revolutionaries and became the main concern for Jews after they were forced to pay the *fiscus iudaicus*.[38] The theme of the resurrection of the dead (Mark 12:18–27) was of particular interest in an atmosphere of extreme violence, and questions about the most important commandment (Mark 12:28–35) could also be revived in a context of hatred.[39] However, it is in the last controversy—the one in which Jesus challenges his adversaries' vision of the messiah (Mark 12:35–37)—where the reference to the Jewish War is most evident. In his reasoning, Jesus uses an exegetical argument to challenge the conviction that the messiah should be a descendant of David. This vision of the messiah, which emerged from the interpretation of some psalms (among then Ps 118 quoted twice in these chapters) and was promoted in the Pharisaic tradition (Pss. Sol. 17), played an essential role in the revolt against Rome. By challenging it, Jesus rejects the logic that led to the Jewish War.[40]

---

36. It seems obvious that the son of the parable is Jesus, who is described as "the beloved son", the title used in the two passages in which a celestial voice reveals his identity: the vision that follows his baptism (Mark 1:11) and the transfiguration (Mark 9:7).

37. Marcus, *Way of the Lord*, 111–29.

38. Zeichmann, "Date of Mark," 432–36.

39. Marcus, *Way of the Lord*, 826 and 835–36.

40. Marcus, *Way of the Lord*, 137–45; Roskam, *Purpose of the Gospel of Mark*, 145–70.

Thus, the narrative of Jesus' activity in Jerusalem evokes the events of the Jewish War in order to detach him from them. The Gospel of Mark argues that Jesus was not one of the messianic pretenders who settled in the city before its destruction. He should not be identified with the kind of messianism they claimed. From the perspective of Mark, all this was a terrible failure. The kingdom of God is something else; it follows a different logic. Therefore, those events should only be remembered to distantiate from them. However, this was not an easy task for the Gospel audience, because the consequences of war remained and affected them directly.

The War and the Disciples (Mark 13)

Jesus' dialogue with his disciples, which Mark has placed at the end of his activity in Jerusalem, is a strange element in his narrative. The teachings of Jesus are not frequent in this gospel. Only here and in parabolic discourse (Mark 4:1–34) does Mark portray Jesus teaching at some length. But the audience for this last teaching is restricted to the four disciples who had followed him from the beginning (Mark 1:16–20). From the perspective of the narrative technique, this chapter is also peculiar because readers are invited to abandon the time of the story and move to their own time.[41]

This change of the time frame is only one of the measures used by the narrator to capture the attention of readers and make them feel directly involved in the story. The discourse contains various allusions that remind readers and listeners that Jesus is speaking to them. Thus, although initially his teachings are addressed to a reduced group of disciples, in the end it becomes clear who the real addressees are: "what I say to you, I say to all" (Mark 13:36). This "all" to whom Jesus directs his teaching is the "generation" mentioned before—that is, "this generation" that "will not pass away until all these things have taken place" (Mark 13:30). The first readers and hearers of the gospel, who belonged to this generation, are directly addressed by the narrator: "let the reader understand!" (Mark 13:14).[42]

---

41. The Gospel of Mark refers frequently to future events (see the list elaborated in Fritzen, *Von Gott verlassen?*, 134–35), but only in some cases are those events outside the story: the coming of the Son of Man (Mark 8:38), the spreading news of the transfiguration (Mark 9:9), the disciples' situation in the future world (Mark 10:29–31), and the encounter between the disciples and Jesus in Galilee (Mark 14:28; 16:7). Mark 13 refers to events that are supposed to be outside the story told in the gospel (Mark 14:3–9).

42. Balabanski, "Mark 13," 62–63. On the different possible meanings of this expression, see Fowler, *Let the Reader Understand*, 83–84.

The Gospel of Mark as Progressive Narrative

However, despite its many peculiarities, the discourse is not a strange element in Mark's story. It is closely related to the previous chapters, especially to the episodes in which Jesus prophetically announces the temple's destruction with the symbolic action of the cursing of the fig tree (Mark 11:12–26). Jesus refers to this same destruction in the initial dialogue with his disciples (Mark 13:2), and the whole discourse is apparently intended to unveil the moment and how such an event will take place (Mark 13:4).

The teaching of Jesus also has a close relationship with the story of the passion that comes afterward.[43] The verb *paradidōmi* is used to speak about the handing over of both the disciples and Jesus (Mark 13:9, 11, 12; 14:11, 18, and so forth). Moreover, the announcement that the disciples will be taken to the Sanhedrin and brought before governors (Mark 13:9) is echoed in the passion of Jesus (Mark 14:55–65; 15:1–5), while the announcement that close relatives will hand over the disciples (Mark 13:12) is fulfilled in the handing over of Jesus by one member of his new family (Mark 14:43–47; 3:31–35). Likewise, the exhortation to the disciples to watch (Mark 13:35, 36) anticipates a similar warning that Jesus addresses to those who join him while he prays in Gethsemane (Mark 14:34, 38). Finally, the "hour" announced by Jesus as something unknown (Mark 13:32) arrives when he is arrested (Mark 14:41).

Accordingly, the signs that will precede the coming of the Son of Man (Mark 13:24–25) will become apparent at the moment of Jesus' death (Mark 15:33). Furthermore, this coming is announced with almost the same words in the discourse and in the confession of Jesus before the high priest (Mark 13:26; 14:62). Finally, the destruction of the temple, which is the central theme of the discourse, will also reappear in the accusations against Jesus and in the mockery of the crucified (Mark 14:55–59; 15:29–30) and will be carried out symbolically on the moment of his death with the tearing of the temple's curtain (Mark 15:38).

All these connections show that Mark 13 is part of Mark's narrative and is perfectly integrated into it. Nevertheless, the change of genre and the time shift suggest that the narrator is no longer telling the story of Jesus but the story of Mark's addressees. At the same time, the connections with what follows helps readers understand that there is a deep relationship between the crisis they are experiencing and the trauma of Jesus' passion. Thus, this final dialogue does not feature an eschatological announcement about what

---

43. This relation was already observed by Lightfoot, *Gospel Message*, 48–59; see also Balabanski, "Mark 13," 66–69; and Lücking, "Zerstörung des Tempels," 157–61.

will happen at the end of time. Although it uses apocalyptic images to describe the dramatic situation lived out by the Gospel's audience, it is not an apocalyptic discourse. This composition is rather a kind of *farewell discourse*[44] that rhetorically anticipates the situation lived by the addressees.[45]

Formally, the teaching of Jesus is presented as an answer to the disciples' question about the moment of the temple's destruction and the signs that will precede it (Mark 13:4). His answer follows a temporal sequence that distinguishes three phases: the beginning of labor pains (Mark 13:5–8), the tribulation (Mark 13:9–23), and the events that will happen after the tribulation (Mark 13:24–27). This sequence concludes with an exhortation to watch and discern the signs. It assures that everything will happen in "this generation," emphasizing the need to watch (Mark 13:28–37). In the description of the two first phases, exegetes have easily recognized the situation experienced by the Gospel's audience.[46] But the third part also belongs to the things that will happen in "this generation."

The main event of this third phase is the coming of the Son of Man (Mark 13:24–27). Readers might recognize in this announcement previous ones in which Jesus has alluded to himself as the Son of Man who "will come with the glory of his Father with the holy angels" (Mark 8:38), or even the prediction that the Son of Man will rise from the dead (Mark 9:9). In the context of Mark's story, the new announcement of his coming in the future reinforces these previous ones. However, this is not the last word about that event, because as the narrative progresses, we witness a dramatic redefinition of this prophecy. During his passion, Jesus will associate this announcement with himself when he acknowledges in front of the high priest that he is the Son of Man who will come in the clouds (Mark 14:62). In this passage, his coming with power refers to his resurrection.[47] Further

---

44. The literary genre of Mark 13 is disputed. Regarding its characterization as *farewell discourse*, see Hatina, "Focus of Mark 13:24–27," 45–48; Fritzen, *Von Gott verlassen?*, 135–36.

45. Vaage, *Trauma, Erzählung, Befreiung*, 125–50, develops this point of view in a chapter titled "The Apocalypse Is Already Over: How Do You Enter the Kingdom of God Now?," which confirms that everything Jesus announced in this chapter was, for the Gospel audience, something that had already happened. Collins, "Apocalyptic Rhetoric," proposes a similar reading of Mark 13. More recently, Fritzen, *Von Gott verlassen?*, 135–52, has argued in favor of it.

46. Balabanski, "Mark 13," 97–100. Especially in Mark 13:9–13, we can see a manifestation of the tribulations that the addressees of the gospel were going through: van Iersel, "Failed Followers."

47. According to Vaage, *Trauma, Erzählung, Befreiung*, 134–42, from the first

on, at the end of Mark's story, a new reference to the future vision of Jesus will clarify what this announcement means for his followers. The angel's words to the women at the tomb explain that they will see Jesus in Galilee (Mark 16:7).[48]

In Mark's farewell discourse, the situation of the Gospel audience is described as a combination of tribulations and hope. In its literary and theological complexity, this discourse reveals that the experience of the Jewish War was traumatic for them. Jesus' followers have lived through terrible events in their environment (wars and famine). They have been prosecuted by courts and kings, and some of them have been handed over to death by their relatives and by other believers (Mark 13:9–13).[49] These events have marked their consciousness indelibly as a group. The consequences of the war have destabilized the pillars on which their society was based: the abomination of desolation is where it should not be.

However, this pessimistic view of the war's consequences is not the last word. According to Mark, this situation is already over (Mark 13:24), and now his audience should look to the future to construct a new identity and a new project. Jesus' final teaching creates a pause that allows readers to distance themselves from their situation.[50] The experienced trauma is not the last word but an opportunity to recover the past creatively and construct a new future.

In this process of reflection, Mark recovers the cultural trauma of the passion in order to elaborate a progressive narrative. This narrative will help the group of Jesus followers to assimilate their traumatic situation in a constructive manner. The connections between the final discourse and the

---

announcement of the passion, Jesus identifies himself as Son of Man, who, after suffering the passion, will rise from the dead. On the other hand, the signs that announce the arrival of the Son of Man (Mark 13:24–25) are recalled at the moment of Jesus' death (Mark 15:33). In this way, the link between the passages is reinforced. Finally, the expression "sitting at the right hand of the Power" belongs to the traditional language of the confession of faith that presupposes the resurrection (Acts 2:25, 34).

48. Mark 13:26; 14:62; and 16:7 are the only three instances of *oraō* in the future tense in the Gospel of Mark. The three announcements refer to seeing Jesus in the future.

49. On the situation of the addressees, see Fritzen, *Von Gott verlassen?*, 364–66.

50. In the words of Balabanski, "Mark 13 breaks the breathless onward movement of the narrative prior to the climactic events of the passion. This gives readers the opportunity to orientate themselves in relation to the central narrative of their faith by recognizing themselves as addressed, and thus in a sense as part of what is to follow . . . The story is thus no longer experienced as 'objective' history to be observed from the outside, but rather as a reality into which one enters" (Balabanski, "Mark 13," 69).

passion narrative that follows relate both experiences. In this way, readers can understand the passion of Jesus as his own story and can understand their own experiences in the light of Jesus' passion (a chosen trauma), which is the founding experience of the group.[51]

A New Identity Shaped by the Passion of Jesus (Mark 14–16)

The interpretation of Mark 11–13 outlined in the previous pages situates the passion narrative in a particular framework. Seen from the perspective of Mark's story, this final narrative does not provide a historical chronicle of the last moments of Jesus' life. Instead, its goal is to propose a model to readers in their traumatic situation,[52] helping them to redefine their collective identity. Mark's story does not look to the past, but to the future; and if it recalls the past, it is to construct a new beginning.

Looking at the passion narrative from the readers' perspective provides a better understanding of why the whole Gospel of Mark is focused on this narrative. It also helps us understand how this ending is integrated into the beginning, which includes the entire gospel (Mark 1:1: "The *beginning* of the good news . . ."). This beginning arises from the creative recovery of a social trauma: the passion and death of Jesus. The first followers had already elaborated such an event as a cultural trauma. There was news about this event and most likely an oral narrative that perhaps might have been written down. However, now those memories are read in the light of the experience lived by Mark's audience in the aftermath of the Jewish War in order to develop a progressive narrative in which the old trauma becomes a source of inspiration to create a new social identity and to open a new path.[53]

---

51. Lücking states: "The parallels between the discourse on the last days and the passion of Jesus put the fate of the disciples—and with it the current crisis experience of the Christian communities—in the context of Jesus' suffering and death. In this way, readers experience their own story in the passion of Jesus. The experience of the Jewish War and the destruction of the Jerusalem temple is dealt with in Mark's Gospel through the updated retelling of the suffering and death of Jesus. Both experiences of crisis interpret each other" (Lücking, "Zerstörung des Tempels," 161, my translation).

52. Dormeyer, *Passion Jesu als Verhaltensmodell*, already highlighted the exemplarity of Jesus' conduct in the passion narrative.

53. Fritzen shows that the time of the narrative and the time of the reader merge in Mark, and that, thanks to this time fusion, the time of the reader can be read into the time of Jesus, in such a way that "his/her situation, questions and challenges are reflected in the world being narrated, and (vice versa) he or she finds himself or herself involved

The marked connections between the farewell discourse of Jesus and the story of his passion reveal the logic of this reading. We find the first key at the end of the discourse when Jesus encourages his disciples to watch (Mark 13:33–36). This appeal has particular relevance, as it is addressed not only to those who at that moment are listening to Jesus but also to everybody (Mark 13:37). The imperative: "Watch!" is repeated twice in that context and is emphasized by the parable of the servant, in which the master asks the porter to "keep watch!" (Mark 13:33). The same invitation returns—this time within the passion narrative—in the scene in Gethsemane (Mark 14:32–42). Here Jesus also warns the small group of disciples that join him to be awake, twice repeating the imperative: "Keep watch!" This exhortation is situated at a critical moment in the passion story: at the moment when Jesus accepts, even without understanding it, the will of the Father, the cup of distress that will be his passion. The failure of the disciples, who are unable to pray with Jesus, explains why one of them will betray him, another one will reject him, and all of them will abandon him.[54]

The way Mark portrays Jesus' closest followers shows that they are not a good example for his readers. Although in the beginning they follow Jesus unconditionally (Mark 1:16–20; 3:13–19; and so forth), their attitude towards him, his mission, and his destiny becomes more distant, and their failure to understand Jesus' way, more evident (Mark 8:14–21; 8:32; 9:33–37; and so forth). Now, at the end of Jesus' life, in the critical moment of his passion, his disciples abandon him.[55] This portrayal of the disciples conceals a criticism of the historical project led by the Twelve. This presentation is also a literary device to show readers that if the path once followed by the Twelve might have been the correct one, now it is not anymore. In this new situation, readers should not take the disciples as their model, but Jesus. Jesus is, in fact, the protagonist of the passion story. Although he hardly speaks, and his attitude becomes increasingly passive, readers are encouraged to pay attention to him; his behavior; and his way of facing betrayal, unfair verdicts, insults, and death. Readers and listeners

---

in the world being narrated" (Fritzen, *Von Gott verlassen?*, 260).

54. Fritzen, *Von Gott verlassen?*, 312–21, has shown correctly the relation between those passages. He points out that the sequence of the four hours of the night in Mark 13:35 (in the evening, at midnight, at cockcrow, at dawn) correspond with the moments when Jesus is betrayed, abandoned, and rejected by the disciples (Mark 14:17: "when evening came"; 14:43–49: later on the night; Mark 14:72: "the cock crows"; 15:1: "as soon it was morning").

55. Guijarro, *Camino del discípulo*, 37–83.

of Mark's Gospel come into the narrative with their own experience and discover in Jesus a way to face it.[56]

The connection between Jesus and Mark's audience becomes evident in the narrative through the shared identity of "being handed over." To the readers, Jesus announces: "you will be handed over to councils . . ." (Mark 13:9), and "brother will hand over brother to death" (Mark 13:12, my translation). The verb "to hand over" describes the situation of uncertainty and the risk of death that threatens them in the context of the Jewish War.[57] This is also Jesus' situation at the beginning of the passion narrative, when Judas, one of the members of his new family (Mark 3:31–35), is planning to hand him over (Mark 14:11). During the dinner with his disciples, Jesus is aware of this threat (Mark 14:18), which will be fulfilled in Gethsemane (Mark 14:41). From that moment on, his journey will be marked by various handovers (Mark 15:1, 15). Jesus and his disciples are "handed over" to the Sanhedrin and have to appear before the governor. His situation is a replica of the circumstances experienced by the addressees of the gospel because he, like they, must face the menace of suffering and death. By portraying Jesus undergoing the same tribulations they are suffering (Mark 15:1, 15), the narrator invites the readers to pay attention to him and to read their situation in that of Jesus.

Paying attention to Jesus, readers will notice that he is becoming more and more a passive character. Seen from this perspective, the passion narrative comprises four different moments. In the first one, Jesus is under threat of being handed over and shows an active attitude (Mark 14:1–50). In the second, he has been handed over and appears silently before the Sanhedrin and the Roman prefect (Mark 14:51—15:15). In the third moment, after being convicted, he suffers mockery and dies on the cross (Mark 15:16–41). Finally, during the fourth moment, Jesus is put in the tomb (Mark 15:42—16:8).

During the first moment, Jesus is under threat of being handed over.[58] This handing over has been announced (Mark 14:11), and Jesus knows

---

56. As Hatina notes: "The positioning of the discourse prior to Jesus' arrest, trial, beatings, humiliation, and death encourages the audience to understand how the anticipated suffering is to be faithfully endured by the followers of Jesus" (Hatina, "Focus of Mark 13:24–27," 48).

57. Van Iersel, "Failed Followers," 256–58. The way Flavius Josephus describes the situation of menace faced also by the sympathizers of the Hebrews (*Jewish War* 2.461–463) allows us to understand better what exactly the menace of being handed over signified.

58. It is interesting to observe that most of the episodes that precede the arrest are

that what has been announced will take place (Mark 14:18). According to Mark 13:9–13, this is the situation lived by the Gospel's addressees. During this stage, Jesus is more active than in the subsequent ones. It is a moment of distress and temptation, as his prayer in Gethsemane reveals (Mark 14:34–35). In this first moment Jesus accepts the death that awaits him. In Bethany, he interprets the woman's gesture as an anticipated unction of his body "for his burial" (Mark 14:8). During the dinner with his disciples, the bread and the cup of wine he shares with them symbolically anticipate his death (Mark 14:22–25). However, it is in the scene in Gethsemane where his attitude is revealed with more details.[59] Readers are taken into the inner experience of someone confronted with such a situation, and this makes them understand that Jesus faced it, accepting God's will. During the first passion prediction, Jesus reproached Peter for thinking humanly and not according to the logic of God (Mark 8:33); now Jesus faces this dilemma and, although he chooses to follow the will of God and not his own will, he does so with intense anxiety (Mark 14:34).

In the second moment, when Jesus is handed over by one of his disciples, he has to appear before courts headed by the high priest and the Roman prefect. Also in this case, his situation is similar to that of the addressees of the Gospel (Mark 13:9: "they will hand you over to councils, and you will be beaten in synagogues, and you will stand before governors and kings"). Jesus' attitude at that moment is more passive. During the two interrogations, he is silent and does not answer the accusations against him (Mark 14:60; 15:4). Only before the high priest does Jesus acknowledge that he is the "Messiah Son of the Blessed." Jesus is not a Davidic messiah like those who provoked the Jewish War, but is one who renounces doing his own will in order to do his Father's.[60] Moreover, in this answer, Jesus recalls the announcement of the coming of the Son of Man with power and glory (Mark 13:26), thus connecting this announced event with his future resurrection[61]

---

not part of the Johannine passion narrative. Most of them contain traditional notices but only in Mark do they take place under the menace of the delivery. Probably Mark included them here to offer his readers a manner to face the threat. Regarding the Markan redaction of these passages, see Guijarro, *Jesús y sus primeros discípulos*, 174–76.

59. About the centrality of this scene in Mark's story of the passion see Feldmeier, *Krisis des Gottessohnes*.

60. Marcus, "Mark 14:61," has shown that "the Son of the Blessed" is a restrictive apposition that specifies the meaning of "the Messiah."

61. The farewell discourse mentions a vision of the "Son of Man coming with the clouds with power and glory" (Mark 13:26). The answer given to the high priest explains

Finally, when Pilate hands Jesus over to be flogged and crucified, he faces mockery, suffering, and death with a passive attitude. This was a situation that some of his followers were living or had lived through, because some of them had also been delivered to authorities to be killed (Mark 13:12). In these scenes, Jesus has to endure silently being condemned for being what he is not: the King of the Jews (Mark 15:26), the Messiah, King of Israel (Mark 15:32). It is impossible to explain to those who accuse him and those who condemn him that Jesus has nothing to do with the messianism that triggered the Jewish War and caused death and hatred in the country. Jesus accepts the unfair verdict of men, but at that decisive moment it is for him more difficult to accept the concealment of God. That is why he breaks the silence, and his voice resonates with force (Mark 15:34) to make God present in the drama of his abandonment. It is not easy to explain the significance of Jesus' cry, which repeats the opening words of Ps 22, probably because they enclose at the same time a reproach and an attitude of confidence.[62] This ambiguity dominates the scene of Jesus' death because it is not clear if the darkness is a sign of the presence of the divine, or if it conceals that presence (Mark 15:33); nor is it evident whether the fact of the tearing of the temple's curtain announces a disaster or a saving event (Mark 15:38).[63] The death of Jesus, as well as the death of his followers during and after the Jewish War, provokes an atmosphere of darkness and confusion, and makes Jesus and his followers ask themselves why God does not intervene. At this moment, the Gospel reaches its climax. The announced death of Jesus has finally taken place. His life trajectory has concluded in this failure. Those who read and listen to the Gospel of Mark might identify themselves with Jesus. But, how does this identification help them to face the experience they are going through?

The ambiguity of the details that surround the death of Jesus, including his own cry/prayer, opens the possibility for a nonfatalistic (nonapocalyptic) reading of the trauma of his death. This ambiguity had been resolved

---

that the Son of Man who comes is "sitting at the right of Power." These expressions allude to the divine enthronement of Jesus, as stated in Hurtado, "Early Christological Interpretation."

62. Regarding the different interpretations of this verse and how they are influenced by the situation of the reader, see Van Oyen and Van Cappellen, "Mark 15:34 and the Sitz im Leben."

63. Fritzen, *Von Gott verlassen?*, 323–59, links the scene with Jesus' prayer in Gethsemane, and adds the words of the centurion to the mentioned ambiguities, because it is not clear whether his words entail a confession of faith or another mockery.

somehow in the passion predictions because all of them ended with the announcement of his future resurrection (Mark 8:31: "and after three days he will rise"; see: 9:31; 10:34). At the beginning of the passion narrative, Jesus announces that his disciples will abandon him (Mark 14:27), and he informs them that after his resurrection he will precede them to Galilee (Mark 14:28). The narrative reveals an explicit interest in reminding the readers of this promise, whose fulfillment is repeated in the final scene of the Gospel by the divine messenger, who adds that the purpose of the promised encounter will be "seeing" Jesus (Mark 16:7: "there you will see him"). However, the narrative concludes in an enigmatic way, as fear prevents the women from spreading this message. In the narrative, these women are the only ones who know the good news. However, outside the narrative, readers also hear the message, and it is to them that the narrator is addressing it.[64] They should go to Galilee to see Jesus there and to start a new life inspired by the logic of God, a logic that constructively integrates the experience of suffering and death.[65]

Conclusion

In his study about the development of the Afro-American identity, Ron Eyerman explains how the trauma experienced by the slaves in the United States of America until the Civil War was elaborated by successive generations of Black intellectuals to finally become the main feature of their identity. The creation of a progressive narrative was crucial in this process. The narrative recognized slavery as an inheritance, a tradition worthy of being kept, a collective past that was fundamental to maintaining the group's identity, and a cultural resource that could be explored and taken advantage of.[66]

The Gospel of Mark reflects a similar process. In this case, the experience of the past, the passion and death of Jesus, had already been elaborated as a cultural trauma by his disciples. The Gospel of Mark (and the group of disciples behind it) assumed and rephrased this foundational experience

---

64. About the possible reactions of readers to this scene see Whitenton, "Feeling the Silence."

65. In the Gospel of Mark, this other possible life is the one that Jesus proposes to his disciples when he creates with them a new family that embodies an ascetic way of life; see Vaage, "Other Home."

66. Eyerman, "Cultural Trauma," 84–97; Eyerman, "The Past in the Present," 163–66.

of the past as an essential part of their identity. The experience that triggered this process was the dramatic situation provoked by the Jewish War in the Syro-Palestinian region. In this distressing situation, the followers of Jesus created a progressive narrative in which the original trauma was creatively elaborated to redefine their group identity. The Gospel of Mark is this progressive narrative. It defines itself as "the beginning of the good news" (Mark 1:1). The entire narrative is this new beginning, although it is at the end of the story that this newness is best perceived. This final part takes place in a section in which narrative place and time are much more precise than in the rest of the Gospel (Mark 11–16). These indications facilitate the merging of what happens in the narrative (Jesus' action) and the situation lived by the addressees (the aftermath of the Jewish War). By playing with these different temporal levels, the narrator invites readers to understand the situation they are living by means of a creative recovery of the memory of Jesus.

The story narrated in these final chapters of the Gospel has to do with the readers. The actions of Jesus in Jerusalem (Mark 11–12) are certainly something from the past. However, the way they are told makes readers remember what happened in the Jewish War, and shows that Jesus did not follow the logic of those who provoked the disaster. This way of telling the story makes the readers also distance themselves from the human logic of war, although this will not spare them its consequences. These consequences are remembered in Jesus' farewell discourse (Mark 13), in which he announces what his disciples will experience. Nevertheless, for the Gospel audience, this was not something that would happen in the future, but the disturbing situation they were undergoing. In that situation, they are invited to recall the memory of Jesus' passion (Mark 14–16), not only to discover the relationship that exists between their experience and that foundational event in the life of the group, but also to discover the possibility of a new beginning. The invitation to go to Galilee opens the possibility of meeting the risen Jesus and being part of a new beginning.

Mark's rhetoric is oriented to this new beginning (Mark 1:1), which is suggested in the open ending of the Gospel (Mark 16:7–8). However, his narrative does not include a well-defined proposal of what this new beginning should be like. The Gospel is only an initial answer based on the conviction that the logic governing the life of the Jesus followers must change. The human logic (that is, the logic that led to the disaster of the war) should be rejected. Instead, the disciples should follow the logic of God, (that is, the logic that led Jesus to behave as his obedient Son).

Conclusion
Why the Context Matters

THIS BOOK HAS TRIED to show that knowledge of the social context in which the Gospel of Mark was written is of paramount importance for understanding this narrative born in a distant time and culture. The necessity of knowing the context in order to understand the text has its origin in the social nature of language—that is, in the fact that words name the reality as perceived by a particular society. This understanding of the context as a *social context* is a significant advance over the traditional understanding of the life context (*Sitz im Leben*) as defined by form and redaction criticism. In the view of form and redaction critics, the life context was something external, a circumstance of the text that explained the composition and transmission of oral traditions or texts. For contextual analysis, instead, the social context is a reality embedded in the text since the text cannot be adequately understood without it.

This new vision of the context and its importance for proper understanding of texts makes contextual analysis a particularly useful instrument for exegesis. If the task of exegesis consists in explaining the original meaning of the text, then the exegetical task cannot be achieved by just describing the history of the text's formation, or by analyzing it at the literary level. These two tasks are essential, but they cannot fulfill the goal of exegesis if they are not complemented by a study of the context that helps to ascertain the meaning of these texts. An explanation of Mark's Gospel that does not take into account the society and culture in which this story arose can easily lead to an anachronistic or ethnocentric reading of it, because into such a reading, readers will inescapably introduce their own worldviews. Hence, in order to understand Mark's Gospel on its own terms we need models that help us to reconstruct its context. The real alternatives are not to use models or not to use models. The real alternatives are instead to use models unconsciously or to use models consciously—and using them consciously has the advantage that we can control them.

The studies gathered in this volume have tried to show, from different perspectives, how the kind of reading that recovers the contextual connotations of some passages from the Gospel of Mark may contribute to explaining this early Christian writing in its original context, bringing to light values, institutions, and roles that these texts presuppose. This contextual reading does not exclude but rather complements the historical-critical and literary analysis, helping us understand these texts in a more respectful and considerate way.

Recovering the context in which the texts were born allows them to be explained more respectfully. This approach recognizes the temporal and cultural distance that separates us from these works and makes us aware of our condition as foreigners to them. This methodological distance, which is a requirement of exegesis, is at the same time the starting point for a creative dialogue between readers and text. This dialogue belongs to hermeneutics, but it should be deep-rooted in a sound exegesis. Therefore, methodological detachment that favors contextual analysis is not an obstacle for a hermeneutical (Christian) reading of the Bible but rather a requirement for it.

The studies presented in Chapters 2–7 of this volume offer some examples of how contextual analysis proceeds. In each case, research has started by identifying a social aspect (a value, an institution, a relationship) presupposed in the text, which initially seems crucial to understanding a particular text segment in its original context. The second step in the research has been to reconstruct the social scenario of that particular aspect with the help of models elaborated in different fields of the social sciences. When the aspect identified as crucial is an *emic* one, I have used models elaborated by comparative studies of Mediterranean societies in the field of cultural anthropology. However, in the cases where the chosen aspect was an *etic* one, I have used models elaborated in the fields of sociology or social psychology. These models are, so to speak, the raw material of reading scenarios. Reading scenarios, in fact, are the result of refining such models by contrasting them with data from the particular social context of the text to be studied. Once the reading scenarios are elaborated, the third step in the research consists of reading the chosen text in this new framework. If the reading scenarios are appropriate, they will not only contribute to

CONCLUSION

explaining the texts but will also bring to light aspects that were known to their authors and readers but that are unknown to us. This explanatory and heuristic potential of reading scenarios makes them a valuable tool for the exegesis of ancient texts.

The advantages of reading Mark's narrative and other biblical texts within the adequate social scenarios are manifest. However, elaborating such reading scenarios is not an easy task because it requires some acquaintance with social models, both *emic* and *etic*, elaborated in different fields of the social sciences. It also demands from the interpreter the ability to choose suitable models and refine them to elaborate the appropriate reading scenarios. Nevertheless, in this task, competent scholars from these other fields of knowledge assist the exegete in understanding the biblical text more accurately and respectfully. With the introduction of contextual analysis, the exegetical task has become more interdisciplinary. This new approach makes exegesis a more complex task, but at the same time, it makes it a fascinating one.

Bibliography

Alexander, Jeffrey C. "Towards a Theory of Cultural Trauma." In *Cultural Trauma and Collective Identity*, edited by Jeffrey C. Alexander et al., 1–30. Berkeley: University of California Press 2004.
Anderson, Graham. *Sage, Saint, and Sophist: Holy Men and Their Associates in the Early Roman Empire*. London: Routledge, 1994.
Assmann, Jan. "Collective Memory and Cultural Identity." *New German Critique* 65 (1995) 125–33.
———. "Cultural Memory: Script, Recollection, and Political Identity in Early Civilizations." *Historiography East and West* 1 (2003) 154–77.
Avalos, Hector. *Health Care and the Rise of Christianity*. Peabody, MA: Hendrickson, 1999.
———. *Illness and Health Care in the Ancient Near East. The Role of the Temple in Greece, Mesopotamia and Israel*. HSM 54. Atlanta: Scholars, 1995.
Bailey, Kenneth. "Informal Controlled Oral Tradition and the Synoptic Gospels." *Asia Journal of Theology* 5 (1991) 34–54.
Balabanski, Vicky. "Mark 13: Eschatological Expectation and the Jewish War." In *Eschatology in the Making: Mark, Matthew, and the Didache*, 55–100. SNTSMS 97. Cambridge: Cambridge University Press, 1997.
Bar-Tal, Daniel. *Intractable Conflicts: Socio-Psychological Foundations and Dynamics*. Cambridge: Cambridge University Press, 2013.
Baumgarten, Albert I. "Finding Oneself in a Sectarian Context: A Sectarian's Food and Implications." In *Self, Soul and Body in Religious Experience*, edited by Albert I. Baumgarten et al., 125–47. Studies in the History of Religions 78. Leiden: Brill, 1998.
———. *The Flourishing of Jewish Sects in the Maccabean Era: An Interpretation*. JSJSup 55. Leiden: Brill 1997.
Bernhard, Andrew E. *Other Early Christian Gospels: A Critical Edition of the Surviving Greek Manuscripts*. T. & T. Clark Library of Biblical Studies. LNTS 315. London: T. & T. Clark, 2007.
Boismard, Marie-Émile. "Betzata ou Siloé?" *RB* 106 (1999) 206–18.
Bond, Helen K. *The First Biography of Jesus: Genre and Meaning in Mark's Gospel*. Grand Rapids: Eerdmans, 2020.
Borg, Marcus J. *Jesus, A New Vision: Spirit, Culture, and the Life of Discipleship*. San Francisco: Harper & Row, 1987.
Borgen, Peder. "Miracles of Healing in the New Testament: Some Observations." *ST* 35 (1981) 91–106.

BIBLIOGRAPHY

Boring, M. Eugene. "Mark 1:1–15 and the Beginning of the Gospel." *Semeia* 52 (1990) 43–81.

Bourdieu, Pierre. "The Sentiment of Honor in Kabile Society." In *Honour and Shame: The Values of Mediterranean Society*, edited by John G. Peristiany, 191–241. The Nature of Human Society Series. Chicago: University of Chicago Press, 1966.

Breytenbach, Ciliers. "MNHMONEYEIN. Das 'Sich-Erinnern' in der urchristlichen Überlieferung. Die Bethanienepisode (Mk 14:3–9 / Jn 12:1–8) als Beispiel." In *John and the Synoptics*, edited by Adelbert Denaux, 548–57. BETL 101. Leuven: Leuven University Press, 1992.

Broadhead, Edwin K. *Prophet, Son, Messiah: Narrative Form and Function in Mark 14–16*. JSNTSup 97. Sheffield: Sheffield Academic, 1994.

Brown, Raymond E. *The Death of the Messiah: From Gethsemane to the Grave; A Commentary on the Passion Narratives in the Four Gospels*. 2 vols. ABRL. New York: Doubleday, 1994.

Bultmann, Rudolf. *The History of the Synoptic Tradition*. Translated by John Marsh. Oxford: Blackwell, 1963.

Burridge, Richard A. "Gospel Genre, Christological Controversy and the Absence of Rabbinic Biography: Some Implications of the Biographical Hypothesis." In *Christology, Controversy, and Community: New Testament Essays in Honor of David R. Catchpole*, edited by David G. Horrell and Christopher M. Tuckett, 137–56. NovTSup 99. Leiden: Brill, 2000.

———. *What Are the Gospels? A Comparison with Graeco-Roman Biography*. SNTSMS 70. Cambridge: Cambridge University Press, 1992.

Campbell, William S. "'Why Do You Abandon me?' Abandonment Christology in Mark's Gospel." In *The Trial and Death of Jesus: Essays on the Passion Narrative in Mark*, edited by Geert van Oyen and Tom Shepherd, 99–117. Contributions to Biblical Exegesis and Theology 45. Leuven: Peeters, 2006.

Capes, David B. "*Imitatio Christi* and the Gospel Genre." *BBR* 13 (2003) 1–19.

Cardeña, Etzel, and Michael J. Winkelman, eds. *Altering Consciousness: Multidisciplinary Perspectives*. Santa Barbara: Praeger, 2011.

Chancey, Mark A. *Greco-Roman Culture and the Galilee of Jesus*. SNTSMS 134. Cambridge: Cambridge University Press, 2005.

Chronis, Harry L. "To Reveal and to Conceal: A Literary- Critical Perspective on 'the Son of Man' in Mark." *NTS* 51 (2005) 459–81.

Clements, Ronald E. "Patterns in the Prophetic Canon: Healing the Blind and the Lame." In *Canon, Theology, and Old Testament Interpretation: Essays in Honor of Brevard S. Childs*, edited by Gene M. Tucker et al., 189–200. Philadelphia: Fortress, 1988.

Coakley, J. F. "The Anointing at Bethany and the Priority of John." *JBL* 107 (1988) 241–56.

Collins, Adela Yarbro. "The Apocalyptic Rhetoric of Mark 13 in Historical Context." *BR* 41 (1996) 5–36.

———. *The Beginning of the Gospel: Probings of Mark in Context*. Minneapolis: Fortress, 1992.

Collins, John J. *The Scepter and the Star: The Messiahs of the Dead Sea Scrolls and Other Ancient Literature*. New York: Doubleday, 1995.

Connerton, Paul. *How Societies Remember*. Themes in the Social Sciences. Cambridge: Cambridge University Press, 1989.

Craffert, Pieter F. "Jesus and the Shamanic Complex: First Steps in Utilizing a Social Type Model." *Neot* 33 (1999) 321–42.

Bibliography

———. *The Life of a Galilean Shaman: Jesus of Nazareth in Anthropological-Historical Perspective*. Matrix 3. Eugene, OR: Cascade Books, 2008.

———. "Re-Visioning Jesus' Resurrection: The Resurrection Stories in a Neuro-Anthropological Perspective." In *The Gospels and Their Stories in Anthropological Perspective*, edited by Joseph Verheyden and John S. Kloppenborg, 253–82. WUNT 409. Tübingen: Mohr/Siebeck, 2018.

Cribiore, Raffaella. *Gymnastics of the Mind: Greek Education in Hellenistic and Roman Egypt*. Princeton: Princeton University Press, 2001.

Crossan, John D. *The Cross that Spoke: The Origins of the Passion Narrative*. 1988. Reprint, Eugene, OR: Wipf & Stock, 2008.

Croy, N. Clayton. "Where the Gospel Text Begins: A Non-Theological Interpretation of Mark 1:1." *NovT* 43 (2001) 105–27.

DeMaris, Richard E. "Possession Good and Bad—Ritual, Effects and Side-Effects: The Baptism of Jesus and Mark 1.9–11 from a Cross-Cultural Perspective." *JSNT* 80 (2000) 3–30.

Derrett, J. Duncan M. "The Evil Eye in the New Testament." In *Modelling Early Christianity: Social-Scientific Studies of the New Testament in Its Context*, edited by Philip F. Esler. 65–72. London: Routledge, 1995.

Destro, Adriana, and Mauro Pesce. "Continuity or Discontinuity between Jesus and Groups of His Followers? Practices of Contact with the Supernatural." In *Los comienzos del cristianismo*, edited by Santiago Guijarro, 53–70. Biblioteca Salmanticensis. Estudios 284. Salamanca: Publicaciones de la Universidad Pontificia, 2006.

Devillers, Luc. "Une Piscine peut en cacher une autre: à propos de Jean 5,1–9a." *RB* 106 (1999) 175–205.

Dewey, Joanna. "The Literary Structure of the Controversy Stories in Mark 2:1–3:6." *JBL* 92 (1973) 394-401.

———. "The Survival of Mark's Gospel: A Good Story?" *JBL* 123 (2004) 495–507.

Dibelius, Martin. *From Tradition to Gospel*. Translated by Bertram L. Woolf. Library of Theological Translations. Cambridge: Clarke, 1971.

Dodds, Eric Robertson. *The Greeks and the Irrational*. Sathor Classical Lectures 25. Berkeley: University of California Press, 1951.

Dormeyer, Detlev. "Mk 1,1–15 als Prolog des ersten Idealbiographischen Evangeliums von Jesus Christus." *Bib Int* 5 (1997) 181–211.

———. *Die Passion Jesu als Verhaltensmodell*. NTAbh, n.f. 11. Münster: Aschendorf, 1974.

Douven, Igor. "Abduction." In *The Stanford Encyclopedia of Philosophy* (website), edited by Edward N. Zalta, https://plato.stanford.edu/archives/sum2021/entries/abduction/.

Downing, F. Gerald. "A Genre for Q and a Socio-Cultural Context for Q: Comparing Sets of Similarities with Sets of Differences." *JSNT* 55 (1994) 3–26.

Dube, Zorodzai. "Jesus' Death and Resurrection as Cultural Trauma." *Neot* 47 (2013) 107–22.

Duprez, Antoine. *Jésus et les dieux guerisseurs*. Cahiers de la Revue biblique 12. Paris: Gabalda, 1970.

Dvorjetski, Estée. "Medical Hot Springs in Eretz Israel and in the Decapolis during the Hellenistic, Roman and Byzantine Periods." *ARAM Periodical* 4 (1992) 425–49.

Edwards, James R. "Markan Sandwiches: The Significance of Interpolations in Markan Narratives." *NovT* 31 (1989) 193–216.

Elliott, James K. "The Anointing of Jesus." *ExpTim* 85 (1974) 105–7.

Bibliography

Elliott, John H. "The Fear of the Leer: The Evil Eye from the Bible to Li'l Abner." *Forum* 4/4 (1998) 42–71.
———. *What Is Social-Scientific Criticism?* GBS. Minneapolis: Fortress, 1993.
Elliott-Binns, Leonard E. *Galilean Christianity*. SBT 1/16. Naperville: Allenson, 1956.
Epstein, Isidore, ed. *The Babylonian Talmud*. Vol. 3, *Seder Kodashim*. 6 vols. London: Soncino, 1948.
Esler, Philip F. *Conflict and Identity in Romans: The Social Setting of Paul's Letter*. Minneapolis: Fortress, 2003.
Eyerman, Ron. "Cultural Trauma: Slavery and the Formation of African American Identity." In *Cultural Trauma and Collective Identity*, edited by Jeffrey C. Alexander et al., 60–111. Berkeley: California University Press, 2004.
———. "The Past in the Present: Culture and the Transmission of Memory." *Acta Sociologica* 47 (2004) 159–69.
Eyerman, Ron, et al., eds. *Narrating Trauma: On the Impact of Collective Suffering*. London: Routledge, 2015.
Fander, Monika. "Frauen in der Nachfolge Jesu: Die Rolle der Frau im Markusevangelium." *EvT* 52 (1992) 413–32.
———. "'Mein Gott, mein Gott, warum hast Du mich verlassen?' (Mk 15,34): (Kriegs-) Traumatisierung als Thema des Markusevangeliums." In *Christologie im Lebensbezug*, edited by Elisabeth Moltmann-Wendel and Renate Kirchhoff, 116–56. Göttingen: Vandenhoeck & Ruprecht, 2005.
———. *Die Stellung der Frau im Markusevangelium: unter besonderer Berücksichtigung kultur- und religionsgeschichtlicher Hintergründe*. 2nd ed. Münsteraner theologische Abhandlungen 8. Altemberge: Telos, 1990.
Feldmeier, Reinhard. *Die Krisis des Gottessohnes: Die Gethsemaneerzählung als Schlüssel der Markuspassion*. WUNT 2/21. Tübingen: Mohr/Siebeck, 1987.
Fentress, James, and Chris Wickham. *Social Memory. New Perspectives on the Past*. Oxford: Blackwell, 1992.
Focant, Camille. *L'évangile selon Marc*. Commentaire biblique. Nouveau Testament 2. Paris: Cerf, 2004.
———. *The Gospel according to Mark: A Commentary*. Translated by Leslie Robert Keylock. Eugene, OR: Pickwick Publications, 2012.
Fowler, Robert M. *Let the Reader Understand: Reader-Response Criticism and the Gospel of Mark*. 1991. Reprint, Harrisburg, PA: Trinity, 1996.
Freyne, Seán. "The Geography of Restoration: Galilee-Jerusalem Relations in Early Jewish and Christian Experience." *NTS* 47 (2001) 289–311.
Frickenschmidt, Dirk. *Evangelium als Biographie: Die vier Evangelien im Rahmen antiker Erzählkunst*. Texte und Arbeiten zum neutestamentlichen Zeitalter 22. Tübingen: Francke, 1997.
Fritzen, Wolfgang. *Von Gott verlassen? Das Markusevangelium als Kommunikationsangebot für bedrängte Christen*. Stuttgart: Kohlhammer, 2008.
Funk, Robert W. "The Watershed of the American Biblical Tradition: The Chicago School, First Phase, 1892–1920." *JBL* 95 (1976) 4–22.
Garber, David G. "Trauma Theory and Biblical Studies." *CurrBR* 14 (2015) 24–44.
Gelardini, Gabriella. *Christus Militans: Studien zur politisch-militärischen Semantik im Markusevangelium vor dem Hintergrund des ersten jüdich-römischen Krieges*. NovTSup 165. Leiden: Brill, 2016.

Bibliography

Gilmore, David D. "Anthropology of the Mediterranean Area." *Annual Review of Anthropology* 11 (1982) 175–205.

Gilmore, David, ed. *Honor and Shame and the Unity of the Mediterranean. A Special Publication of the American Anthropological Association 22.* Washington, DC: American Anthropological Association, 1987.

Gnilka, Joachim. *Das Evangelium nach Markus.* Vol. 1. EKKNT. Zurich: Benzinger, 1978.

———. *Das Evangelium nach Markus.* Vol. 2. EKKNT. Zurich: Neukirchener. 1979.

González Echegaray, Joaquín. *Arqueología y evangelios.* Estella, Spain: Verbo Divino, 1994.

Good, Byron J., and Mary Jo Delvecchio-Good. "The Meaning of Symptoms: A Cultural Hermeneutic Model for Clinical Practice." In *The Relevance of Social Science for Medicine,* edited by Leon Eisenberg and Arthur Kleinman, 165–96. Culture, Illness, and Healing 1. Dordrecht: Reidel, 1980.

Goodman, Martin. "Diaspora Reactions to the Destruction of the Temple." In *Jews and Christians: The Parting of the Ways AD 70 to 135,* edited by James D. G. Dunn, 27–38. WUNT 6. Tübingen: Mohr/Siebeck, 1992.

———. *The Ruling Class of Judaea: The Origins of the Jewish Revolt against Rome A.D. 66–70.* Cambridge: Cambridge University Press, 1987.

Graham, Susan L. "Silent Voices: Women in the Gospel of Mark." *Semeia* 54 (1991) 145–58.

Grant-Davie, Keith. "Rhetorical Situations and their Constituents." *Rhetoric Review* 15 (1997) 264–79.

Grassi, Joseph A. "The Secret Heroine of Mark's Drama." *BTB* 18 (1988) 10–15.

Green, Joel B. "The Gospel of Peter: Source for a Pre-Canonical Passion Narrative?" *ZNW* 78 (1987) 293–301.

Green, William S. "Palestinian Holy Men: Charismatic Leadership and Rabbinic Tradition." *ANRW* II.19.2 (1979) 619–47

Guijarro, Santiago. *El camino del discípulo: Seguir a Jesús según el Evangelio de Marcos.* Colección Nueva alianza 230. Salamanca: Sígueme, 2015.

———. "La composición del evangelio de Marcos." *Salmanticensis* 53 (2006) 5–33.

———. "Cultural Trauma, Collective Memory, and Social Identity: The Gospel of Mark as 'Progressive Narrative.'" In *Reading the Gospel of Mark in the Twenty-First Century: Method and Meaning,* edited by Geert Van Oyen, 141–69. Leuven: Peeters, 2019.

———. *Fidelidades en conflicto: La ruptura con la familia por causa del discipulado y de la misión en la tradición sinóptica.* Penitudo temporis 4. Salamanca: Publicaciones Universidad de la Pontificia de Salamanca, 1998.

———. "The First Disciples of Jesus in Galilee." *HvTSt* 63 (2007) 885–908.

———. *Jesús y sus primeros discípulos.* Asociación Bíblica Española 46. Estella, Spain: Verbo Divino, 2007.

———. "Healing Stories and Medical Anthropology: A Reading of Mark 10:46–52." *BTB* 30 (2000) 102–12.

———. "The Politics of Exorcism: Jesus' Reaction to Negative Labels in the Beelzebul Controversy." *BTB* 29 (1999) 118–29.

———. "La primera generación en Judea y Galilea." In *Así empezó el Cristianismo,* edited by Rafael Aguirre, 101–38. Agora 28. Estella, Spain: Verbo Divino, 2010.

———. "The Visions of Jesus and His Disciples." In *The Gospels and Their Stories in Anthropological Perspective,* edited by Joseph Verheyden and John Kloppenborg, 217–31. WUNT 409. Tübingen: Mohr/Siebeck, 2018.

———. "Why Does the Gospel of Mark Begin as It Does?" *BTB* 33 (2003) 28–38.

Guijarro, Santiago, and Ana Rodríguez Láiz. "The 'Messianic' Anointing of Jesus (Mark 14:3–9)." *BTB* 41 (2011) 132–43.
Halbwachs, Maurice. *The Collective Memory*. Translated by Francis J. Ditter, Jr., and Vida Yazdi Ditter. New York: Harper & Row, 1980.
———. *La mémoire collective*. Bibliothèque de sociologie contemporaine. Paris: Presses Universitaires de France, 1968.
Hatina, Thomas R. "The Focus of Mark 13:24–27: The Parousia or the Destruction of the Temple?" *BBR* 6 (1996) 43–66.
Head, Peter M. "A Text-Critical Study of Mark 1:1: 'The Beginning of the Gospel of Jesus Christ.'" *NTS* 37 (1991) 621–29.
Hearon, Holly. "The Story of the Woman Who Anointed Jesus as Social Memory: A Methodological Proposal for the Study of Tradition as Memory." In *Memory, Tradition and Text: Uses of the Past in Early Christianity*, edited by Alan Kirk and Tom Thatcher, 99–118. SemeiaSt 52. Atlanta: SBL, 2005.
Heemstra, Marius. *The Fiscus Iudaicus and the Parting of the Ways*. WUNT 2/277. Tübingen: Mohr/Siebeck, 2010.
Hengel, Martin. *Studies in the Gospel of Mark*. Translated by John Bowden. Philadelphia: Fortress, 1985.
Hogan, Larry P. *Healing in the Second Temple Period*. NTOA 21. Göttingen: Vandenhoek & Ruprecht, 1992.
Holst, Robert. "The One Anointing of Jesus: Another Application of the Form-Critical Method." *JBL* 95 (1976) 435–46.
Horbury, William. "Messianism in the Old Testament Apocrypha and Pseudepigrapha." In *King and Messiah in Israel and the Ancient Near East: Proceedings of the Oxford Old Testament Seminar*, edited by John Day, 402–33. JSOTSup 270. Sheffield: Sheffield Academic, 1998.
Hurtado, Larry W. "Early Christological Interpretation of the Messianic Psalms." *Salmanticensis* 64 (2017) 73–101.
———. "The Gospel of Mark: Evolutionary or Revolutionary Document?" *JSNT* 40 (1990) 15–32.
Iersel, Bas van. "Failed Followers in Mark: Mark 13:12 as a Key for the Identification of the Intended Readers." *CBQ* 58 (1996) 244–63.
———. *Mark: A Reader-Response Commentary*. Translated by W. H. Bisscheroux. JSNTSup 164. Sheffield: Sheffield Academic, 1998.
Ilan, Tal. "'Man Born of Woman . . .' (Job 14:1): The Phenomenon of Men Bearing Metronymes at the Time of Jesus." *NovT* 34 (1992) 23–45.
Incigneri, Brian J. *The Gospel to the Romans: The Setting and Rhetoric of Mark's Gospel*. Bib Int 65. Leiden: Brill, 2003.
Jacobson, Arland D. *The First Gospel: An Introduction to Q*. 1992. Reprint, Eugene, OR: Wipf & Stock, 2005.
Jenni, Ernst, and D. Vetter. "'Áyin, Ojo." In *DTMAT*, 2:336–46.
Jeremias, Joachim. "Die Salbungsgeschichte: Mk 14:3–9." *ZNW* 35 (1936) 75–82.
Jones, Kenneth R. *Jewish Reactions to the Destruction of Jerusalem in A.D. 70: Apocalypses and Related Pseudepigrapha*. JSJSup 151. Leiden: Brill, 2011.
Josephus, Flavius. *The Jewish War*. Translated by Henry St. John Thackeray. 2 vols. Josephus in 9 [10] vols., 2–3. LCL 203, 210. Cambridge: Harvard University Press, 1976–1979.
Kähler Martin. *Der sogenannte historische Jesus und der geschichtliche, biblische Christus*. Newly edited by E. Wolf. TB. Systematische Theologie 2. Munich: Kaiser, 1953.

Bibliography

Kee, Howard Clark. *Medicine, Miracle and Magic in New Testament Times.* SNTSMS 55. Cambridge: Cambridge University Press, 1986.

Keith, Chris. *The Gospel as Manuscript: An Early History of the Jesus Tradition as Material Artifact.* Oxford: Oxford University Press, 2020.

Kelber, Werner H. "Conclusion: From Passion Narrative to Gospel." In *The Passion in Mark: Studies on Mark 14–16*, edited by Werner H. Kelber, 153–80. Philadelphia: Fortress, 1976.

———,ed. *The Passion in Mark: Studies on Mark 14–16.* Philadelphia: Fortress, 1976.

Kennedy, George A., ed. *Progymnasmata: Greek Textbooks of Prose Composition and Rhetoric.* WGRW 10. Atlanta: SBL, 2003.

Kertelge, Karl. *Die Wunder Jesu im Markusevangelium.* SANT 33. Munich: Kösel, 1970.

Kirk, Alan. "Social and Cultural Memory." In *Memory, Tradition and Text: Uses of the Past in Early Christianity*, edited by Alan Kirk and Tom Thatcher, 1–23. SemeiaSt 52. Atlanta: SBL, 2005.

Kirk, Alan, and Tom Thatcher. "Jesus Tradition as Social Memory." In *Memory, Tradition and Text: Uses of the Past in Early Christianity*, edited by Alan Kirk and Tom Thatcher, 25–42. SemeiaSt 52. Atlanta: SBL, 2005.

Klauck, Hans-Josef. *Vorspiel im Himmel? Erzähltechnik und Theologie im Markusprolog.* Biblisch-theologische Studien 32. Neukirchen: Neukirchener, 1997.

Kleinman, Arthur. *Patients and Healers in the Context of Culture: An Exploration of the Borderland Between Anthropology, Medicine and Psychiatry.* Comparative Studies of Health Systems and Medical Care 3. Berkeley: University of California Press, 1980.

Kloppenborg Verbin, John S. *Excavating Q: the History and Setting of the Sayings Gospel.* Minneapolis: Fortress, 2000.

Kloppenborg, John S. "*Evocatio Deorum* and the Date of Mark." *JBL* 124 (2005) 419–50.

Kuhn, Heinz-Wolfgang. *Ältere Sammlungen im Markusevangelium.* SUNT 8. Göttingen: Vandenhoeck & Ruprecht, 1971.

Kutsch, Ernst. *Salbung als Rechtsakt im Alten Testament und im altem Orient.* BZAW 87. Berlin: Töpelmann, 1963.

Latourelle, René. *Milagros de Jesús y teología del milagro.* Verdad e imagen 112. Salamanca: Sígueme, 1990.

Le Donne, Anthony. "Theological Memory Distortion in the Jesus Tradition. A Study in Social Memory Theory." In *Memory in the Bible and Antiquity: The Fifth Durham-Tübingen Research Symposium (Durham, September 2004)*, edited by Loren T. Stuckenbruck et al., 164–77. WUNT 212. Tübingen: Mohr/Siebeck, 2007.

Legault, André. "An Application of the Form-Critique Method to the Anointings in Galilee and Bethany." *CBQ* 16 (1954) 131–45.

Lenski, Gerhard E. *Power and Privilege A Theory of Social Stratification.* McGraw-Hill Series in Sociology. New York: McGraw Hill, 1966.

Leon-Dufour, Xavier, ed. *Los milagros de Jesús segun el Nuevo Testamento.* Translated by Alfonso de la Fuente Adánez. Colección biblica y lenguaje 5. Madrid: Cristiandad, 1979.

Lieb, Michael. *The Visionary Mode: Biblical Prophecy, Hermeneutics, and Cultural Change.* Ithaca: Cornell University Press, 1991.

Lightfoot, R. H. *The Gospel Message of Saint Mark.* Oxford: Clarendon, 1950.

Linnemann, Eta. *Studien zur Passionsgeschichte.* FRLANT 102. Göttingen: Vandenhoeck & Ruprecht, 1970.

Bibliography

Lloyd, G. E. R. *Being, Humanity, and Understanding: Studies in Ancient and Modern Societies.* Oxford: Oxford University Press, 2012.

Lohmeyer, Ernst. *Galiläa und Jerusalem.* FRLANT 52. Gottingen: Vandenhoeck & Ruprecht, 1936.

Lücking, Stefan. *Mimesis der Verachteten: Eine Studie zur Erzählweise von Mk 14,1–11.* SBS 152. Stuttgart: Katholisches Bibelwerk, 1993.

———. "Die Zerstörung des Tempels 70 n. Chr. als Krisenerfahrung der frühen Christen." In *Zerstörungen des Jerusalemer Tempels: Geschehen—Wahrnehmung—Bewältigung*, edited by Johannes Hahn, 140–65. WUNT 147. Tübingen: Mohr/Siebeck, 2002.

Lüdemann, Gerd. *Die Auferstehung Jesu: Historie, Erfahrung, Theologie.* Göttingen: Vandenhoeck & Ruprecht, 1994.

———. *The Resurrection of Jesus: History, Experience, Theology.* Translated by John Bowden. Minneapolis: Fortress, 1994.

Mack, Burton L. "The Anointing of Jesus: Elaboration within a Chreia." In *Patterns of Persuasion in the Gospels*, edited by Burton L. Mack and Vernon K. Robbins, 85–106. Foundations & Facets. 1989. Reprint, Eugene, OR: Wipf & Stock, 2008.

Macknik, Stephen L., et al. *Sleights of Mind: What the Neuroscience of Magic Reveals about Our Brains.* London: Profile, 2011.

Malbon, Elizabeth Struthers. "Ending at the Beginning: A Response." *Semeia* 52 (1990) 175–84.

———. "Fallible Followers: Women and Men in the Gospel of Mark." *Semeia* 28 (1983) 29–48.

———. *In the Company of Jesus: Characters in Mark's Gospel.* Louisville: Westminster John Knox, 2000.

———. *Narrative Space and Mythic Meaning in Mark.* BibSem 13. Sheffield: Sheffield Academic, 1991.

Malina, Bruce J. *The New Testament World: Insights from Cultural Anthropology.* Rev. ed. Louisville: John Knox, 1993.

———. *The New Testament World: Insights from Cultural Anthropology.* 3rd ed. Louisville: John Knox, 2001.

———. "Reading Theory Perspective: Reading Luke-Acts." In *The Social World of Luke-Acts: Models for Interpretation*, edited by Jerome H. Neyrey, 3–23. Peabody, MA: Hendrickson, 1991.

Malina, Bruce J., and Jerome H. Neyrey. "First-Century Personality: Dyadic not Individual." In *The Social World of Luke-Acts: Models for Interpretation*, edited by Jerome H. Neyrey, 67–96. Peabody, MA: Hendrickson, 1991.

———. "Honor and Shame: Pivotal Values of the Mediterranean World." In *The Social World of Luke-Acts: Models for Interpretation*, edited by Jerome H. Neyrey, 25–65. Peabody, MA: Hendrickson, 1991.

———. *Portraits of Paul: An Archaeology of Ancient Personality.* Louisville: Westminster John Knox, 1996.

Malina, Bruce J., and Richard L. Rohrbaugh. *Social-Science Commentary on the Gospel of John.* Fortress: Minneapolis, 1998.

———. *Social-Science Commentary on the Synoptic Gospels.* Minneapolis: Fortress, 1992.

———. *Social-Science Commentary on the Synoptic Gospels.* 2nd ed. Minneapolis: Fortress, 2003.

Malzoni, Cláudio V. "Da cabeça aos pés. A unção de Jesus em Betânia, em Mc 14:3–9 e nos textos afins na tradição evanglica." *Perspectiva Teológica* 30 (1988) 95–106.

Bibliography

Marcus, Joel. "The Jewish War and the *Sitz im Leben* of Mark." *JBL* 111 (1992) 441–62.

———. *Mark 1-8: A New Translation with Introduction and Commentary.* AB 27. New York: Doubleday, 2000.

———. *Mark 8-16: A New Translation with Introduction and Commentary.* AYB 27A. New Haven: Yale University Press, 2009.

———. "Mark 14:61: 'Are You the Messiah-Son-of-God?'" *NovT* 31 (1989) 125–41.

———. *The Way of the Lord: Christological Exegesis of the Old Testament in the Gospel of Mark.* Louisville: Westminster John Knox, 1992.

Marxsen, Willi. *Mark the Evangelist: Studies on the Redaction History of the Gospel.* Translated by James Boyce et al. Nashville: Abingdon, 1969.

Maunder, Chris J. "A *Sitz im Leben* for Mark 14:9." *ExpTim* 99 (1987) 78–80.

McKnight, Edgar V. *What Is Form Criticism?* GBS. Philadelphia: Fortress, 1969.

McVann, Mark. "Reading Mark Ritually: Honor-Shame and the Ritual of Baptism." *Semeia* 67 (1994) 179–98.

———. "Rituals of Status Transformation in Luke-Acts. The Case of Jesus the Prophet." In *The Social World of Luke-Acts: Models for Interpretation*, edited by Jerome H. Neyrey, 333–60. Peabody, MA: Hendrickson, 1991.

Meier, John P. *A Marginal Jew: Rethinking the Historical Jesus.* Vol. 1, *The Roots of the Problem and the Person.* 4 vols. ABRL. New York: Doubleday, 1991.

———. *A Marginal Jew: Rethinking the Historical Jesus.* Vol. 2, *Mentor, Message and Miracles.* 4 vols. ABRL. New York: Doubleday, 1994.

Mell, Ulrich. "Jesu Taufe durch Johannes (Markus 1,9–15). Zur narrativen Christologie vom neuen Adam." *BZ* 40 (1996) 161–78.

Mendels, Doron. *Memory in Jewish, Pagan, and Christian Societies of the Graeco-Roman World.* LSTS 45. London: T. & T. Clark, 2004.

———. "Societies of Memory in the Graeco-Roman World." In *Memory in the Bible and Antiquity: The Fifth Durham-Tübingen Research Symposium (Durham, September 2004)*, edited by Loren T. Stuckenbruck et al., 143–67. WUNT 212. Tübingen: Mohr/Siebeck, 2007.

Merkur, Daniel. "Cultivating Visions through Exegetical Meditations." In *With Letters of Light: Studies in the Dead Sea Scrolls, Early Jewish Apocalypticism, Magic, and Mysticism in Honor of Rachel Elior*, edited by Daphna V. Arbel and Andrei A. Orlov, 62–91. Ekstasis 2. Berlin: de Gruyter, 2011.

Michaelis, Wilhelm. "ὁράω κτλ." In *TDNT* 5 (1967) 315–82.

Miller, Susan. *Women in Mark's Gospel.* JSNTSup 259. London: T. & T. Clark, 2004.

Miquel Pericás, Esther. *Amigos de esclavos, prostitutas y pecadores: El significado sociocultural del marginado moral en las éticas de Jesús y de los filósofos cínicos, epicúreos y estoicos.* Asociación Bíblica Española 47. Estella, Spain: Verbo Divino, 2007.

———. "The Impatient Jesus and the Fig Tree: Markan Disguised Discourse against the Temple." *BTB* 45 (2015) 144–54.

———. *Jesús y los espíritus: Aproximación antropológica a la práctica exorcista de Jesús.* Biblioteca de estudios bíblicos. Minor 13. Salamanca: Sígueme, 2009.

———. "Del movimiento de Jesús al grupo de Q. Un estudio sobre la localización social de la moral." In *Los comienzos del Cristianismo*, edited by Santiago Guijarro, 93–115. Biblioteca Salmanticensis. Estudios 284. Salamanca: Publicaciones de la Universidad Pontificia, 2006.

Bibliography

Müller, Ulrich B. *Die Entstehung des Glaubens an die Auferstehung Jesu: Historische Aspekte und Bedingungen.* SBS 172. Stuttgart: Katholisches Bibelwerk, 1998.

Naluparayil, Jacob C. *The Identity of Jesus in Mark: An Essay on Narrative Christology.* SBFA 49. Jerusalem: Franciscan, 2000.

Navarro, Mercedes. *Ungido para la vida: Exégesis narrativa de Mc 14:3–9 y Jn 12: 1–8.* Asociación Bíblica Española 36. Estella, Spain: Verbo Divino, 1999.

Neirynck, Frans. "The Redactional Text of Mark." *ETL* 57 (1981) 144–62.

Nepos, Cornelius. *Life of Epaminondas.* In *The Book on the Great Generals of Foreign Nations*, 164–83. Translated by J. C. Rolfe. LCL. Cambridge: Harvard University Press, 1929.

Neufeld, Dietmar. "Eating, Ecstasy, and Exorcism (Mark 3:21)." *BTB* 26 (1996) 152–62.

Neyrey, Jerome H. "Ceremonies in Luke-Acts: The Case of Meals and Table-Fellowship." In *The Social World of Luke-Acts. Models for Interpretation*, edited by Jerome H. Neyrey, 361–87. Peabody, MA: Hendrickson, 1991.

———. "Clean/Unclean, Pure/Polluted and Holy/Profane: The Idea and the System of Purity." In *The Social Sciences and New Testament Interpretation*, edited by Richard L. Rohrbaugh, 80–104. Peabody, MA: Hendrickson, 1996.

———. *An Encomium for Jesus: Luke, Rhetoric, and the Story of Jesus.* New Testament Monographs 40. Sheffield: Sheffield Phoenix 2020.

———. *Honor and Shame in the Gospel of Matthew.* Louisville: Westminster, 1998.

———, ed. *The Social World of Luke-Acts: Models for Interpretation*, Peabody, MA: Hendrickson, 1991.

Neyrey, Jerome H., and Eric S. Stewart, eds. *The Social World of the New Testament: Insights and Models.* Peabody, MA: Hendrickson, 2008.

Noorda, Sijbolt J. "Illness and Sin, Forgiving and Healing. The Connection of Medical Treatment and Religious Beliefs in Ben Sira 38:1–15." In *Studies in Hellenistic Religions*, edited by Maarten J. Vermaseren, 215–24. EPRO 78. Leiden: Brill, 1979.

Novenson, Matthew V. *The Grammar of Messianism: An Ancient Jewish Political Idiom and Its Users.* Oxford: Oxford University Press. 2017.

Öhler, Markus. *Elia im Neuen Testament: Untersuchungen zur Bedeutung des alttestamentlichen Propheten im frühen Christentum.* BZNW 88. Berlin: de Gruyter, 1997.

Olick, Jeffrey K., and Joyce Robbins. "Social Memory Studies: From 'Collective Memory' to the Historical Sociology of Mnemonic Practices." *Annual Review of Sociology* 24 (1998) 105–40.

Orlov, Andrei. *The Glory of the Invisible God: Two Powers in Heaven Traditions and Early Christology.* Jewish and Christian Texts in Context and Related Studies. London: T. & T. Clark, 2019.

Oyen, Geert Van, and Patty Van Cappellen. "Mark 15:34 and the *Sitz im Leben* of the Real Reader." *ETL* 91 (2015) 569–99.

Peppard, Michael. *The Son of God in the Roman World: Divine Sonship in Its Social and Political Context.* Oxford: Oxford University Press, 2011.

Peristiany, John G., ed. *Honour and Shame: The Values of Mediterranean Society.* Chicago: University of Chicago Press, 1966.

Perrin, Norman. "The High Priest's Question and Jesus' Answer (Mark 14,61–62)." In *The Passion in Mark: Studies on Mark 14–16*, edited by Werner H. Kelber, 80–95. Philadelphia: Fortress, 1976.

———. *What Is Redaction Criticism?* GBS. Philadelphia: Fortress. 1969.

Bibliography

Pierre, Marie-Joseph, and Jourdain-Marie Rousée. "Sainte Marie de la Probatique." *Proche Oriente Chretienne* 31 (1981) 23–42.

Pilch, John J. "Altered States of Consciousness in the Synoptics." In *The Social Setting of Jesus and the Gospels*, edited by Wolfgang Stegemann et al., 103–15. Minneapolis: Fortress, 2002.

———. *Flights of the Soul: Visions, Heavenly Journeys, and Peak Experiences in the Biblical World*. Grand Rapids: Eerdmans, 2011.

———. *Healing in the New Testament: Insights from Medical and Mediterranean Anthropology*. Minneapolis: Fortress, 2000.

———. "Sickness and Healing in Luke-Acts." In *The Social World of Luke-Acts. Models for Interpretation*, edited by Jerome H. Neyrey, 181–209. Peabody, MA: Hendrickson, 1991.

Poole, Ross. "Memory, History and the Claims of the Past." *Memory Studies* 1 (2008) 149–66.

Pseudo-Cicero. *Rhetorica ad Herennium*. Translated by Harry Caplan. LCL 403. Cambridge: Harvard University Press, 1954.

Reed, Jonathan L. *Archaeology and the Galilean Jesus: A Re-Examination of the Evidence*. Valley Forge, PA: Trinity, 2000.

Rhoads, David M., and Donald Michie. *Mark as Story: An Introduction to the Narrative of a Gospel*. Philadelphia: Fortress, 1982.

Rhoads, David M., et al. *Mark as Story: An Introduction to the Narrative of a Gospel*. 2nd ed. Minneapolis: Fortress, 1999.

———. *Mark as Story: An Introduction to the Narrative of a Gospel*. 3rd ed. Minneapolis: Fortress, 2012.

Robbins, Vernon K. "Social-Scientific Criticism and Literary Studies: Prospects for Cooperation in Biblical Interpretation." In *Modelling Early Christianity. Social-Scientific Studies of the New Testament in Its Context*, edited by Philip F. Esler, 274–89. London: Routledge, 1995.

Robinson, James M. et al., eds. *The Critical Edition of Q: Synopsis Including the Gospels of Matthew and Luke, Mark and Thomas with English, German, and French Translation of Q and Thomas*. Hermeneia—A Critical and Historical Commentary on the Bible. Supplements.. Minneapolis: Fortress. 2000.

Rodríguez Láiz, Ana. *El Mesías hijo de David: El mesianismo dinástico en los comienzos del cristianismo*. Asociación Bíblica Española 65. Estella, Spain: Verbo Divino, 2016.

Roh, Taeseong. *Die familia Dei in den synoptischen Evangelien: Eine redaktions- und sozialgeschichtliche Untersuchung zu einem urchristlichen Bildfeld*. NTOA 37. Göttingen: Vandenhoeck & Ruprecht, 2001.

Rolin, Patrice. *Les controverses dans l'Évangile de Marc*. Etudes bibliques n.s. 43. Paris: Gabalda, 2001.

Roskam, Hendrika N. *The Purpose of the Gospel of Mark in Its Historical and Social Context*. NovTSup 114. Leiden: Brill, 2004.

Rowland, Christopher. *The Open Heaven: A Study of Apocalyptic in Judaism and Early Christianity*. 1982. Reprint, Eugene, OR: Wipf & Stock, 2002.

Rowland, Christopher, et al. "Visionary Experience in Ancient Judaism and Christianity." In *Paradise Now: Essays on Early Jewish and Christian Mysticism*, edited by April D. De Conick, 41–56. SBLSymSer 11. Atlanta: SBL, 2006.

Sacks, Oliver. *Hallucinations*. New York: Vintage, 2012.

Bibliography

Saldarini, Anthony J. *Pharisees, Scribes and Sadducees in Palestinian Society: A Sociological Approach*. Grand Rapids: Eerdmans, 1988.
Sanders, E. P. *Jesus and Judaism*. Philadelphia: Fortress, 1985.
Sankey, Paul J. "Promise and Fulfilment: Reader-Response to Mark 1:1–15." *JSNT* 17 (1995) 3–18.
Sawicki, Marianne. *Seeing the Lord: Resurrection and Early Christian Practices*. Minneapolis: Fortress, 1994.
Scarborough, John. "Medicine." In *Civilization of the Ancient Mediterranean*, edited by Michael Grant and Rachel Kitzinger, 1227–48. New York: Scribner, 1988.
Schenke, Ludger. *Das Markusevangelium*. Berlin: Kohlhammer, 1988.
———. *Die Urgemeinde: Geschichtliche und theologische Entwicklung*. Stuttgart: Kohlhammer, 1990.
Schröter, Jens. *Erinnerung an Jesu Worte: Studien zur Rezeption der Logienüberlieferung in Markus, Q und Thomas*. WMANT 76. Neukirchen: Neukirchener, 1997.
Seybold, Klaus, and Ulrich B. Mueller. *Sickness and Healing*. Translated by Douglas W. Stott. Biblical Encounters Series. Nashville: Abingdon, 1978.
Shaw, Brent D. "The Myth of the Neronian Persecution." *JRS* 105 (2015) 73–100.
Sjoberg, Gideon. *The Preindustrial City, Past and Present*. New York: Free Press, 1960.
Soards, Marion L. "Appendix IX: The Question of a Premarcan Passion Narrative." In *The Death of the Messiah: From Gethsemane to the Grave; A Commentary on the Passion Narratives in the Four Gospels*, edited by Raymond E. Brown, 1492–1524. 2 vols. ABRL. New York: Doubleday, 1994.
Stone, James V. *Vision and Brain: How We Perceive the World*. Cambridge: MIT Press, 2012.
Swartley, Willard M. "The Role of Women in Mark's Gospel: A Narrative Analysis." *BTB* 27 (1997) 16–22.
Tajfel, Henry. *Human Groups and Social Categories: Studies in Social Psychology*. New York: Cambridge University Press, 1981.
Tannehill, Robert C. "The Disciples in Mark: The Function of a Narrative Role." in *The Interpretation of Mark*, edited by William Telford, 134–57. Issues in Religion and Theology 7. Philadelphia: Fortress, 1985.
Tart, Charles T. *States of Consciousness*. New York: Dutton, 1975.
Theissen, Gerd. *The Gospels in Context: Social and Political History in the Synoptic Tradition*. Translated by Linda M. Maloney. Minneapolis: Fortress, 1991.
———. *Lokalkolorit und Zeitgeschichte in den Evangelien: Ein Beitrag zur Geschichte der synoptischen Tradition*. NTOA 8. Göttingen: Vandenhoeck & Ruprecht, 1989.
———. *The Miracle Stories of the Early Christian Tradition*. Translated by Francis McDonagh. Edited by John Riches. SNTW. Edinburgh: T. & T. Clark, 1983
———. *Urchristliche Wundergeschichten*. SNT 8. Gütersloh: Mohn, 1974.
Théon, Aelius. *Progymnasmata*. Text prepared and translated by Michel Patillon; with the assistance, for the Armenian, of Giancarlo Bolognesi. Collection des universités de France. Paris: Belles Lettres, 1997.
Tiemeyer, Lena-Sofia. *Zechariah and His Visions: An Exegetical Study of Zechariah's Vision Report*. T. & T. Clark Library of Biblical Studies. LHBOTS 605. London: Bloomsbury, 2015.
Triandis, Harry C. *Individualism & Collectivism*. New Directions in Social Psychology. Boulder, CO: Wesview, 1995.

Bibliography

Trocmé, Étienne. *La formation de l'Évangile selon Marc*. Etudes d'histoire et de philosophie religieuses 57. Paris: Presses Universitaires de France, 1963.

———. *The Formation of the Gospel according to Mark*. Translated by Pamela Gaughan. Philadelphia: Westminster, 1975.

———. *The Passion as Liturgy: A Study in the Origin of the Passion Narratives in the Four Gospels*. London: SCM, 1983.

Turner, Victor W. *The Ritual Process: Structure and Anti-Structure*. The Lewis Henry Morgan Lectures 1966. Chicago: Aldine, 1969.

Vaage, Leif E. "An Other Home: Discipleship in Mark as Domestic Asceticism." *CBQ* 71 (2009) 741–61.

———. *Trauma, Erzählung, Befreiung: Das Markusevangelium aus amerikanischer Perspektive*. Theologie interkulturell Series 26. Düsseldorf: Patmos, 2017.

———. "Violence as Religious Experience in the Gospel of Mark." In *Experientia*. Vol. 2, *Linking Text and Experience*, edited by Colleen Shantz and Rodney A. Werline, 119–35. EJL 35. SBLSymSer 40. Atlanta: SBL, 2012.

Van Eck, Ernest. "The Baptism of Jesus in Mark: A Status Transformation Ritual." *Neot* 30 (1996) 187–215.

Vermes, Geza. *Jesus the Jew: A Historian's Reading of the Gospels*. Minneapolis: Fortress, 1981.

Vironda, Marco. *Gesù nel Vangelo di Marco: Narratologia e cristologia*. Bologna: Dehoniane, 2003.

Volkan, Vamik D. "Transgenerational Transmissions and Chosen Traumas: An Aspect of Large-Group Identity." *Group Analysis* 34 (2001) 79–97.

Wardle, Timothy. "Mark, the Jerusalem Temple and Jewish Sectarianism: Why Geographical Proximity Matters in Determining the Provenance of Mark." *NTS* 62 (2016) 60–78.

Weber, Thomas. "Thermal Springs, Medical Supply and Healing Cults in Roman-Byzantine Jordan." In *Studies in the History and Archaeology of Jordan*, edited by Gahzi Bisheh, 6:331–8. Amman: Department of Antiquities 1997.

Wedderburn, Alexander J. M. *A History of the First Christians*. Understanding the Bible and Its World. London: T. & T. Clark, 2004.

Weeden, Theodore J. *Mark: Traditions in Conflict*. Philadelphia: Fortress, 1971.

Wells, Louise. *The Greek Language of Healing from Homer to the New Testament Times*. BZNW 83. Berlin: de Gruyter, 1988.

Whitenton, Michael R. "Feeling the Silence: A Moment-by-Moment Account of Emotions at the End of Mark (16:1–8)." *CBQ* 78 (2016) 272–89.

Wolf, Eric. *Peasants*. Foundations of Modern Anthropology. Englewood Cliffs, NJ: Prentice-Hall, 1966.

Worsley, Peter. "Non-Western Medical Systems." *Annual Review of Anthropology* 11 (1982) 315–48.

Xenophon. *Hiero; Agesilaus; Constitution of the Lacedaemonians; Ways and Means; etc.* Translated by C. E. Marchant and G. W. Bowersock. LCL 183. Cambridge: Harvard University Press, 1925.

Young, Allan. "The Anthropologies of Illness and Sickness." *Annual Review of Anthropology* 11 (1982) 257–83.

Zeichmann, Christopher B. "Loanwords or Code-Switching? Latin Transliteration and the Date of Mark's Composition." *JJMJS* 4 (2017) 42–64.

Bibliography

———. "The Date of Mark's Gospel apart from the Temple and Rumors of War: The Taxation Episode (12:13–17) as Evidence." *CBQ* 79 (2017) 422–37.

AUTHOR INDEX

Alexander, Jeffrey C., 124, 124n13, 124n14, 125, 125n16, 125n128, 149
Anderson, *Graham*, 88n17, 149
Assmann Jan, 59, 60n31, 107, 107n13, 125n17, 149
Avalos, Hector, 84n3, 87n10, 90n23, 91n26, 149

Bailey, Kenneth, 57, 57n20, 58n21
Balabanski, Victoria, 26n42, 132n42, 133n43, 134n46, 135n50, 149
Bar-Tal, Daniel, 126n20, 149
Baumgarten, Albert I., 61n35, 61n36, 62n37, 62n38, 64, 64n40, 65n41, 149
Bernhard, Andrew, 53n10, 149
Boismard, Marie-Émile, 88n13, 149
Bolognesi, Giancarlo, 36n16, 149
Bond, Helen K., 42n36, 149
Borg, Marcus J., 47, 47n43, 149
Borgen, Peder, 84n3, 149
Boring, M. Eugene, 31n2, 32n6, 150
Bourdieu, Pierre, 40n29, 150
Breytenbach, Ciliers, 102n1, 150
Broadhead, Edwin K., 117n36, 150
Brown, Raymond E., 11n3, 150
Bultmann, Rudolf, 2, 101n1, 150
Burridge, Richard A., 22n27, 24n23, 33, 33n8, 33n10, 33n11, 34, 34n13, 34n14, 35n15, 38, 38n23, 150

Campbell, William S., 13n9, 150
Cappellen, Patty Van, 140n62, 158
Capes, David B., 29n48, 150
Cardeña, Etzel, 72n11, 150
Chancey, Mark A., 56n15, 150
Chronis, Harry L., 115n31, 150
Clements, Ronald E., 97n40, 150
Coakley, J. F., 102n1, 150
Collins, Adela Yarbro, 11n1, 26n42, 134n45, 150
Collins, John J., 110n24, 114n29, 150
Connerton, Paul, 107n12, 108n17, 150
Craffert, Pieter F., 47, 47n44, 48n47, 69n4, 70n5, 150
Cribiore, Raffaella, 36n16, 151
Crossan, John D., 11n3, 151
Croy, N. Clayton, 41n33, 151

Delvecchio-Good, Mary Jo, 85n5, 92n27, 92n28, 153
DeMaris, Richard E., 32n3, 151
Derrett, J. Duncan M., 96n37, 151
Destro, Adriana, 81n38, 151
Devillers, Luc, 88n13, 151
Dewey, Joanna, 21n25, 51n4, 151
Dibelius, Martin, 2, 101n1, 151
Dodds, Eric R., 74, 74n19, 151
Dormeyer, Detlev, 31n2, 33, 33n7, 136n52, 151
Douven, Igor, 8n12, 151
Downing, F. Gerald, 22n29, 151
Dube, Zorodzai, 125n19, 151

AUTHOR INDEX

Duprez, Antoine, 88n13, 151
Dvorjetski, Estee, 88n15, 151

Edwards, James R., 117n36, 151
Elliott, James K., 101n1, 151
Elliott, John H., 5n7, 96n37, 152
Elliott-Binns, Leonard E., 50n1, 152
Epstein, Isidore, 111n26, 152
Esler, Philip F., 58n23, 152
Eyerman, Ron, 123n11, 126, 126n23, 126n24, 127n25, 141, 141n66, 152

Fander, Monika, 19 5n6, 105n8, 105n9, 109n19, 113n27, 129n30, 152
Feldmeier, Reinhard, 139n59, 152
Fentress, James, 107n12, 152
Focant, Camille, 69n3, 81n37, 152
Fowler, Robert M., 132n42, 152
Freyne, Seán, 56n17, 152
Frickenschmidt, Dirk, 22n27, 22n30, 23n32, 33n10, 152
Fritzen, Wolfgang, 129n31, 132n41, 134n44, 134n45, 135n49, 136n53, 137n54, 140n63, 152
Funk, Robert W., 2n1, 152

Garber, David G., 123n12, 152
Gelardini, Gabriella, 26n38, 152
Gilmore, David D., 6n8, 7n10, 39n25, 96n36, 153
Gnilka, Joachim, 52n6, 80n36, 153
González Echegaray, Joaquín, 109n20, 153
Good, Byron J., 85n5, 92n27, 92n28, 153
Goodman, Martin, 122n8, 123n9, 153
Graham, Susan L., 102n2, 153
Grant-Davie, Keith, 24n34, 153
Grassi, Joseph A., 102n2, 153
Green, Joel B., 11n3, 153
Green, William S., 76n28, 88n18, 94n30, 153
Guijarro, Santiago, 9n14, 9n15, 9n16, 10n17, 10n18, 10n19, 10n20, 12n5, 41n31, 46n42, 53n9, 56n18, 58n21, 60n32, 87n8, 116n33, 137n55, 139n58, 153

Halbwachs, Maurice, 107n12, 154
Hatina, Thomas R., 134n44, 138n56, 154
Head, Peter M., 41n33, 154
Hearon, Holly, 106n10, 154
Heemstra, Marius, 123n9, 154
Hengel, Martin, 25n35, 25n36, 154
Hogan, Larry P., 91n25, 154
Holst, Robert, 101n1, 154
Horbury, William, 110n23, 110n25, 154
Hurtado, Larry W., 19, 20n23, 140n61, 154

Iersel, Bas van, 102n2, 134n46, 138n57, 154
Ilan, Tal, 38n21, 154
Incigneri, Brian J., 25n35, 154

Jacobson, Arland D., 23n31, 154
Jenni, Ernst, 95n32, 154
Jeremias, Joachim, 103n5, 154
Jones, Ken, 123n10, 154

Kähler Martin, 20n24, 154
Kee, Howard C., 87n11, 155
Keith, Chris, 22n28, 23n32, 34n14, 155
Kelber, Werner H., 11n2, 19, 19n21, 19n22, 155, 158
Kennedy, George A., 37, 155
Kertelge, Karl, 93n29, 155
Kirk, Alan, 107n12, 107n14, 155
Klauck, Hans-Josef, 32n6, 33, 33n9, 155
Kleinman, Arthur, 84, 84n4, 86n6, 86n7, 89n19, 90n22, 153, 155
Kloppenborg, John S., 26n39, 50n1, 151, 153, 155
Kuhn, Heinz-Wolfgang, 21n26, 51, 51n3, 127n26, 155
Kutsch, Ernst, 109n21, 155

AUTHOR INDEX

Latourelle, René, 83n1, 155
Le Donne, Anthony, 109n18, 155
Legault, André, 101n1, 155
Lenski, Gerhard E., 6n8, 6n9, 155
Leon-Dufour, Xavier, 83n1, 155
Lieb, Michael, 74, 74n20, 75, 75n23, 75n24, 75n25, 76n26, 78n30, 155
Lightfoot, Robert H., 133n43, 155
Linnemann, Eta, 11n2, 155
Lloyd, Geoffrey E. R., 70n5, 156
Lohmeyer, Ernst, 50n1, 156
Lücking, Stefan, 27n43, 102n3, 105n8, 118n37, 120n3, 128n27, 133n43, 136n51, 156
Lüdemann, Gerd, 69n2, 156

Mack, Burton L., 102n3, 156
Macknik, Stephen L., 71n8, 156
Malbon, Elisabeth Struthers, 14n11, 14n13, 31n1, 31n2, 32n5, 42n34, 102n2, 156
Malina, Bruce J., 4n5, 4n6, 7n11, 39n26, 39n27, 41n32, 43n37, 58n26, 59n29, 96n33, 96n35, 97n38, 109n20, 156
Malzoni, Cláudio V., 102n1, 156
Marcus, Joel, 15n15, 18n17, 25, 25n37, 26n38, 26n41, 27n43, 27n44, 28n46, 32n4, 42n35, 52n6, 61n33, 80n36, 81n39, 117n34, 117n35, 121n5, 130n33, 131n37, 131n39, 131n40, 139n60, 157
Marxsen, Willi, 12n6, 13n7, 17n16, 51n2, 157
Maunder, Chris J., 106n11, 157
McKnight, Edgar V., 2n3, 157
McVann, Mark, 32n3, 44n39, 110n22, 157
Meier, John P., 37n19, 88n18, 157
Mell, Ulrich, 31n2, 157
Mendels, Doron, 107n14, 108n15, 157
Merkur, Daniel, 76, 76n27, 157
Michaelis, Wilhelm, 95n31, 157
Michie, Donald, 159

Miller, Susan, 102n2, 157
Miquel, Esther, 66n43, 77n29, 103n4, 130n35, 157
Müller, Ulrich B., 69n1, 158

Naluparayil, Jacob C., 31n2, 158
Navarro, Mercedes, 102n2, 158
Neirynck, Frans, 105n7, 158
Neufeld, Dietmar, 77n29, 158
Neyrey, Jerome H., 7n11, 8n13, 34n12, 37n18, 38n20, 39, 39n26, 39n27, 40n28, 40n30, 41n32, 43n38, 58n26, 59n29, 61n34, 96n35, 97n38, 156, 157, 158, 159
Noorda, Sijbolt J., 87n9, 158
Novenson, Matthew V., 114n29, 158

Öhler, Markus, 63n39, 158
Olick, Jeffrey K., 107n12, 158
Orlov, Andrei, 78n31, 80n36, 157, 158
Oyen, Geert Van, 140n62, 158

Patillon, Michel, 36n16, 160
Peppard, Michael, 42n36, 158
Peristiany, John G., 6n8, 39n25, 150, 158
Perrin, Norman, 14n14, 158
Pesce, Mauro, 81n38, 151
Pierre, Marie-Joseph, 88n14, 159
Pilch, John J., 47, 47n45, 47n46, 48n47, 72n10, 72n10, 73n18, 74n21, 80n35, 84n3, 88n16, 96n34, 159
Poole, Ross, 108n16

Reed, Jonathan L., 56, 56n16, 56n17, 159
Rhoads, David, 3n4, 21n25, 31n2, 159
Robbins, Joyce, 107n12, 158
Robbins, Vernon K., 2n2, 156, 159
Robinson, James M., 19n20, 159
Rodríguez Láiz, Ana, 10n19, 28n46, 154, 159
Roh, Taeseong, 52n7, 159

AUTHOR INDEX

Rohrbaugh Richard L., 43n37, 109n20, 156, 158
Rolin, Patrice, 52n5, 52n7, 52n8, 159
Roskam, Hendrika N., 26n38, 131n40, 159
Rousée, Jourdain-Marie, 88n14, 159
Rowland, Christopher, 76, 76n26, 78n31, 159

Sacks, Oliver, 71n9, 159
Saldarini, Anthony J., 56n15, 66n43, 160
Sanders, Ed P., 13n8, 160
Sankey, Paul J., 31n2, 160
Sawicki, Marianne, 105n8, 160
Scarborough, John, 87n11, 160
Schenke, Ludger, 25n37, 50n1, 122n7, 160
Schröter, Jens, 18, 19, 19n20, 20, 160
Seybold, Klaus, 87n11, 88n12, 88n17, 160
Shaw, Brent D., 25n35, 160
Sjoberg, Gideon, 6n8, 160
Soards, Marion L., 12n4, 160
Stewart, Eric S., 8n13, 160
Stone, James V., 70n7, 160
Swartley, Willard M., 102n2, 160

Tajfel, Henry, 58n23, 58n24, 59n27, 59n28, 124, 125n15, 160
Tannehill, Robert C., 14n13, 160
Tart, Charles T., 72n11, 72n13, 72n14, 72n15, 72n16, 72n17, 78n33, 160

Theissen, Gerd, 25, 25n37, 26n38, 26n39, 36n40, 36n41, 55n14, 58n22, 83n1, 122n7, 160
Thatcher, Tom, 107n14, 154, 155
Tiemeyer, Lena-Sofia, 74n22, 75n23, 160
Triandis, Harry C., 58n25, 59n30, 160
Trocmé, Étienne, 11n1, 18, 18n18, 18n19, 20, 161
Turner, Victor, 44, 44n39, 45n41, 161

Vaage, Leif E., 119n1, 134n45, 134n47, 141n65, 161
Vermes, Geza, 88n18, 161
Vetter, D., 95n32, 154
Vironda, Marco, 114n30, 116n32, 117n34, 161
Volkan, Vamik D., 125, 126n21, 161
Van Eck, Ernest, 32n3, 44n40, 160
Wardle, Timothy, 27n45, 161

Weber, Thomas, 88n15, 161
Wedderburn, Alexander J. M., 65n42, 161
Weeden, Theodore J., 81n39, 161
Wells, Louise, 90n24, 161
Whitenton, Michael R., 141n64, 161
Wickham, Chris, 107n12, 152
Winkelman, Michael J., 72n11, 150
Wolf, Eric, 6n8, 154, 161
Worsley, Peter, 84n2, 84n4, 85n5, 161
Young, Allan, 85n2, 89n20, 90n21, 161

Zeichmann, Christopher B., 28, 28n47, 131n38, 161

INDEX OF ANCIENT DOCUMENTS

OLD TESTAMENT/HEBREW BIBLE

Genesis
15:1.12	75
15:12	75

Exodus
3:6	117
15:26	95
24	75, 80n36, 81n37
24:1	80
24:6	80
24:9	80
24:12–18	80

Numbers
12:6	75

Leviticus
13—15	91
21:18	97
24:5–9	35n12

1 Samuel
9:16	110, 111
10:1	110, 111, 112
15:16	75
16:13	110, 111, 112
21:1–7	53n12
21:2–7	63, 64
24:7	110
26:16	110

2 Samuel
1:14	110
1:16	110
2:4	111, 112
5:3	111
5:6–8	97
16:13	110
19:22	110

1 Kings
1:32–48	110
1:33–34;	111
1:39	110, 111, 112
17—2 Kings 2	63
17:7–24	63
17:17–24	94
19:19–21	53n9, 60n32, 63
19:9–18	60

2 Kings
4:8–37	94
5:1–19	94
6:3	111, 112
9:3	110, 111
9:6–9	112
9:6	110, 111, 112
11:12–20	110
11:12	110, 111, 112
23:30	111

Isaiah
29:7	75
Isa 56:7	27, 130
Isa 63:19	78

INDEX OF ANCIENT DOCUMENTS

Jeremiah

7:11	27

Exekiel

1—3	74n21, 76n26, 78
16	60-61

Hosea

2	60

Zechariah

1—6	74
9:9	130n32

Job

4:13	75

Lamentations

4:20	110

Psalms

22:5	109
118	130, 131
118:22–23	131
22:5	09

Psalms LXX

2:2-6	111
17:50-55	111
44:8	111
88:21	111
131:10	111
131:17	111

୭

APOCRYPHA

Ben Sira

38:1–15	87
48:3–5	63
49:8	75

୭

PSEUDEPIGRAPHA

1 Enoch

48:8–10	110

2 Baruch

29:3	110
30:1	110

3 Baruch 123

4 Baruch 123

4 Ezra

	123
12:32	110

Apocalypse of Abraham 123

Psalms of Solomon

17	131
17:32	110
18:5	110
18:7	110

Sybiline Oracles

4–5	123

୭

NEW TESTAMENT

Matthew

	18, 23, 30, 31, 34, 34n14, 37, 102, 104, 130n32
1:16	38
5:27–28	95
5:29	95
6:22–23	95
12:22	95
13:15	95
13:55	38n22

INDEX OF ANCIENT DOCUMENTS

15:15	95	1:30	86
20:5	95, 96	1:39	13n7
23:16	95	1:40–45	46
23:24	05	2:1—3:6	15, 21n26, 46, 50, 51
26:6–13	102	2:1–2	54
		2:3–12	54
Mark		2:3–4	87
1–16	22, 24	2:5–7	115
1–13	11, 12, 14, 15, 17, 18, 19, 19n20, 20, 21, 22, 23, 24, 29, 52	2:6	13
		2:7	15, 52, 115
		2:10	51, 61n33
1:1–15	31, 32, 33n7, 43, 47	2:13–28	52
1:1–13	19, 32, 115	2:13–14	53
1:1–3	32, 41, 48	2:13	52, 53, 54, 55
1:1	34, 41, 41n33, 114, 114n36, 115, 117, 118, 136, 142	2:14–15	53n10
		2:14–15a	53
		2:14	63
1:2–7	22	2:15–17	54
1:2–3	42	2:15	52, 57, 60
1:4–8	32, 41, 42, 43	2:16–17	53
1:4–5	45	2:16	13, 57, 60, 61, 62
1:9–15	32, 42, 43, 44, 48, 49	2:17	87
		2:17b	53n10, 63, 66n44
1:9–11	43, 68	2:17c	53
1:9	23, 37, 42, 44	2:18–22	54
1:10–13	45	2:18–20	53
1:10–11	42, 68, 77	2:18	57, 60, 61
1:10	77	2:19a	63
1:11	79, 114, 115, 117, 131n36	2:20	15, 66n44
		2:21–22	53
1:12–13	43	2:22	52
1:13	32	2:23–27	55
1:14—8:26	115	2:23–24	53
1:14–15	32, 33n9, 43 46	2:23	60
1:14	17, 13n7, 44, 128	2:24	57, 61, 62
1:15	32	2:25–26	53, 63, 87
1:16–20	46, 132, 137	2:27	63
1:16–18	53n9, 116n33	2:28	63, 115
1:16	13n7	3:1–5	51, 54
1:19–20	53n9	3:2	52
1:21–39	46, 54	3:6	15, 51, 128
1:25	115	3:12	115
1:27–28	41	3:13–19	137
1:27	115	3:19	17
1:28	13n7	3:21	79
1:29–31	14n12	3:22–30	45

169

INDEX OF ANCIENT DOCUMENTS

Mark (*continued*)

3:22	13, 41	9:7	79, 115, 131n36
3:31–35	133, 138	9:9	132n41
4:1–34	21n26, 132	9:10	16
4:17	17	9:11–13	16, 17
4:35—5:43	21n26	9:17–18	86
4:38	14	9:30–32	116
4:41	115	9:31	15, 128, 128n28, 141
5:8	115	9:32	17
5:18–20	14n12	9:33–37	137
5:25–27	94	9:33–34	13
5:25–26	87	9:33	17
5:35	14	9:35	14, 116
5:37	13n10	9:47	95
6:3	23, 37, 38	10:17	14
6:6b—8:26	121n6	10:29–31	132n41
6:14–16	114	10:32–34	116, 128
6:15	94	10:33–34	15
6:17–29	17	10:33	128n28, 128n29
6:45—8:10	21n26	10:34	141
6:52	13	10:35–40	13, 17
7:1	13	10:37	116
7:3–4	25	10:38	16
7:5	13	10:43	14
7:24–30	14n12	10:45	14, 16, 118
7:25	86	10:46–52	14n12, 83, 84, 99
8:14–21	13	10:47–48	28, 116
8:27–28	115	10:51	98, 99
8:29–30	115	11—16	26, 119, 128, 142
8:28	94	11—13	16, 116, 136
8:29	115, 117	11—12	129, 142
8:30	115, 116	11:1–11	130
8:31—10:52	82, 93	11:9–10	28, 116
8:31—9:1	116	11:11	130
8:31–33	128	11:12–26	133
8:31–32	15	11:12-14	130
8:31	51, 128n29, 141	11:12	128n28, 133
8:32	13, 137	11:15—12:40	21n26
8:32b	17	11:15–17	27, 112, 130
8:33	139	11:17	27, 121
8:34	14	11:18	16, 126, 128n28, 129
8:38	132n41, 134		
9:1-9	68	11:20-24	130
9:2	13n10, 80	11:21	14
9:4-8	79	11:27—12:40	16
9:4-7	68, 77	11:28	28, 130
9:5	14	12:1–12	28, 131

170

INDEX OF ANCIENT DOCUMENTS

12:8	16	14:1	13, 16, 128
12:10-12	131	14:2–8	105
12:13–17	28, 131	14:3–10	13
12:14	14	14:3–9	12, 101, 101, 103, 132n41
12:18–27	131		
12:19	14	14:3	104, 112
12:28–35	131	14:4	112
12:32	14	14:8	14, 112, 139
12:35–37	28, 112, 116, 131	14:9	105, 106, 113
12:35	116	14:10–12	12, 112
12:41–44	14n12	14:10–11	13
12:42	25	14:10	15, 128n28
13	10, 19, 22, 26n42, 129, 132, 132n41, 133, 133n43, 134n43, 134n45, 135n50, 142	14:11–12	13
		14:11	133, 138
		14:12	12
		14:14	14
		14:17	137n54
13:1–2	26	14:18	133, 138, 139
13:2	26, 133	14:20–21	13
13:4	129, 133, 134	14:21	14
13:5–8	134	14:22–25	12, 139
13:9–23	134	14:25	52
13:9–13	26, 134n46, 135, 139	14:27	13, 17, 141
		14:28	12, 132n41, 141
13:9	128n28, 133, 138, 139	14:29	15, 17
		14:30	13
13:12	133, 138, 139	14:32	12
13:14	26, 121, 132	14:32–42	12, 13, 113, 118, 137
13:24–27	134, 13n44		
13:24–25	133	14:34–35	139
13:24	135	14:34	133, 139
13:26	68, 133. 135n48, 139, 139n61	14:38	133
		14:41	133, 138
13:28–37	134	14:43–50	16
13:30	129, 132	14: 43-49	137n54
13:32	133	14:43–47	133
13:33–36	137	14:43	12, 13
13:33	137	14:44	17
13:35	133 137n54	14:45	14
13:36	132, 133	14:46	13
13:37	137	14:50	13, 17, 116
14–16	11, 12, 17, 18, 19, 20, 23, 24, 29, 129, 136, 142	14:51—15:15	138
		14:51–52	12
		14:53–65	16
14:1–50	138	14:53	13
14:1–11	101	14:53b	13
14:1–2	12, 112	14:55–65	133

INDEX OF ANCIENT DOCUMENTS

Mark (*continued*)
14:55–59	133
14:55	13, 133
14:55b	12
14:57–58	14
14:58	26, 27
14:60	13, 139
14:61–62	117, 118
14:61b–62	12
14:61	14
14:61b	15
14:62–63	115
14:62	133, 134, 135n48
14:63	13
14:64	52, 117
14:66–72	13
14:66-69	116n33
14:66-68	116
14:70	23, 37
14:72	137n54
15:1–5	16, 133
15:1	13, 15, 137n54, 138
15:2	14
15:3–4	52
15:4	139
15:9	14
15:10	12
15:12	14
15:15–20	16
15:15	138
15:16–41	138
15:16–20a	12
15:16	25
15:21–32	16
15:21	12, 14
15:22b	12
15:26	140
15:27	12
15:29–30	133
15:31–32	12
15:31	13
15:32	140
15:33	133, 135n47, 140
15:34	140
15:38	133, 140
15:39	12, 14, 15
15:40–41	12, 14
15:42—16:8	138
15:42–47	14
15:42b	12
15:43b	12, 14
16:1-8	14, 16
16:7-8	12, 142
16:7	12, 132n41, 135, 135n48, 141

Luke
	18, 23, 30, 31, 34, 34n14, 37, 79, 102, 103, 104, 106, 109
1:1–4	34
1:1	34
4:22	38
4:25-26	63
4:26	94
6:39	95
7:7-8	87
7:36-50	102, 103, 109
7:46	109
10:18	68, 79
16:23	95
18:15	95
24:16	95

John
	11, 79, 102, 103, 104, 106
1:21	94
1:33-34	77
1:46	37
1:51	68
1:52	79
2:19	26
2:25	135n47
2:34	135n47
5:2-9	88n13
5:5-7	94
6:5	95
7:52	37
9:2	95
12:1-8	102, 103
12:3	104
12:34	135n47
12:40	95

INDEX OF ANCIENT DOCUMENTS

17:1	95

Acts

2:39	121n6
7:56	79
10:11	79
21:21	121n6
2827	95

Romans

2:19	95

1 Corinthians

2:9	95

Galatians

2:11–15	65

Ephesians

1:18	95
2:13	121n6
2:17	121n6

1 Peter

5:13	25

2 Peter

1:17-18	79n34

1 John

2:16	95

Revelation

4—5	74
4:1–2	79

↩

PHILO AND JOSEPHUS

Philo

Life of Moses

1:1–4	34
1:1	38
1:3	38
1:5–31	35

Josephus

Antiquities of the Jews

15.245–246	87
17.171	88
19.157	87

Life

1–12	35
1.6	38
404	87

Jewish War

2.135-157	13n34
2.266–270	121
2.344	130n32
2.409–410	120
2.409	27, 130
2.434	120n4
2.444	130n32
2.457–459	121
2.461–464	26
2.461–463	122
4.135–157	27

↩

DEAD SEA SCROLLS

4QComGen A (4Q252)	110, 111
4QMMT	52–57, 97n39
11QT^a 45:12-14	97n39

↩

RABBINIC WRITINGS

b. Ker. 5a–6a	111

↩

INDEX OF ANCIENT DOCUMENTS

GRECO-ROMAN WRITINGS

Aristotle
Poetics
1452b   118

Cicero
De legibus
1:26–27   95

De officiis
1:150   38n22

De oratore
3:221   95

Rhetorica ad Herenium
3:10   36
3:13   36

Cornelius Nepos
Life of Atticus
1:1–4   35
1:1–4   35

Life of Epaminondas
1:4   36

Homer
Odyssey
1:1–21   33

Lucian of Samosata
Demonax
2   38
3–4   35

Plato
Symposium
109n20   109n20

Plutarch
Cato Minor
1–4   35

Mullierum Virtutes
242e–263c   109

Quintus Curtius Rufus
Historiae Alexandri Magni
8.9.27   109n20

Tacitus
Life of Agricola
4–5   35
4   38

Annals
15:44, 2–3   25

Theon
Progymnamata
78   37
110   37

Xenophon
Hiero
7:3   40

EARLY CHRISTIAN WRITINGS

Q Document   18, 19n20, 20, 22, 23, 23n31, 66n43
3:2b—4:14   19
3:7–9   22
3:16b–17   22
17:23—22:30   19

Gospel of Thomas
31   87
47c   53n11
104   53n11

INDEX OF ANCIENT DOCUMENTS

Eusebius
Ecclesiastical History
3:39,15   24

Papyri
POxy 1244   53n10

www.ingramcontent.com/pod-product-compliance
Lightning Source LLC
Chambersburg PA
CBHW020851160426
43192CB00007B/875